East Asia, Globalization, and the New Economy

T0330676

The world economy is being transformed as a result of East Asia's competitive production costs and the IT/e-business revolution. Modern logistics that have reduced communication and transportation costs are shifting the locus of production from West to East. East Asia, China in particular, is fast becoming the industrial center of the world.

East Asia, Globalization, and the New Economy analyzes this global growth process. The book is particularly concerned with overcoming the "digital divide," the current and future impact of technology policies, and the potential benefits and difficulties posed by this growth pattern. It takes a systematic look at prospects for the future. Will the IT/e-business revolution help sustain East Asian growth?

Written by a recognized expert in the area of global economics, this book offers the first book-length treatment of IT/e-business prospects in the region and questions whether these developments will renew and sustain the rapid economic development of East Asia. This up-to-date study will interest scholars, researchers, and practitioners in business and economic development.

F. Gerard Adams is visiting Professor in the College of Business Administration at Northeastern University in Boston and Professor Emeritus at the University of Pennsylvania.

Routledge Studies in the Growth Economies of Asia

East Asia, Globalization, and the New Economy

F. Gerard Adams

Routledge
Taylor & Francis Group

LONDON AND NEW YORK

First published 2006
by Routledge
2 Park Square, Milton Park, Abingdon, Oxon OX14 4RN

Simultaneously published in the USA and Canada
by Routledge
711 Third Avenue, New York, NY 10017

Transferred to Digital Printing 2006

Routledge is an imprint of the Taylor & Francis Group, an informa business

First issued in paperback 2013

© 2006 F. Gerard Adams

Typeset in Times New Roman by
Newgen Imaging Systems (P) Ltd, Chennai, India

British Library Cataloguing in Publication Data
A catalogue record for this book is available from the British Library

Library of Congress Cataloging in Publication Data
A catalog record for this book has been requested

ISBN 13: 978-0-415-76991-4 (hbk)
ISBN 13: 978-0-415-64730-4 (pbk)

Contents

Illustrations

Figures

Maps

Tables

Preface

This book is focused on the implications of the globalization and information and communications technology (ICT) revolutions for the economic development of East Asia. The technological and business management transformation that started principally in the United States is today shaping manufacturing and business operations all over the world. It is an integral ingredient of globalization. It is widely seen as the driver of change for sustaining East Asia's rapid growth.

Several years have passed since the financial crisis in East Asia in 1997 and since so many information and telecommunication technology firms in the United States crashed and burned in 2000 and 2001. Globalization has made further strides, linking East Asia ever more closely to the Western economies and their advanced technologies. Today, most observers are once again optimistic about the *new economy*'s impact on East Asia. This is a good time to take stock.

The countries of East Asia differ greatly in their participation in this global transformation. Some are already on the cusp of the ICT world, rapidly approaching new technological and business frontiers. Others are making significant progress, becoming increasingly dominant in the consumer products, even in those that rely heavily on sophisticated manufacturing techniques. And others, still, have a long way to go to take advantage of the new hard and soft technologies that make up the ICT/e-business revolution. Critical barriers, termed the "digital divide," impede the transformation of some important East Asian economies from labor-intensive manufacturing to high technology and e-business. Such barriers as insufficient education and lacking communications infrastructures are being overcome in East Asia as in other parts of the world. The special requirements of the new fields for entrepreneurship, advanced technical skills, manufacturing experience, and, even, competence in the English language represent more challenging impediments. Yet, many experts and politicians expect that the new technology, communication, and business setting will be the basis for further globalization and continued rapid progress in East Asia.

This book asks the following questions. How will the IT/e-business revolution sustain East Asian economic growth? What does economic thinking tell us about the advantages that high technology, networked communication, and computerized automation offer to the increasingly global economy? What have been the developments in IT and e-businesses in East Asia? Does the ICT/e-business revolution really create new opportunities for East Asia that will sustain rapid growth related to the technological promise of computers and networks? What are the appropriate public policy strategies? What opportunities does this new world offer and how may entrepreneurs participate in the East Asian development?

This project grew out of a series of lectures to executive MBA students at Northeastern University in Boston, at the Sasin Graduate Institute of Business Administration in Thailand, at the Johns Hopkins—Nanjing University Center in China. It is also based on extensive discussions in the United States and abroad with business people and academic colleagues about the e-business revolution and its implications for the world economy.

The material is addressed to several audiences.

1   A general *professional/business audience* concerned with IT and e-business with focus on East Asia. These are people who wish to inform themselves about what is going on in the business world, generally, and in East Asia, specifically. Is it really a different world from what it was? In what particulars? How do the changes related to advanced technology, globalization, and the Internet impact on business opportunities and on the aggregate economy? How do they affect development prospects in East Asia: the future of the East Asian growth *miracle*?

2   An *audience of business managers* in East Asia and in the Western countries who directly face the problems and opportunities brought about by rapidly changing technology and a sea change in competition. How can their business operations be adapted to this twenty-first century world? What investments should they make in knowledge and in IT hardware and software to participate in the e-business world? What parts of their businesses can gain from computerization and what parts call for good old-fashioned personal contacts and elbow grease? These issues apply not just to the budding IT/e-business entrepreneurs in East Asia but also to American and European business managers who are competing in an increasingly competitive world and who might want to take advantage of the new opportunities in the region.

3   An *academic audience*—The topics of globalization and of the "new economy" are central to current discussions of economic development and growth. East Asia, the most rapidly growing region of the world, also represents an important interest. The book provides useful background for study of current economic developments, worldwide. Globalization represents a tremendous gain to the people of the East Asian region and elsewhere, but it is sometimes seen as a threat in the advanced countries of Europe and the United States. The book may be the basis for an exciting course in East Asian economics and business. The material may also serve as readings and research support in other university courses at the MBA or advanced undergraduate levels in international management and entrepreneurship. Emphasis on broad contemporary trends and on economics makes these materials suitable for use in economics and social science courses as well such as introductory economics, economic development, world economic history, international economic policy, and technological change.

Biography

F. Gerard Adams is Visiting Professor in the College of Business Administration at Northeastern University in Boston and Professor Emeritus at the University of Pennsylvania.

After receiving his PhD from the University of Michigan in 1956, he was a business economist in the petroleum industry and served in government at the Council of Economic Advisors in Washington and at the Organization for Economic Cooperation and Development in Paris. He spent 38 years on the faculty of the University of Pennsylvania, where he was Professor of Economics. He has taught and lectured abroad in many locations, most recently in Bangkok, Thailand, and Nanjing, China. In addition to his teaching he is active in business consulting and forecasting. He was one of the founders of Wharton Econometric Forecasting Associates, now Global Insight, and has long been associated with Project LINK, a worldwide forecasting project based at the United Nations. He has traveled widely and has spent extensive periods living and working in Europe and East Asia.

Adams has been primarily concerned with empirical and policy applications of economics. He has worked on a broad range of studies, including models of nations, regions, commodity markets, energy, industries, and firms and the linkages between these models. In recent years he has been concerned with the economics of development in East Asia, and, particularly, with the implications of the IT/e-business revolution.

Adams is author of numerous articles and editor or author of a number of books, among them *An Econometric Model of International Trade; Industrial Policies for Growth and Competitiveness; Modeling the Multiregional Economic System; Commodity Exports and Economic Development; The Business Forecasting Revolution; The Macroeconomic Dimensions of Arms Reduction, Economic Activity, Trade, and Industry in the US–Japan-World Economy; East Asian Development: Will the East Asian Growth Miracle Survive?; Public Policies in East Asian Development*; and *Macroeconomics for Business and Society*. Most recently he published *The E-Business Revolution and the New Economy*.

Abbreviations

B2B	business to business
B2C	business to consumer
BIBF	Bangkok International Banking facility
BOI	Board of Investment
BoT	Bank of Thailand
BPO	business process outsourcing
CAT	Communication Authority of Thailand
DLD	Domestic Liability Dollarization
ERSO	Electronics Research and Service Organization
FDI	foreign direct investment
GDP	Gross Domestic Product
ICT	Information and communications technology
IMF	International monetary fund
MITI	Ministry of international trade and industry
NAFTA	North American Free Trade Area
NITC	National Information Technology Committee
NRI	Network Readiness Index
NUS	National University of Singapore
OECD	Organization for economic cooperation and development
PPP	Purchasing power parity
RFID	radio frequency identification tags
SEZ	Special Economic Zones
TSMC	Taiwan Semiconductor Manufacturing Corporation
UMC	United Microelectronics Corporation
WEF	World Economic Forum
WTO	World Trade Organization

Part I
East Asia, globalization, and the new economy

1 Introduction

The challenge of sustaining East Asian growth

In the past 40 years, the developing countries of East Asia have shown remarkable economic growth. All the world admires what has been achieved in the region. Countries that were dirt poor not so long ago grew rapidly and achieved Western-style living standards. Countries that used to rely on oxcart agriculture have become manufacturing powerhouses. Many entrepreneurs from the region and from the advanced countries have directed their attention and, in many cases, their investments into the East Asian region. The East Asian *miracle*[1] has been based largely on the development of manufacturing, much of it exports to the West. Growing domestic markets, high rates of domestic saving and investment, and modernization have also made important contributions.

East Asian development has been closely linked with the globalization of world production and trade. There has been a radical geographic reorientation of industrial production from high-wage countries in North America and Europe toward East Asia. Specifically, mass production products, at first simple ones, like apparel and toys, and then more complex ones, like automobiles and computers, are increasingly being sourced in East Asia. Huge advantages in labor cost, favorable exchange rates, growing production experience, and recent improvements in local technology have established the competitiveness of the East Asian countries in world markets. With reference to China, the headline in the *Financial Times* (February 04, 2003) summarizes these developments neatly: "How cheap labor, foreign investment and rapid industrialization are creating a new workshop of the world."

The microeconomics of the export-competitive industries are traditional—manufacturing with high labor content, often assembly, done on production lines that have substantial economies of scale. They involve relatively standard products—in some cases, standardized "commodities," and in others trademarked goods that are differentiated but still call for known and widely available technology. Much of this production is being done with the backing of foreign direct investors and with foreign management, although increasingly local capital and acquired skills have supported such projects.

In 1997, the East Asian growth momentum was rudely interrupted by, what has since been called, the East Asian Financial Crisis. The crisis called into question the ability of several East Asian countries to compete effectively and to participate in a world of open capital markets. Since then, some countries in East Asia have had to struggle to get back on a sustained steady growth track, although others such as China and South Korea have continued to achieve steady and rapid growth.

Today, the world economy faces new challenges. The dot-com crash in 2000–1 and the recent worldwide economic slowdown now appear to have been only short-term interruptions in more fundamental long-term development trends. Globalization is extending its reach. Financial and entrepreneurial flows continue to revolutionize the geography of world production, trade, and financing. Rapid technological progress in computers and networks lies behind these developments. Indeed, in recent years, the pace of technical change seems to have accelerated. New information and communications technology (ICT) promises radical reductions in the costs of carrying on international transactions. Lower communication and transportation costs reduce the disadvantages of distance: the world is getting smaller and more interrelated. Manufacturing of many products is increasingly outsourced to developing countries providing opportunities for export industries and employment in many parts of the world. East Asia has been a leader in these developments. The mix of products originating in East Asia is evolving from traditional labor-intensive export goods to technically advanced products such as computers and chips. Electronic networks are taking over many of the tasks of coordinating the ever more complex supply chain. Service functions that can take advantage of telecommunications, even in some cases sophisticated knowledge-intensive activities like research and engineering, are being relocated to low-wage countries. The ongoing changes are organizational as well as technical. The ICT/e-business revolution promises to alter further where and how enterprises do their business.

The East Asian development process has been going on for many years, expanding East Asia's export markets, building efficient new industrial centers, and rapidly raising living standards. Many experts argue that this growth pattern is likely to continue. Indeed, this process will be facilitated by increased computerization and reductions in transportation costs. New communication and networking technologies enable East Asian countries to participate more easily, more effectively, and more widely in the "new economy" and e-business world. However, the technical characteristics of some new economy products are significantly different from the old economy products, requiring much higher capital intensity and technological sophistication. That may make a difference for some East Asian countries but not for others.

The developments in technology and business are likely to have a major impact in East Asia. Technical and organizational changes have facilitated the process of globalization. This broadening of relationships across the world offers some important advantages but also poses substantial risks: a more global world economy means that each country is more and more dependent on what is going on in other countries.

On the one hand, exposure to advanced management and technology promotes rapid economic progress, as the East Asian experience demonstrates. And foreign capital and entrepreneurship, often originating with overseas East Asians, have facilitated this kind of development. Competitiveness in world markets requires product quality and specifications that are usually well ahead of products designed for home markets. Participation in export markets builds modern industry. Competition from abroad keeps domestic producers on their toes.

On the other hand, increasing integration throughout the world economy also has its dangers. The saying goes, "when the United States economy sneezes, the rest of the world catches cold."[2] Indeed, when the United States and Europe catch cold, some East Asian countries catch pneumonia! If major markets such as Japan, the United States, and Europe were to slow down or if protectionism were again to limit trade flows, suppliers in East Asia could sink into recession. As financial markets become more open, there is also renewed fear of international financial crises such as the East Asian financial crisis of 1997. There is even concern that linkages between the producing and consuming countries might cause isolated crises to engulf the entire world economy.

Paradoxically, the enormous size of China also raises fears among people in the developed countries. China is already a superpower, an important geopolitical force, and its influence will increase as it grows. China will dominate the East Asian region.[3] Indeed, China may dominate markets for manufactures worldwide. Even today, competition from China's low-cost industries is challenging producers across the world, some from other developing countries.

The leading East Asian countries are taking advantage of some of the newest technology. They have become major producers of consumer electronics and related equipment. Korea's Samsung and China's Lenovo (Allen 2002), power-houses in flat screen TVs and PCs, respectively, are good examples. On the other hand, East Asia shows somewhat less competitive strength in the software and e-business dimensions of the IT revolution. Some East Asian countries are finding the new technologies and e-businesses a daunting challenge, since they have not yet attained a stage of technological and educational development that permits them to lead or at least to operate competitively in these new fields. As the advanced countries progress to still more sophisticated high-tech systems, some developing countries fear that they may be left behind.

The issue is whether and how the East Asian countries can participate in the new economy. Can they use it to continue to leverage themselves on their rapid growth path?

This book is concerned with East Asia, Globalization, and "New Economy." What have been the underpinnings of the East Asian growth process and how are they affected by ongoing changes in world business? How do the East Asian countries fit into a larger globally integrated economy? Has the ICT/e-business revolution influenced growth in East Asia? How does it affect the competitive advantage of various East Asian countries? After the 1997 East Asian financial crisis, did participation in the new technology and in e-business offer opportunities to revive the East Asian growth process? How can ICT/e-business development sustain the growth in East Asia over the coming decades? What should be the role of private entrepreneurship and of public policy?

In Part I, we introduce the fundamentals of the ICT/e-business revolution, the "new economy," and globalization. How do they relate to East Asia?

Part II considers the so-called growth miracle in East Asia and the relative position of the various East Asian countries. Whereas there are important common elements in East Asian development, the situation of each country is somewhat different. They are spaced widely along the steps of the development ladder. They differ considerably in their relative strengths and weaknesses: domestic market size, advancement of technology, education and culture, and cultural links abroad. Most important for our discussion, they differ in their position with respect to the "digital divide."

Part III is concerned with policy. There are important commonalities and differences in each country's development strategy. How has government policy played a role in East Asian development in the past and what might be its role looking forward? What are the technological challenges associated with IT-based development and what are the special policies required to advance the ICT revolution in East Asia?

Part IV deals with the future and introduces the opportunities being created in East Asia. As we look ahead, for a few years and, then, for many years, what can we expect to see in East Asia as a result of the changes in technology and business organization that are taking place today? What elements of the ICT/e-business revolution offer comparative advantage to various East Asian countries? What are the implications from a geopolitical perspective? What kinds of policies will advance East Asia's transition to this "new economy"? What kinds of strategies can businesses use to take advantage of the new opportunities? How will the ICT/e-business revolution sustain East Asian economic growth?

2   The ICT/e-business revolution

A new economy?

Important technological changes lie behind the fundamental transformation and globalization of the world economy that have been taking place in the past few years. The new technology leads to an entirely different perspective on *what* to produce, *how* to produce, and, importantly, *where* to produce. It affects business strategy and organization. It changes traditional ways of looking at economies and at economic development. It influences public policy decisions. We begin by asking about the nature of these technical changes: what is the ICT/e-business revolution? What are its implications? In short, what is new about the "new economy?"

First, this chapter is concerned with the profound changes that are revolutionizing the world's production, distribution, and management systems. Later, we pose the question about how the IT/e-business revolution is changing the character of the world economy. How may East Asia be affected?

There is wide agreement that the world economy has been undergoing a revolution, one that has produced a bright future. The MIT economist, Lester Thurow summarizes it:

> We now live in a period of time historians of the future will call the third industrial revolution. Leaps forward and interactions between six key technologies (microelectronics, computers, telecommunications, manmade materials, robotics, and biotechnology) are once again sending the economy off in new directions. Collectively, these technologies and their interactions are producing a knowledge-based economy that is systematically changing how we conduct our economic and social lives.[4]

(2003: 30)

Improved technology has been a central force for economic progress and change, in East Asia as in the rest of the world. Economic and technical change is an ongoing process that affects production, and, importantly for East Asian growth, influences economic development and trade patterns. Much modern technology connected with electronics and computers has been with us for a while. The mainframe computer has been around for almost 50 years; the PC, now in almost everyone's home, has been available for more than 20 years. In advanced countries, most firms have automated production processes and most have computerized a large part of their back-office business operations. In East Asia, as well, some countries have already moved far up on the technological scale. In fact, South Koreans are one of the most "wired" or "wireless" people in the world. Nevertheless, until now, much of East Asia's growth still reflects the region's comparative advantage in labor-intensive manufacturing. As labor costs in the advanced world have risen, production of labor-intensive products like apparel, shoes, and toys has been transferred to East Asia.

The ICT/e-business revolution has added new dimensions to the globalization process. Since the mid-1990s, there has been a sea change in communication and networking. The pace of technical progress applications accelerated, translating many high-tech innovations into practical and widely used new products and services. The "virtual" or "digital" economy appears to have arrived. Many experts in the United States believe that we have reached a new era, a "New Economy." A "fun" definition of the "new economy" appears in the *Encyclopedia of the New Economy* on the web:

> When we talk about the new economy, we're talking about a world in which people work with their brains instead of their hands. A world in which com- munications technology creates global competition—not just for running shoes and laptop computers, but also for bank loans and other services that can't be packed into a crate and shipped. A world in which innovation is more important than mass production. A world in which investment buys new concepts or the means to create them, rather than new machines. A world in which rapid change is a constant. A world at least as different from what came before it as the industrial age was from its agricultural predecessor. A world so different its emergence can only be described as a revolution.
>
> (Browning and Reiss 1998)

Despite the romantic sound of this definition, it includes important real world elements, conceptual, technical, and organizational:

- brain work and investment in knowledge creation;
- communications network linking together various users;
- continued technical change and innovation;
- worldwide competition.

For a while, the dot-com crash and the recent worldwide economic slowdown cooled enthusiasm for the "new economy," but the underlying technological trends in hardware and software applications are continuing. Even the United States is only a part of the way toward the long-run potentials widely foreseen for the ICT/e-business revolution. Other regions of the world, including most of East Asia, are following in the footsteps of the more advanced countries. Some of the smaller East Asian countries—Singapore, Korea, and Taiwan—are IT leaders, but the most populous countries in the region such as China and Indonesia still lag behind in the transformation process. But, perhaps, not for long!

In this chapter we ask: "What are the essential elements of the new economy?" In later chapters, we focus on East Asia and the actual and potential impact of the ICT/e-business revolution in that part of the world.

Essentials of the ICT/e-business revolution

The setting for business and manufacturing activity has been changing rapidly across the world in recent years. These changes greatly affect the potentials for various industries in East Asia. What are the distinguishing microeconomic characteristics? While we focus on a small number of central developments, we define the revolution broadly, looking beyond technical innovations to the structure of organizations and management, the relationships between market participants, the declining cost of communication and transportation, the geography of the world production system, the impact of global finance, and the role of government.

We discuss the microeconomic forces that drive the IT/e-business revolution and their impact on the operation and organization of business along the following lines:

- communication and network interconnectivity
- technological change and knowledge
- economies of scale
- externalities
- reduced transaction costs
- dynamic competition
- entrepreneurship and finance.

Communication and network interconnectivity

If one were to pick one new principal driver of change, the big technical difference that accounts for the ongoing changes in the world economy is the *information network*. Businesses worldwide can be linked together in a giant computerized communication and control system, irrespective of geographic distance or national boundaries.

Not so long ago, computers were stand alone operations. Businesses built their computer systems for internal use. Specialized programs running on mainframe computers were meant to operate within the confines of the business and were not accessible to outsiders by design and for technical reasons. Today, interconnection is available to business firms, governments, and consumers worldwide making it possible to connect a variety of computers and programming systems in a world-encompassing network. Important technical developments lie behind the networked economy:

- The development of astonishing electronic technology, unthinkable in the first half of the twentieth century. (The transistor was not invented at Bell Labs until 1948.) Today's VLSI chips contain millions of transistors, yet progress at miniaturization still appears to have some time to go.

- The enormous expansion of computing power and its wide diffusion. (We will consider the question of the "digital divide" that separates the advanced countries from the laggards in Chapter 7.)
- The improvement and cost reduction of communication through broadband, fiber optics, and satellites.
- Improved shipping and logistics shipment tracking operations.
- The development of computer languages and programs that permit different systems to communicate with each other (Java). The development of the Internet.[5]
- The refinement of applications programs ranging from business supply chain management and accounting to end-user programs such as word processing.
- The integration of these program systems to manage business transactions with a minimum of human intervention.

These are only a few examples of the technical developments that are making possible a revolution in technology and business. Friedman describes these developments as follows:

> Do you recall "the IT revolution" that the business press has been pushing for the last 20 years? Sorry to tell you this, but that was just the prologue. The last 20 years have been about forging, sharpening and distributing all of the new tools to collaborate and connect. Now the real information revolution is about to begin as all the complementarities among these collaborative tools start to emerge.
>
> (2005: 36)

Like previous industrial revolutions, networked computers represent a new technology with general applicability useful for a wide range of tasks. Where earlier phases of the industrialization represented the substitution of mechanical power for human muscle, today's computer network revolution largely substitutes capital goods and software for human intervention. Many transactions that used to require people talking to each other or written documents—bills, confirmations, letters in hard copy form, often with numerous carbons—can be carried out automatically and instantaneously by computers. These changes are altering production processes and the way in which business is organized and carried out between firms (B2B) and between business firms and consumers (B2C). The e-business revolution will result in important changes in the structure and location of business, changes in production, transportation, and management that broadly affect the world's economic system.

Some classic examples of the changes that are taking place are as follows:

- Technically sophisticated production processes, usually highly automated, are being used to fabricate advanced chips, fiber optic cables, computers, electronic storage, and switches.
- Interaction from the production site to the point of sale is the key to optimal supply chain management.

- Information needs are met seamlessly across continents and oceans. Communication has been vastly facilitated and greatly reduced in cost. Imagine the contrast between the old days when a business would send a written order abroad, by steamship, taking perhaps six weeks, and after some delay the supplier would finally ship the product on a freighter taking months, as compared to today's instantaneous communications and high-speed shipping.
- With the growth of cell phones and fiber optic networks, telephone charges have declined drastically and phone availability has mushroomed even in many developing countries. Communications are available at any time and practically at any place.
- E-mail has become a standard means of communication, replacing "snail mail," phone messages, and the fax machine, itself a relatively recent innovation. Cellular telephone use is growing rapidly in East Asia as well as elsewhere in the world, taking the place of limited land-based systems. Advanced communication often makes possible geographically broader market access and, as a result, improves market efficiency. Of course, e-business operations are very much dependent on rapid network connections.
- Communication systems also make possible distance sourcing for products that can be transmitted electronically—videos and music, call centers, programming, engineering, and R&D in low-wage countries serving companies in advanced high-wage countries.
- Transportation costs have been falling steadily as containerized shipping through large ports with fast ships has cut shipping costs and speeded deliveries. Many products can be shipped economically via air freight.
- Computer control using bar codes (an issue in recent US West Coast port labor disputes) has facilitated logistics. Radio frequency identification tags (RFID) promise to be the next stage of technical development for logistical control. Low transportation cost and more rapid shipment have facilitated the transfer of the locus of production in many industries from Europe and the United States to East Asia.

Reductions in transaction costs and the changing optimal scale of production are changing the structure of industry. On the one hand, as firms can reach and control farther, a higher optimal scale of production puts a premium on large scale, even a global scale of operation. Large-scale operations meet worldwide product requirements from a small number of very large production sites. Paradoxically, with sophisticated control systems, there is also a greater possibility to customize products to meet the users' specific preferences. In economic terminology, there are advantages to "horizontal integration." On the other hand, greater automation and reduced cost of carrying out transactions means that operations at other stages of the production process can be "outsourced," so there is less need for "vertical integration." We are now seeing the changes in industrial structure and geography that are implicit in these "new economy" developments.

In the vast field of business to business (B2B) transactions, management of the supply chain and of inventories can be automated. The paper-based and human interaction systems of the past entailed enormous labor costs. Today, most of this work can be handled automatically, keeping track of the transactions on the computer from the inputs of raw materials to the point-of-sale. Optimization algorithms keep the product in stock and supply just enough to meet purchaser needs. The savings in terms of reduced service staff and inventory holdings are potentially very large, although in practice it often takes time and capital to make the necessary investments in equipment and trained manpower and to "shake out" the difficulties of the new approaches. Many other aspects of business operations including accounting, human resource management, banking, and financial services have also been computer automated.

In the business to consumer (B2C) area, in the advanced countries, substantial business is being done over the web as consumers select the products they require from Internet sites and order them directly on the computer—"Let your computer mouse do your walking." The need for sales personnel or contact persons is greatly reduced. Some consumer operations have switched rapidly to the Internet—airline tickets and hotel reservations, stock market transactions, and orders for books, for example. It is more difficult to computerize markets for other products, but even goods that call for accurate sizes such as clothing are being successfully marketed on the Internet.

Some experts are disappointed, however, as most consumer goods are still purchased at conventional brick and mortar stores. Perhaps they were overly optimistic. Most retail business will continue to be carried out at the shopping mall. For many people, shopping is apparently its own reward, after all. Even so, the volume of consumer e-business was increasing rapidly in the advanced countries even during a time of recession. In developing countries, even in major countries like China, Internet links are not yet sufficiently developed to provide widespread direct access to consumers. Moreover, for many products the physical tasks of fulfillment—delivery of the product, payments for the transaction, returns—must still be handled in conventional ways.

So far, the network economy is making its biggest mark in commerce and industry. In these sectors, the possibilities for automating are being applied increasingly, on one end, linking demand and production and, on the other end, sourcing parts and materials. But there are still many unused opportunities that will yield gains in productivity for some years to come.

An interesting example related to international trade finance is described in the *Wall Street Journal* (June 4, 2004) with the headline "Financing Goes Just-in-Time." The reference is to the fact that "Even today, buyers and sellers predominantly settle their payments by a paper-heavy method called the *letter of credit*, first popularized by the Medici banking family of Florence more than four centuries ago." Every time a firm issues a purchase order from one of its suppliers, say in China, it requests its bank to open a letter of credit. The letter, sometimes written on bond paper, along with numerous supporting logistics and customs clearance documents, is sent by courier to China. Payment is made when the requisite papers have been checked and when there is confirmation that the shipment has been made. This procedure takes as long as two weeks and incurs substantial cost estimated in the aggregate to be 5 percent of the total value of world trade. Today, systems have been developed to do these transactions instantaneously over electronic networks at minimal cost. But a large fraction of international trade finance is still carried out by banks using the old-fashioned letter of credit procedures, in part because it is the way the banks provide credit to finance the transaction. Eventually the letter of credit will go the way of the dodo bird, but not quite yet.

There are also enormous potentials for extending the electronic network into other aspects of daily life. Already many governments including China are talking about e-government, although few have yet to enable electronic systems to carry out a large part of their operations. The same can be said for education where, except for the corporate training market, there is still more talk than effective action with regard to distance learning or e-learning. Other vast potentials lie in health care patient records, digital photography, publishing, entertainment such as video-on-demand, and instant messaging and peer-to-peer file sharing.

It may be some time, however, before the heavy costs of adaptation are absorbed and the potentials of the new systems are fully realized. This is true even in the advanced countries where consumer e-business is well advanced. Elsewhere, in much of the world, only the first steps in the new developments are apparent. New approaches, perhaps based on wireless connections, are being developed. It is clear that in the future there will be vast possibilities.

Technological change and the knowledge economy

In contrast to traditional export commodities, the products of the IT revolution are characterized by rapid technological change. A good example is the development and use of the new technologies in microelectronics—the transistor, the integrated circuit, glass fiber communication networks, and their applications in consumer products such as cell phones and Internet services. Similar development sequences apply to software algorithms. Technological change influences production processes and may result in rapid and, sometimes, abrupt product change. When advanced technology is introduced product differentiation is likely, but as products mature generic versions often become available built to standard specifications, because they must be able to interact with related products. Competitiveness depends greatly on a firm's skill in using new technologies to improve its products and to reduce production costs. The current wave of electronic and communications innovation has produced enormous progress. Its potential is far from being exhausted.

Intellectual content is an important ingredient of the new economy products. This may take the form of technical knowledge embodied in machines or production processes. It may also be intellectual property in computer programs or video or music. Trade may occur in patent licenses, consulting, and financial intermediation rather than physical commodities. Issues of intellectual property protection are important. Some countries do not provide adequate patent, trademark, or copyright protection and there is widespread "piracy." In turn, firms that value their patents and trade secrets may avoid doing business or making investments in countries where "knockoffs" are manufactured and intellectual property rights are not adequately enforced.

Improved knowledge is more central than ever to economic progress. Technological improvement has always been based on advances in knowledge and skill—the modern lathe or milling machine and learning how to use it, for example.[6] Setting up and maintaining today's digital or computer-operated controls require a level of technical competence and knowledge that is far more advanced than what was needed for using earlier generations of machinery. The reader will be all too aware of the difficulties of getting a personal computer to operate consistently without crashing. On a professional level, the challenges are frequently much greater. For hardware, advanced technological processes, like chip fabrication, may require special facilities: a "clean room" and highly qualified technicians. For software, program integration and smooth running operations of a computer network call for a special kind of skill. Innovating with new hardware and software are highly specialized crafts. They require an advanced level of technical education, and in many cases, a knowledge of English in order to understand the complex instructions. The same is true of setting up e-business operations, though once the system is operational, it should be—but often is not—relatively intuitive to operate.

Innovation depends greatly on what has been done earlier. In physicist Isaac Newton's words: "If I have seen further, it is by standing on the shoulders of giants." (in a letter to Robert Hooke (February 5, 1675)). Accumulated knowledge and experience serve as a base for further progress. Fortunately, the accumulation of knowledge is a one-way street. Once knowledge or skills have been acquired, they do not wear down with use. Knowledge does not decline, though technological progress may make a particular piece of knowledge or a specialized skill obsolete as new technologies take its place. A classic example is the substitution of digital electronics for the analog systems that came earlier. An entire generation of engineers was rendered obsolete at least until they acquired the new skills necessary for digital. On the other hand, digital electronics has become the basis for systems that would simply not have been possible with the old technology. Moreover, knowledge does not have to be worked out from scratch. Once ideas have been developed, perhaps in the leading countries, they may be transferred to other users, unless they are subject to intellectual property protection like patents or unless they are kept as trade secrets. (We discuss the questions of intellectual property protection at greater length in Chapter 9.)

Imitation is not just a form of flattery. It is a way to advance technology in a country that is not quite at the technological frontier. That has been a way for East Asian firms to enter advanced industries. There may also be possibilities for leapfrogging, that is, skipping stages of technological development, to jump in one long leap to a leading edge technology. At least that has been the hope of many East Asian officials, although few organizations have actually been successful at making a leap into unfamiliar technological territory.

Skills, too, can be transferred from developed to developing countries. This is where foreign direct investment (FDI) plays an important role. FDI does more than provide capital—typically, direct foreign investors operating their own plants or participating in a joint venture supply knowledge and skill. That may involve providing modern machinery, itself a form of technology transfer. It may call for training of the machine operators and teaching managers advanced management techniques. Some of that training may occur in the company's home office and some of it may take place in the field. Ultimately, experience, economists call it "learning-by-doing" (Arrow 1962), is the best teacher.

In the new economy, there is a premium on technical skill and knowledge. An advanced level of scientific expertise is necessary to get projects started, to make them competitive, and to provide maintenance. A lengthy period of learning improves production performance. The learning curve that shows how costs fall as experience accumulates stretches over many years. Specialized skilled workers and supplies are the essential ingredients. Often, these are concentrated in technologically specialized geographic centers, so-called clusters, where new industries tend to gather.

Diminishing costs and large optimal scale

Many of the products of IT industries are characterized by very low marginal costs of production and distribution. The large fixed costs of product development and plant construction are offset by low variable costs. Economists speak of "economies of scale." Large-scale producers are also low-cost producers. As a result, there is a premium on attaining a very large scale of production.

Markets for sophisticated products or services are often dominated by a small number of global players who sell advanced products, have brand recognition, or provide specialized services. Examples are IBM, Lenovo, Nokia, Intel, Sony, and Samsung (Allen 2002). Some of these huge firms are American, but others are European and, increasingly, they are also East Asian. Their large size allows them to manufacture at optimum scale. Perhaps, even more importantly, they gain economies of scale in management, finance, and commercial operations. Some of these leading firms were the original developers of advanced new products, but others, who were not leaders at the start, were simply the first ones to attain large efficient production and distribution volumes. Paradoxically, once large dominant producers have been established, the large volume required to attain cost economies represents a barrier to the entry of newcomers.

In technically complex products, a dominant firm may be able to control the technical "standard" for certain products or services. This can provide a substantial degree of monopoly power. As in the case of Microsoft "Windows," ownership of the industry technical standard may mean control of almost the entire market and the ability to drive out competitors in markets for related applications. Some economists have argued that such control may impede further product development and technological progress.

Externalities

Knowledge-based product and production processes typically generate *externalities*. The knowledge gained by the research or experience of one firm eventually leaks out to benefit other firms as well. Externalities are typical of knowledge acquisition from R&D or from learning-by-doing. They may be the basis for still further technical advance or for building competitive businesses. In East Asia, new technologies introduced by foreign enterprises are quickly adopted by domestic competitors.

By definition, externalities are not captured by the initial researchers. The anticipated benefit to the society exceeds the benefit that can be captured by the firm investing in R&D. As a result, there may not be as much incentive for research on new products or processes as is justified by the anticipated value of the new development. The argument for public subsidies or for industrial policies promoting specific kinds of high-tech industries is frequently made on the ground that these industries must overcome initial barriers and that they will ultimately yield important knowledge externalities benefiting other producers in the same area. Once a high-tech base has been established, externalities and learning-by-doing (and large scale) will promote efficiency and further growth. A broader but more practical view of externalities is to focus on the linkages between firms. In the course of social and business interaction, firms draw on other firms for information and skills, a process that Lall (1999) calls *collective learning*. The East Asian experience provides some support for these ideas, the success of electronics in industrial clusters in Taiwan and Malaysia, for example. But there is also some negative evidence such as the failure of aircraft construction in Indonesia and the difficulties of establishing an operational chip foundry in Thailand.

Transaction cost economics and the global management chain

As we have noted, the cost of doing business related to carrying out and implementing business transactions can be greatly reduced by computer network automation and high-speed communication. These reduce the need for human interaction in business transactions and frequently allow the work to be carried on at a distance. Many links between firms are automated or carried out electronically, accounting for large productivity gains in the supply chain and in wholesale and retail distribution, for example. E-commerce may add further gains.

To these computer-based improvements in business productivity, Nobel Prize winner Ronald Coase (1937) has added another dimension. Focusing on the transaction costs involved in making and following up on business agreements, Coase argued that such costs influence the structure of business organizations. Operations that involve high transaction costs—negotiation, repeated ordering, discussion of quality and performance, for example—are best handled by employees within an integrated firm. Low transaction cost relationships that are routine or automatic or that are subject to defined management or legal rules can be handled at arms's length between separate firms.

In recent years this has led to the outsourcing phenomenon, the delegation of specific business functions to specialized independent firms. Outsourcing is being extended to entire technically specialized operations such as data processing and logistics. Much of this work is sent abroad. This is frequently called business process outsourcing (BPO). It has made possible the creation of firms like computer seller Dell Inc. that sell a high-profile product but have no manufacturing facilities of their own, only some limited assembly operations to meet specific customer needs. *The Economist* (April 9, 2005: 66) writes: "What economists call 'vertical' FDI allows firms to locate different stages of production wherever they are best suited: marketing where customers are close at hand, research and development where workers are smart, assembly where they are cheap." Usually, the responsibilities for product design, marketing, and sales remain in the hands of the lead company, often, but not always, in an advanced country, whereas physical production and logistics are carried out by foreign affiliates, merchant producers, and logistics firms in East Asia. The global value chain, as it is called, calls for production and management split up between many firms and spread over many countries, taking advantage of their competitive strengths.

A much simplified example is shown in Figure 2.1. At the top of the diagram is the entrepreneurship and management function. Below, we show the production and distribution process, where the product is handled physically. At the left is the raw material phase, in the middle are the manufacturing and assembly operations, and to the right is distribution and marketing. The production operations and assembly operations are frequently carried out in East Asia, although raw materials, manufacturing, and assembly may be sited at different locations. Distribution and marketing are functions that are sited at the market; their location depends on whether the product is for export to advanced countries or is sold directly in the developing world. The critical elements in this picture are the communications links from and to the management headquarters, the thin double headed lines, and the transportation links between the different phases of the production process,

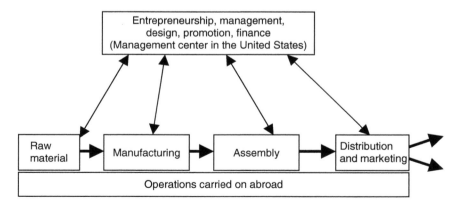

Figure 2.1 The virtual enterprise.

the thick arrows. In the past, these links were very costly. As communication and transportation costs have declined and as transportation has become faster and cheaper, the different elements of the production process can be separated and located where they can be carried out most economically. Control remains with the central entrepreneurship and management.

The share of value-added going to production and assembly, the labor intensive aspects of the production process that loom large in the diagram, may be small relative to the share going to designers, managers, and marketers. Trefler (2003) suggests an allocation of value added as follows: Substantial value added goes to the entrepreneurs, managers, and designers of the product. Very little goes to the production and assembly phases in the middle. After all, production of many products is a "commodity" activity that can be carried on by many unbranded highly competitive contract manufacturers who pay low wages in East Asia and who take away only modest profits. Finally, the marketing and distribution phase carried on in the developed countries and protected by brand names, takes a large part of the product value. A good example is the brand name shirt purchased by the consumer in the United States. A high-quality brand shirt might sell at retail for $50. It is cut, assembled, and packaged in China. Given Chinese wages, it probably costs no more than $5 to produce. The remaining $45 go for entrepreneurship, capital, and design activity by the brand name firm in the United States and for the costs of shipping, distribution, marketing, retail and distributors' margins, etc. Manufacturing costs may only account for 10 percent of the total value.[7] The process described relies heavily on inter-firm relationships. These relationships based on low transactions costs and long distance communication are very different from traditional relationship-based business linkages thought to be prevalent in East Asia.

Dynamic competition

The IT/e-business fields are characterized by dynamic competition. The classic ideas of Joseph Schumpeter about monopolistic competition and "creative destruction" (Schumpeter 1942) apply with a vengeance. Schumpeter saw a world of monopolistic competition in which entrepreneurs "differentiated" their products. Competitors would introduce new products and services. A few are radical innovations. Most of them are differentiated only sufficiently to establish a profitable market position by trade marks, differences in quality, or special features. The market is the ultimate arbiter of success. New products that survive the market test are presumably improvements and expand the market or, sometimes, drive out the old.[8] Schumpeter refers to this process eloquently:

> the competition from the new commodity, the new technology, the new source of supply, the new type of organization... —competition which commands a decisive cost or quality advantage and which strikes not at the margins of the profits and outputs of the existing firms but at their foundations and their very lives.
>
> (Schumpeter 1975 edition: 84)

Importantly, the competitive search for profit inspires newcomers to introduce new technologies and management systems, but it also forces existing producers to remain on their toes, to keep their products up to date with the latest technology, and to maintain their quality. Even a monopoly product like Microsoft's Windows faces an "ever-present threat" (Schumpeter's words) from competing operating systems.

The change to digital electronics and miniaturization that occurred during the 1970s and 1980s was the basis for a veritable deluge of new applications reaching the market in the 1990s and since then. These included ever smaller and more powerful computer processors, cellular telephones, the Internet and broadband communication, and the almost infinite number of new products and services they spawned. This was an example of product differentiation and creative destruction that went way beyond the prediction, possibly, even beyond the imagination of Joseph Schumpeter.

Publicity materials from IBM title a section "The Relentless Forces of Innovation and Commoditization."

> From its start, the IT industry has been characterized by the cycle of innovation and commoditization... Companies that create new high-demand technologies and services enjoy, for a time, barriers to entry and superior margins and pricing power, for the simple reason that there are few or no other providers of that technology or service. However, alternative technologies or capabilities inevitably emerge, decreasing or eliminating the innovator's advantages. In short, that segment of the industry commoditizes... Winners can be the innovators—those with the capacity to invest, manage, and leverage the creation of intellectual capital—or the commodity players, who differentiate through low price, economies of scale, and efficient distribution of other parties' intellectual capital... Perhaps the greatest risk is to get squeezed in the middle.
>
> (IBM 2005: 15)

Physical product differentiation becomes more difficult as products mature, but differentiation through quality, advertising, design, and trade marks, remains an important factor in establishing market position. It is interesting to note that until recently Western firms have assumed the role of the innovator and commoditization has been the strength of East Asian producers. However, more recently, we also see the emergence of East Asian producers successfully establishing distinct and frequently innovative market identities.

Entrepreneurship, risk, and venture capital

Dynamic competition is ultimately a matter of entrepreneurship and finance. The new IT economy is the product of an entrepreneurial society. Disruptive innovations (Christenson 2000) that radically change the standard way of operating or significantly alter widely used products have typically been initiated by new entrepreneurial companies. Such efforts involve a high level of risk. One of the advantages of the initial stages of the new industries in the United States has been the willingness of venture capitalists, in Silicon Valley, for example, to take on the high risks, and presumably high rewards, of innovative ventures. During the 1980s and 1990s, the United States had a unique advantage, a highly entrepreneurial business society, and the availability of venture capital financing. This made possible effective innovation spurred on by the efforts of small new firms, many started by young men in a garage (Jobs and Wozniak at Apple Computers) or an upstairs bedroom (Gates at Microsoft). Some of these rapidly became national and, even, global enterprises. Some of these firms have displaced earlier giants. They have established strong positions, in some cases a large degree of market dominance or control, so that in some lines they are becoming increasingly difficult to challenge. The classic case, as we have noted, is Microsoft.

The combination of available risk-bearing capital and entrepreneurship has been a significant advantage for the development of new IT and e-business firms in the United States. Such funding has not been as widely available in the rest of the world. Some East Asian countries have relied heavily on financing by leading families and by banks. A transition economy like China is unusual in that much of industry is still partially publicly owned, often by provincial and local governments, and is heavily supported by the banks. Korea has followed the Japanese example of large industrial groups in contrast to small- and medium-size enterprises in Taiwan. Just to prove that one rule does not always hold, both Taiwan and Korea have been technological leaders.

What is advantageous at the early stages of a new industry when rapid technical change is taking place may not be so useful when the industry matures. Today, opportunities for radical innovation may be more limited than they were earlier in the information technology revolution. Indeed, few of the small companies that initiated the ICT/e-business revolution remain. Many small pioneering firms have disappeared or have been absorbed by their larger competitors. A few have become immense firms, producing and marketing products that are the standards of their industries and that are no longer undergoing rapid change.

As the information technology and e-business fields mature, the frenzied pace of technical innovation may slow. But, from a technological perspective, most experts believe that there is still room for important new developments. And from a commercial point of view many applications are still in their early stages. There is need to refine services that are already available to better integrate various approaches being used. Some illustrations are the rapid changes occurring in hardware such as cell phones, HDTV, WiFi, systems integration, business management and communications programs, etc. Applications in some e-business fields still have huge potentials for more development. Supply chain management, video and audio entertainment, health care information, e-government, and e-commerce are applications in some e-business fields that have great promise. The technological frontier is still beyond current real world applications and their diffusion. Many technologies are available but are not yet widely applied even in the advanced countries. Importantly for our discussion of East Asia's potentials, the revolution is much farther along in some parts of East Asia than in others.

A "new economy?"

There have been many changes in technology and in the world business environment. Can we say that we are now in a "new economy?" Do these changes fundamentally change the character of economics and of the economic system? How does the new economy, if there is one, affect East Asia?

The economic theory perspective

The issue of whether there is a "new economy" has divided the economics profession. Of course, much depends on what one means by the term. There is no doubt when we see the world from a new technology perspective that it is very much a *new* economy. An ICT/e-business revolution is under way that promises to have big impacts on the East Asian countries as well as on the rest of the world. But is it a "new economy" from an economist's perspective? Do the changes that are occurring create a vastly changed economic system? Are the traditional laws of economics still valid? Can you still think in terms of traditional supply and demand curves?

The new economy is more competitive, more flexible, and more global than the old, but, in many respects, its theoretical underpinnings are little changed. From a theory perspective, what are the elements that remain the same and what are the ones that are different?

- The new economy is very much a capitalist free enterprise system. Even in countries that have traditionally placed great emphasis on planning and public sector ownership, the new economy industries are largely entrepreneurial and profit-seeking. The competitive dynamics of these fields thrive best under private enterprise control. Transitional economies like China have been building market economy IT industries even when a large part of ownership still remains in state hands, as we have noted. The managers of these enterprises have been remarkably entrepreneurial.
- Resource allocation and markets in the new economy operate as they always have. But the scope of competition, the speed of market responses, and the flexibility of the system has been greatly increased. The decline in transaction costs has made possible wider participation by potential competitors, at home and from abroad. This has tended to increase the intensity and scope of competition.
- Faster innovation and technological development can translate into more rapid growth of productivity, a significant positive factor since productivity is the basis for improving living standards.
- The new economy is increasingly global with greater potentials for allocating different parts of the production process between countries and with greater mobility of capital than in the past. (Globalization is discussed in Chapter 3.)

The new economy has sometimes been promoted as more productive, less inflationary, and less likely to have business cycles than the old. Theoretical analysis provides only a little support for such thinking. Gains in productivity may help to reduce inflationary pressures. Uncertainties may be reduced to the extent that more precise calculations of future prospects can be made. On the other hand, the increased dynamic of technical change and increased openness may make it difficult to forecast and to stabilize the economy.

The changes associated with the ICT/e-business revolution may also mean that we must view the economies of the poor countries, those usually referred to as less developed, differently than we have in the past. Must we rethink the theory of economic development? We believe that much of the traditional framework of economic thought about economic growth and development is still relevant. (This framework is discussed with reference to East Asia in Chapter 5.) Indeed, the changes in the economy related to the introduction of IT support some of the ideas about the nature of the competitive economy that go way back to Adam Smith's *Wealth of Nations* in 1776 and, of course, more recent thinking about growth, technical change, and development (Romer 1986). But we will also note that many global trading and financial relationships are undergoing change and that these changes are having profound impacts on the location of production and on trade relationships between countries.

The *new economy*, notwithstanding, a new economic science does not replace standard theory, though it may influence the importance or magnitude of the relationships observed. Whether and how the economy has changed must be treated as a quantitative or qualitative issue, a question of degree.

What does the evidence show?

Do the data support the idea that we have a new economy? Developments must be considered at the level of the world's major producing regions—the United States, a leader in the IT/e-commerce fields, the other advanced countries, and the developing countries particularly in East Asia.

We may take a broad statistical approach, measuring whether there have been significant changes in the economy's performance as a result of the introduction of new IT and its implications for business. When we do that, things are not as certain as when we marvel at the vast technology-based innovations, as we did above. We see some changes in statistical trends that clearly reflect the impact of technological change on the overall economy? In the United States, the "Goldilocks" economy of the late 1990s provided a few years when the high productivity growth, low inflation, and the absence of recession suggested that economic conditions in the new economy would be "just right." But the dot-com crash of 2000–1 and the recession that followed proved that the business cycle was not dead after all. Indeed, these developments suggested to opponents of the new economy hypothesis (Kiley 1999; Gordon 2000)[9] that much of what we had seen in the 1990s could be attributed to a speculative boom. Since then the debate has continued as economic historians and statisticians have sifted through the data and as new information on productivity gains is coming in (Oliner and Sichel 2000, 2002; Jorgenson 2001, 2002; Baily 2002; Jorgenson *et al.* 2002a,b; Brynjolfsson and Hitt 2003).

Today, the statistics for the United States are no longer inconclusive. Business sector productivity data during the 1996 to 2005 period were considerably higher then in the previous 20 years, 3.2 percent per year as compared to 1.5 percent per year. The very latest productivity data over the 2001 recession and the recent business cycle recovery have remained higher than we would anticipate on the basis of historical experience. The productivity gains have been particularly large in finance and retail and wholesale trade, sectors that have been taking advantage of the e-business technology. In the United States, the ICT/e-business revolution is making a difference!

In the other advanced economies, in Europe and Japan, the broad statistical basis for arguing that there is a new economy is less clear.[10] The data do not yet show much support for the new economy hypothesis. Recent OECD studies (OECD 2001, 2003) note that growth has been quite uneven, very slow in Germany and Japan and quite strong in Australia, the Netherlands, and Ireland, in addition to the United States. It is not clear, however, to what extent improvements are owing to the application of advanced technology or whether they reflect other forces. There is no evidence of a worldwide upsurge of aggregate productivity. A recent working paper (Basu *et al.* 2003) is entitled "The Case of the Missing Productivity Growth: Or, Does Information Technology Explain Why Productivity Accelerated in the United States but not the United Kingdom?" IT is a general-purpose technology. For it to make a significant difference in aggregate productivity, it must find application in fields outside the information technology industries, in finance and trade, for example. It takes big investments in hardware and training and much time for new techniques to replace customary labor-intensive business procedures. The authors argue that other advanced countries in Europe, like the United Kingdom, may still be at earlier stages in the IT implementation process—large investments with little productivity gain. They have also been hindered by sluggish economies and by more rigid labor markets than the United States (Baily 2003). The Basu *et al.* study deals specifically with a statistical comparison of the United States and the United Kingdom (Table 2.1). This view is at once pessimistic and optimistic. Whereas until recently these economies have not seen the rapid growth of productivity in service activities as in the United States, the prospect is that in time the new technologies will be applied effectively and will yield increases in productivity.

There is little evidence in the statistics of an improvement in European productivity trends, but there is a lot of evidence to show that Europe and Japan are changing their production systems in line with the IT/e-business revolution, though perhaps a little more slowly than in the United States. Here, too, there are striking exceptions. In some fields, particularly cellular telephones, European companies have been world leaders—Nokia and Phillips. And some smaller countries like Ireland, sometimes known as Europe's Silicon Valley, and Finland have made spectacular leaps into high tech.

Table 2.1 Productivity growth comparison: United States and the United Kingdom (Total factor productivity growth, 1990–2000, percent change, annual rate)

	United States		United Kingdom	
	Pre-1995	*Post-1995*	*Pre-1995*	*Post-1995*
Private non-farm economy	0.59	1.92	1.72	0.78
ICT producing sectors	5.52	11.02	3.82	10.46
Non-ICT producing sectors	0.61	1.54	2.52	0.93
Wholesale trade	1.66	5.37	3.44	3.71
Retail trade	0.83	5.33	0.73	−1.17
Finance and insurance	1.31	4.90	1.89	3.87

Source: Basu *et al.* 2003, tables 3 and 4.

With regard to East Asia, the situation is less clear. On one hand, for many years Gross Domestic Product (GDP) growth in the East Asian region has been much more rapid than in the developed world (see Table 4.2). This rapid pace of growth was interrupted by the 1997 East Asian crisis, except in China, but growth has largely resumed in the region (Collins and Bosworth 1996; Crafts 1999). Some economists have attributed much of the rapid increase in East Asian GDPs to increases in inputs of labor and capital. But a close look at the data suggests that in most East Asian countries there have been significant gains in productivity. In recent years, growth of labor productivity has ranged from 7 percent per year in China to 3 percent in South Korea, Indonesia, and Thailand and 1–2 percent in the other countries. On the other hand, in most of East Asia, the high rate of productivity growth was only indirectly related to the IT/e-business revolution. Production of IT-related products has been growing rapidly, but much production still represents labor-intensive activities for making conventional consumer products and for assembling consumer electronics (Adams and Shachmurove forthcoming). The productivity gains represent shifting of production from low-productivity activities to higher productivity manufacturing, increasing capital intensity of production, the result of high rates of investment, and improvements in technology (Adams and Shabbir forthcoming). An important point is that aggregate productivity improves simply when modern efficient industries grow more rapidly than tradition-bound activities and account for a larger share of aggregate output. This would occur even if there were no improvement in productivity in each of the underlying industries.

Many of the technological innovations in East Asia represent "catching up" or imitative technology and shifts out of low-productivity fields like agriculture into modern industry. But, in most East Asian countries, only a small part of the technological improvement represents the application of new economy technology, except directly in the production of IT products. Most of these gains represent improvements in traditional production or assembly technology, already well known in the West. The improvements in production methods have often been relatively simple steps. Whereas some of these gains are clearly a consequence of technological improvement along with industrialization, it would not be correct to link this long-run trend directly with much more recent sophisticated developments in the IT fields. There is no doubt, however, that some countries—Singapore, Taiwan, South Korea, and Malaysia—have made tremendous strides particularly as producers of chips, consumer electronic equipment, and related advanced technology products. Finally, the transfer of manufacturing to East Asia owes much to the economies associated with the new communication and transportation technologies.

An interesting example of differences in production technology is a new assembly plant I observed on a trip to China some years ago. This firm produced electronic circuit boards, the innards of little electronic pianos. The plant was new, an affiliate of a well-known Japanese company, one of the first in a vast, new, industrial free-trade zone. It was a spacious building, clean and air-conditioned. In the middle, around a long table, sat many workers. On one end, the first worker picked up the plastic board and inserted a transistor. Then she (note that they were all women) would hand the board to the next worker who would solder the transistor and hand it to another worker who would test the connection and so on around the table, until the product was completed at the end of line, having gone through the hands of perhaps 50 workers. This was hand assembly, but in terms of layout, cleanliness, and efficiency it was probably a cut above traditional Chinese factories.

A couple of weeks later, I happened to visit an American plant in the US Middle West making a very similar electronic board. The product was produced entirely automatically untouched by human hands without any direct assembly labor. The plastic base traveled along a conveyor belt. At each stop a robotic arm would insert the appropriate parts. At the end, the board would go through a bath of molten tin for soldering. Finally, the product would be tested automatically and packaged.

It is highly likely that today, only a few years later, the Chinese factory has greatly improved its production methods. But considering that the cost of labor in China remains less than one-tenth that of the United States (Adams and Shachmurove forthcoming), simple labor-intensive production methods remain economic in China (see the discussion in Chapter 10). As more sophisticated products are produced using more advanced methods, productivity improvements are increasingly related to the new technology.

As the East Asian countries have gone from agriculture into manufacturing, more productive high value-added manufacturing industries are replacing older less productive activities. There are important implications

- for employment—fewer workers are needed on the farm and rapid industrial growth is required to absorb the outflow of workers from agriculture;
- for regional location of production—in China, export production has burgeoned along the East Coast and surplus labor is increasing in the agricultural and traditional industrial areas elsewhere. Other East Asian countries are being challenged by Chinese competition;

- for urbanization—cities are growing rapidly and the countryside is losing people. A massive floating population of unemployed or marginally employed workers is appearing in the cities.

Some East Asian countries have gone much further on the scale of economic development than others. As we consider at greater length later, Singapore, Taiwan, and South Korea have jumped wholeheartedly on the new economy bandwagon. Some, like Malaysia, are making important strides. Others, like Vietnam and Indonesia, are aware of the potentials of these developments and taking policy steps to promote them but still face significant barriers.

The technological transformation requires some further steps. It calls for dynamic innovation, more advanced technology, network communication, computer languages, and entrepreneurship. It is skill-biased, meaning that increasingly improvements depend on sophisticated knowledge rather than simply on the application of more unskilled labor and hardware. In some East Asian countries, the new economy will require a paradigm shift away from labor-intensive procedures toward more sophisticated production methods. It will also call for replacing old-fashioned production controls and communication, in the non-IT sectors as well, with applications of new economy approaches to finance and distribution.

3   Globalization

A linked world

Globalization, the increased interconnection of trade and financial flows between all parts of the world, has been the mainstay of East Asia's rapid growth. The growth of exports has turned East Asia into an industrial powerhouse serving the needs of Europe and the United States, What are the connections between the IT/e-business revolution and the globalization process?

International specialization of production and trade goes back a long way— historians might remind us of the spice trade of the seventeenth century. One might take the position, consequently, that globalization is not something new and that it should be seen separately from the IT revolution. But growing international integration of production, finance, and flows of information is also very much a second half of the twentieth-century phenomenon (Fischer 2003; Wolf 2004). In the post-Second World War period, world trade has increased at twice the growth of Gross Domestic Product (GDP). In recent years, the globalization process has speeded up and expanded. As we have noted, the recent technological transformation has greatly improved the means of international communication and trade, reducing costs of transportation and communication and increasing the speed at which international linkages can be maintained. The new means of communication have made possible faster and cheaper trade in goods. They have also facilitated financial transactions and trade in a variety of services that can be transmitted electronically. Reductions in trade barriers and convergence on common cultural norms also increase the geographic range of business.

Thomas Friedman (2005) argues that technical change has created a "flat world," in which relationships between entrepreneurs in the United States and China and India take place on a more "level playing field" than in the past.

What is globalization?

Globalization has become the shorthand term for the increasing integration of global markets. More and more, it is argued, we are living in a global village, one economy that links East and West, rich and poor. The notion of one globally integrated economy is still premature, but, in comparison to only 30 or 40 years ago, the world economy has been increasingly integrated. In the process, we have seen monumental changes in world trade, financial flows, and flows of information, from the mature countries to the developing countries, from the more advanced countries in East Asia to those still at earlier stages of development.

Globalization means that business managers enlarge their horizons from a domestic perspective to a worldwide view. They look far and wide for the most profitable geographic strategies. This means finding places to produce most cheaply and finding profitable markets for their products without (or with little) concern for national boundaries. The result is not only broad new opportunities but also a geographic widening of competition. Traditional patterns of production often maintained by protective walls are breaking down. Gains in productivity and efficient sourcing are likely, however, to come at some cost. Structural adjustments and unemployment are occurring in the traditional manufacturing strongholds. This makes globalization a political "hot button" issue.[11]

Traditional notions of globalization focus on international integration of markets through increased trade in goods. Clearly that has been a dominant feature of recent trends, going from the classical notions of trade in cheese and wine, the basis of David Ricardo's comparative advantage, produced where the climate conditions were most appropriate. More modern ideas of trade competitiveness look at differences in production factor endowments and differences in production technology. (For a discussion of these concepts as applied to East Asian competitiveness, see Chapter 10.)

We used to think mostly of trade in natural resources and agriculture-based products or simple manufactures, like iron ore, coffee, or clothing. Such trade flows remain important—indeed, their scope has increased tremendously. Increasingly better quality consumer manufactures originate in far away countries, in Mauritius and Sri Lanka, as well as in East Asia. The United States and Europe import strawberries and other out-of-season fruit from Latin America during the winter. More and more East to West trade flows have included sophisticated manufactures, like automobiles, TVs, and computers.

A signal change has been the extension of trade to services and intellectual products that do not require physical shipment. These include intellectual property like patent licenses and rights to movies and, most recently, trade in services like computer programming and call center services that can be transmitted electronically. World exchange also includes other dimensions such as financial flows, flows of knowledge and intellectual capital, flows of entrepreneurship, and migration of people.

Finally, it is important to note that "Globalization is much more than an economic phenomenon. The technological and political changes that drive the process of economic development have massive non-economic consequences... globalization is political, technological, and cultural, as well as economic." (Fischer 2003: 5.)

Semi-globalization

The rapid concentration of industrial production in Asia and the growth of exports from that region to the rest of the world are not so much the result of fully internationally integrated markets, as of imperfections in the integration of these markets. Ghernawat (2003) introduces the idea of semi-globalization to explain worldwide economic trends. This is an important innovation, contrasting sharply with less nuanced traditional notions of increasing world integration. It has significant implications for explaining economic history and for making policy. We explore the semi-globalization concept and the relationship between semi-globalization and the IT revolution.

According to Ghernawat, traditional economists have seen the world from two extreme perspectives, an autarchic one and a fully integrated one. In the autarchy case, country markets are separated as if by high walls. To all intents and purposes, activity and prices in one country are independent of activity and prices in other countries. In contrast, fully integrated markets are tightly and smoothly linked, one to another, so that flows between them rapidly wipe out price differentials; the "law of one price" applies. These extremes are far from what we observe in the real world.

There are two central points. First, there remain important barriers between most national markets. Some are high and some low. Trade barriers and tariffs, high transport costs, restrictions on foreign investment, and differences in culture and taste block international exchange. Indeed, many goods and services, like housing or personal services are simply not movable and so are not subject to international shipment and competition. As a result, relationships between national markets are seldom in equilibrium. Some barriers may prevent markets from reaching international equilibrium altogether. Others may mean that it takes a long time to attain equilibrium relationships. Examples of the effect of such barriers are persistent balance of payments deficits, disequilibria between purchasing power parity (PPP) exchange rates, large international differences in real wages and prices, and the classic Feldstein-Horioka saving and investment puzzle.[12,13]

The second point is that globalization has several potential dimensions. We may speak about globalization as international integration of markets for goods and services, but we may also speak about integration of financial markets, of labor markets, and even of technology and knowledge. Some of these markets may be far more integrated than others.[14] Whereas there are clearly still important barriers in markets for goods and services, these impediments have been declining as trade restrictions are reduced and as transportation costs have declined. There have also been favorable changes toward the integration of financial markets and the diffusion of knowledge, although the international integration of these markets remains spotty. On the other hand, labor market integration remains much lower.

If labor markets were fully integrated, workers in the low-wage developing countries would migrate to the advanced countries in vast numbers, *and* there would be a strong tendency for wage equalization. (In a high-wage country, one could say wage reduction). If capital and knowledge were also free to move and if there were no transportation costs, it would make no significant difference to costs in what region of the world goods are produced.[15]

But that is not the way the world works. Populations are not free to move, a matter of restrictions on immigration, languages, housing, and cultural factors. Although there has been much attention on high rates of legal and illegal migration, only a small share of populations actually migrate internationally. Wage differentials between developed and developing countries remain high. There has been some migration, of course. And unskilled workers in the advanced countries complain about the effects of foreign competition leading to failure of wages to rise and unemployment. But these changes have not been nearly enough to equalize wages. On the other hand, capital and, to some extent, knowledge are increasingly mobile and that makes it possible to use labor where it can be obtained most cheaply.

As a result, we observe a shift in the location of industrial production from the "old" industrial countries toward East Asia and, specifically in recent years, toward China. Manufactures are being produced cheaply in East Asia and other low-wage countries for export to the West. This change reflects the increasing integration in international markets for goods, and increasing international flows of finance and knowledge, that have enabled the East Asian developing economies to produce goods competitive in world markets. Feenstra (1998) discusses the international outsourcing process under the title the "Integration of Trade and Disintegration of Production in the World Economy."

The linkage between capital and knowledge transfer in foreign direct investment (FDI) has been an important factor in making this possible. Foreign investors, entrepreneurs, and managers, have gone to East Asia to take advantage of the labor market disequilibrium, the low labor costs in the region relative to wages paid in the advanced Western economies. Mobility of capital, knowledge, and goods have taken the place of mobility of labor. Now that production facilities are established, additional FDI seeks to exploit local markets, for example, the automobile industry in China aimed at the burgeoning Chinese market.[16] Since the Chinese supply of unskilled labor is very large—two-thirds of China's population is still on the farm—it will be a long time before the surplus of unskilled workers in the region is exhausted, though in Eastern China the wages of skilled technicians are already rising rapidly.

Semi-globalization and IT

The IT revolution has a special place in these processes. Rapid improvement in communication and transportation has been a critical issue. Many of today's developments would not have been possible only a generation ago. Orders can be communicated instantaneously, worldwide. Logistic controls, air freight, and fast shipping make it possible to link East Asia directly into the multinational supply chain. Merchandise can be produced in China, packaged—even with price labels—and sent directly to the US wholesale warehouse or to specific retail outlets.

As we have noted, most innovative is the international procurement of services that do not require physical shipment. Bangalore and Hyderabad in India and other areas, where there is an underpaid but highly educated population, have become centers of a rapidly growing software industry. Programming, that would cost more than $100 an hour in the United States, can be obtained in developing countries for $10 an hour. A programming job scheduled at closing time in the United States can be supplied from Asia by next morning.

It is too soon to tell how far these developments will go, since we are only at the early stages of a vastly different and more greatly integrated world economy. (East Asian competitiveness is considered in Chapter 10 and likely future developments are considered in Part IV.)

A linked world

With the IT/e-business revolution, the ties between the world's countries in trade, finance, and technology are becoming ever closer. The world's economies are increasingly intertwined. Much of what happens in East Asia depends not only on decisions that are made there but also on developments that originate in the rest of the world economy. This is not only a matter of trade and financial flows. Importantly, in recent years, East Asian countries have opened their markets to foreign business, sometimes as a condition of joining the WTO. Entrepreneurs from the more advanced countries, often from Taiwan and Singapore have developed manufacturing facilities in the region. Many of these operations are more efficient than local businesses, causing these, too, to switch to more sophisticated production techniques.

The new technology and business organization certainly introduce some important new consideration. The laws of economics still apply. But we live in a greatly changed world and these changes do have important implications for the development strategy. We will be looking more closely at the implications in the chapters that follow. This is after all a new world:

- a world with emphasis on technology, skill, and knowledge
- a changing, dynamic competitive world
- a more open world to trade and financial flows
- a linked global world, a smaller world.

Part II
East Asian development

4 East and Southeast Asia

A dynamic but diverse region—overview

Over the past 40 years, East and Southeast Asia has been the most dynamic region in the world. Its rapid pace of development has surprised economists and policy makers, challenging them to explain the mechanisms of growth—economic, political, and cultural—that have energized developments in East Asia. Most of the countries in the region began as poor countries with few resources—even Singapore, today among the richest, was little more than a backwater in the early 1950s. Today, some of the East Asian countries have achieved advanced country living standards, and others are on the way.

According to the World Bank *World Development Report* (various) real Gross Domestic Product (GDP) in the middle- and low-income countries of the region (East Asia and the Pacific[17]) grew at an annual rate of 7.2 percent per year from 1990 to 2003. Average per capita income increased almost as rapidly at 6.0 percent annually. These statistics compare with real GDP growth of 2.5 percent and per capita income growth of 1.8 percent in the high-income countries, largely Europe and North America. Industry accounted for 49 percent of the value-added of the region's output in 2003 as compared to 27 percent in the high-income countries. Capital formation accounts for approximately one-third of the region's output flow as compared to 19 percent in the high-income countries. Merchandise exports in US dollar terms grew almost 12 percent per year between 1990 and 2001. In 2003, manufactures accounted for 80 percent of the region's merchandise exports. Most of these goods are labor-intensive products taking advantage of the region's comparative advantage in labor costs. Since 2003, trends for rapid export-led growth have continued in most of the region's countries.

We can summarize this introductory picture as follows:

- East Asian growth has been very rapid, far exceeding that prevailing in the advanced Western countries historically or currently.
- East Asian growth has been supported by very high rates of saving and capital formation and to a lesser extent by foreign capital.
- East Asian growth has been energized by exports of manufactures that have been growing almost twice as fast as the growth of GDP.
- East Asian manufactures have been principally labor-intensive goods like clothing, shoes, and toys, taking advantage of the region's low labor costs,

but increasingly some East Asian countries have turned to more sophisticated high-tech products.

• The East Asian economies have become increasingly industrialized so that today they are industrial suppliers to the rest of the world.

In this chapter, we will look closely at the statistics and facts of East Asian development, applying a comparative perspective to the East and Southeast Asian countries. (Geographically and culturally, Japan belongs to the East Asian region. It was, in some sense, a pioneer of East Asian development and plays an important role as an investor and importer of East Asian products. Today, Japan is an advanced country and stands somewhat separate from the path of East Asian development. For this reason, we will focus our discussion on the other East Asian countries, bringing in Japan only when it is relevant to our story.)

Taking a geographic overview (Map 1), in the north, South Korea is an industrial power producing cars and TVs for the world. In the middle, China, the world's most populous country with almost 1.3 billion people, is showing economic growth at an astonishingly rapid rate. China is particularly interesting, since it began as a centrally planned socialist economy and is making a rapid transition to an entrepreneurial market system. Further south, Malaysia, Singapore, and Taiwan are rapidly becoming electronic industry powerhouses. Thailand attracts tourists from all over the world to supplement its booming agriculture and industry. It also has hopes of becoming a center for automobile parts production. The Philippines and Indonesia, troubled by political instability, have seen much

Map 1 East and Southeast Asia: a dynamic region.

labor-intensive and resource-based industry but remain at a somewhat lower level of development. On the periphery, Vietnam, Myanmar, Laos, and Cambodia, countries that are making the transition from central control to the market economy, are predominantly agricultural at an early stage development but are hoping also to participate in the East Asian development process, probably through labor-intensive production and assembly activities.

This quick survey shows that while the outstanding development record represents one of the factors common to the entire region, East Asia is also among the most heterogeneous of the world's regions.

The differences between countries are important in explaining the linked growth process—from the more advanced countries to the ones at lower rungs of development—that we describe later in Chapter 5. The differences include the following:

- level of income and industrial structure
- stage of development and technology
- wages, exchange rate, and competitiveness
- size of the domestic market
- openness to trade and foreign investment
- government intervention and entrepreneurship
- cultural considerations.

A spectacular growth record

Most of the East Asian countries have shared in the spectacular record of the region's growth (Table 4.1). But some, like China, have consistently grown more rapidly than others, like the Philippines and Hong Kong. (We show comparable

Table 4.1 Long-term trends in East Asian economic growth

	Growth of real GDP per year			
	1970–80	*1980–90*	*1990–2001*	*2001–6 (est.)*
Hong Kong	9.2	6.9	3.9	3.2
Singapore	8.3	6.6	7.8	3.5
South Korea	10.1	9.4	5.7	4.6
Indonesia	7.2	6.1	3.8	4.3
Malaysia	7.9	5.3	6.5	5.3
Philippines	6.0	1.0	3.3	5.3
Thailand	7.1	7.6	3.8	6.9
China	5.5	10.2	10.0	8.3
United States	2.8	3.0	3.5	3.7
Japan	4.3	4.0	1.3	1.3

Source: World Bank, *World Development Reports*.

Note
est. = estimate.

data for the United States and Japan where growth was 3.5 percent and 1.3 percent, respectively.)[18]

The movement of GDP, year by year, during the tumultuous period beginning in 1996 is shown in Figure 4.1 and Table 4.2. (The forecast statistics for 2004–6 shown in Table 4.2 are country projections assembled by the Economic and Social Commission for Asia and the Pacific (ESCAP 2004) and the United Nations Department of Economic Affairs Project LINK.) As is apparent, some countries took a serious hit into negative growth in 1997, 1998, and 2001, but some like China and Taiwan were able to maintain their financial stability and continued their rapid growth with hardly an interruption. In the more recent years, most countries in East Asia have shown recovery but the growth of some countries has been precarious, subject to financial uncertainties and cyclical forces and remains somewhat slower than in the spectacular growth decades of the 1980s and 1990s. Nevertheless, the

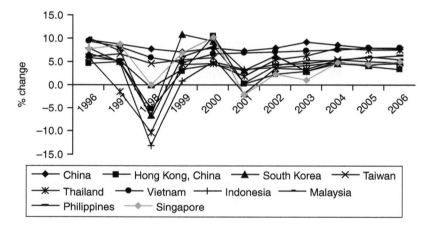

Figure 4.1 Growth of real GDP (percent per year).

Table 4.2 GDP growth (% per year)

	1996	1997	1998	1999	2000	2001	2002	2003	2004[a]	2005[a]	2006[a]
China	9.6	8.8	7.8	7.1	8.0	7.3	8.0	9.1	8.5	8.0	7.8
Hong Kong, China	4.5	5.0	−5.3	3.0	10.5	0.1	2.3	3.0	5.1	4.0	3.4
South Korea	6.7	5.0	−6.7	10.9	9.3	3.0	6.3	3.0	4.5	4.2	5.0
Taiwan	6.1	6.7	4.6	5.4	5.9	−1.9	3.6	3.3	5.4	4.9	4.7
Thailand	5.9	−1.4	−10.5	4.4	4.6	1.8	5.4	6.3	8.0	7.5	7.5
Vietnam	9.3	8.2	5.8	4.8	6.8	6.9	7.0	7.2	7.5	8.0	8.0
Indonesia	7.8	4.7	−13.1	0.8	4.9	3.3	3.7	4.1	4.8	4.4	4.5
Malaysia	10.0	7.3	−7.4	6.1	8.3	0.4	4.1	5.2	5.3	6.0	5.5
Philippines	5.8	5.2	−0.6	3.4	4.4	3.2	4.4	4.5	5.4	5.8	6.3
Singapore	7.7	8.5	−0.1	6.9	10.3	−2.0	2.2	1.1	4.7	4.4	4.9

Source: United Nations Department of Economic and Social Affairs; LINK "Global Economic Outlook," April 2004.

Note

a Forecast.

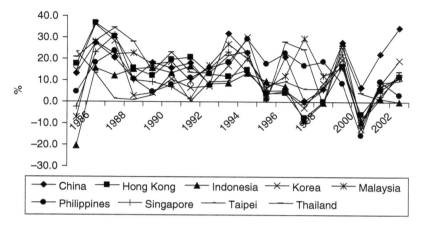

Figure 4.2 Export growth in East Asia, 1988–2003.

continued rapid expansion of China and recovery in many of East Asia's markets have enabled most of the countries in the region to return to a rapid growth mode by 2004.

We begin by asking how successful East Asia has been in its pursuit of international markets. As we have already noted in Chapter 3, the record of East Asian exports has been spectacular, though, in recent years, quite cyclical (Figure 4.2). In all the East Asian countries, exports have been a major driver of growth. Chinese exports have expanded many years by 20–30 percent. In 2002, they are reported to have grown 22.3 percent and even more rapidly, 34.6 percent, in 2003. Other East Asian countries have also shown rapid export growth but, despite substantial devaluations, in recent years many have lagged behind China which in 2003 accounted for $528 billion of exports (including Hong Kong and Macao[19]), about 8.1 percent of world exports and 44 percent of East Asian (other than Japanese) exports.

For a longer-term perspective, for each East Asian developing country, we show total exports (in billions of US$) from 1970 to 2003 and forecasts to 2005 (Table 4.3). The United States and Japan are included for comparison. China has had extremely rapid growth of exports, averaging 15.6 percent per year from 1992 to 2002 to the United States. While growth of Chinese exports to the European Union was slower, their growth compared favorably with that of most other East Asian countries. The growth of exports to Japan was also rapid (10.6 percent per year) in the 1992–2002 period. In recent years, Chinese exports have grown with astonishing rapidity.

In market share terms, Chinese exports have grown steadily. Table 4.4 shows the Chinese share of world exports reaching over 8 percent in 2002. Other East Asian countries show steady increases in their shares of world trade until 1995 and stable or slightly declining shares thereafter. Note that considering their

Table 4.3   Exports, 1970–2005 (in billions of US$)

	1970	1980	1990	1995	2000	2002	2003	2004ᵃ	2005ᵃ
World	298.4	1,921.8	3,377.6	5,079.1	6,387.5	6,478	7,224	8,153	8,728
China	2.3	18.1	62.1	148.8	249.2	325	437	498	548
Hong Kong	2.5	19.8	82.2	173.8	201.9	201.6	227	255	298
Macao	0	0.5	1.7	2	2.5	2.3	2	2	3
China, Hong Kong and Malaysia	4.8	38.4	146	324.6	453.6	528.4	667	755	849
South Korea	0.8	17.5	65	125.1	172.3	162.8	196	233	256
Malaysia	1.7	11.1	29.4	74.1	98.2	93.3	100.5	109.1	115.9
Philippines	1	5.7	8.1	17.5	39.8	35	35.9	38.7	42.3
Thailand	0.7	6.5	23.1	56.5	69.1	63.1	66.1	78.1	85.3
Singapore	1.6	19.4	52.8	118.3	137.8	126.1	145.3	160.1	172.2
Indonesia	1.1	25.2	25.7	45.5	62.1	66	78	85	92
Taiwan	1.4	19.8	76.1	111.6	147.8	138	152	170	184
Japan	19.3	130.4	287.6	443.1	479.2	396.1	427.8	471.8	507
United States	42.7	225.6	393.6	584.7	781.1	711.7	744.5	835.3	937

Source: Computed from International Monetary Fund, *International Financial Statistics*.
Note
a Forecast.

Table 4.4   Shares of world exports (%), 1970–2002

	1970	1980	1990	1995	2000	2002
China, Hong kong and Malaysia	1.6	2.0	4.3	6.4	7.1	8.2
South Korea	0.3	0.9	1.9	2.5	2.7	2.5
Malaysia	0.6	0.6	0.9	1.5	1.5	1.4
Philippines	0.3	0.3	0.2	0.3	0.6	0.5
Thailand	0.2	0.3	0.7	1.1	1.1	1.0
Singapore	0.5	1.0	1.6	2.3	2.2	1.9
Indonesia	0.4	1.3	0.7	0.9	1.0	0.9
Taiwan	0.5	1.0	2.2	2.2	2.3	1.9
Japan	6.5	6.8	8.5	8.7	7.5	6.4
United States	14.3	11.7	11.6	11.5	12.2	10.7

Source: Computed from IMF, *International Financial Statistics*.

relatively small size the trade shares of some East Asian countries such as South Korea (2.5 percent), Singapore (1.9 percent), and Taiwan (1.9 percent) are quite substantial. Japan shows a growing market share until 1990 and loses share, presumably to East Asian competition, thereafter. The United States shows substantial declines in market share (except in 1995–2000) to play a considerably smaller role in world export markets in 2002 than in 1970.

The direction of trade is summarized in Table 4.5. In the 1992–2001 period, exports to the United States were rising rapidly. Export growth from East Asia to the United States has been dominated by China. Growth of Chinese exports to the European Union was much slower, although Chinese exports to Japan grew at

Table 4.5 Direction of trade: long-term growth of East Asian exports (% change per year)

Trade flows from	To United States		To European Union		To Japan	
	1986–92	*1992–2001*	*1986–92*	*1992–2001*	*1986–92*	*1992–2001*
World	6.2	8.4	5.3	1.8	8.1	1.9
Japan	2.6	2.9	11.5	1.4	—	—
China	27.4	15.4	25.7	3.6	3.2	10.6
South Korea	4.2	8.3	13.4	1.6	8.8	3.9
Hong Kong	1.4	−0.2	11.5	1.6	17.7	1.3
Malaysia	16.5	11.0	18.3	3.5	26.0	3.4
Singapore	13.6	3.1	21.1	17.8	17.4	1.4
Thailand	12.6	7.5	18.9	−0.4	27.2	1.5
Indonesia	1.8	8.9	17.0	−5.1	12.3	1.5
Philippines	12.7	10.4	10.6	4.9	19.5	9.4
Vietnam	0	0	35.8	12.5	14.5	15.3
Taiwan	3.2	2.0	17.8	1.6	16.5	1.5

Source: Computed from IMF, *International Financial Statistics*.

10.6 percent per year, much more rapidly than in the 1986–92 period. These statistics are suggestive of the changing patterns of export trade in the East Asian region. Growth of exports is slower in recent years than in the 1986–92 period. But China's exports to the United States and Japan continue to show spectacular growth. Vietnam, operating from a small base, also shows rapid export growth to the European Union and Japan.

We will consider in detail the forces that lie behind the economic development of East Asia in Chapters 5 and 10.

Diversity and growth in East Asia

> An important lesson is that the "East Asian Tigers" are actually a heterogeneous bunch.
>
> (Mahmood and Singh 2003: 1053)

The diversity of East Asian countries is as much an important element of their development process as their commonalities. As we show in (Table 4.6), the countries of East Asia are at very different levels of income and development. This has important consequences, allowing the process of development to sweep from more advanced countries to others at earlier stages.

A summary of the basic statistics for 2004 of the East Asian economies is presented in Table 4.6. Take a look at the enormous range in the size and other characteristics of the countries in the region.

The countries have been ranked in order of per capita income, in US dollars on a purchasing power equivalent basis. The range is approximately from 1 to 10! On one extreme, Singapore, South Korea, and Hong Kong (China) have achieved

Table 4.6 Basic statistics of East Asian countries, 2004

	Income per capita US$ PPP basis	Population (millions)	Area (1000 square km)	Population growth % per year (1990–2003)	% Urban	Education (secondary rate %)		Poverty % of population
						Male	Female	
Hong Kong (China)	25,560	6.7	1.1	1.1	100.0	75	79	—
Singapore	24,910	4.1	0.7	2.2	100.0	128	—	—
Taiwan	20,000 est.	22.4	36.2	0.7	60.0	98	100	0.6
South Korea	18,110	47.3	99.5	0.8	82.5	97	98	7.4
Malaysia	8,340	23.8	328.6	2.4	58.1	93	103	8.1
Thailand	6,550	62.9	510.9	1.8	20.0	87	89	12.9
Philippines	4,360	80.1	298.2	2.2	59.4	77	78	39.4
Indonesia	2,940	213.5	1,811.6	1.3	42.1	77	77	23.4
China	4,260	1,271.1	9,327.4	0.8	38.7	65	58	3.6
Vietnam	2,130	78.9	325.5	1.5	24.5	64	58	37.0

Source: Asian Development Bank, World Bank.

Notes
est. = estimate.
km = kilometers.

per capita income levels almost on a par with the advanced countries—the United States, Europe, and Japan. Many of East Asian countries still remain what the World Bank terms "upper and lower middle income countries."[20] These countries show an average per capita purchasing power only one-third or less than that in the developed world. It would be unrealistic, however, to assume that such countries are entirely low-income rural economies or that all citizens live in poverty. On the contrary, anyone who has seen the modern urban complexes of Bangkok or Shanghai recognizes that even lower middle income countries may have a growing middle class in the big cities, their relatively moderate average income nationwide notwithstanding. Finally, a few East Asian countries—Vietnam, and others not shown, Laos, Cambodia, and Myanmar—are still very low-income countries. Obviously, poverty is closely related to per capita income, and, not surprisingly, the poor countries tend to be predominantly rural and to have low levels of educational participation. It is important to note the inverse relationship between size and income in East Asia. The high-income countries are very small. The large countries in East Asia, particularly the most populous, China, Indonesia, and Vietnam are still at the lower end of the income scale.

As we will see in more detail in Chapter 10, the per capita income data provide important insights about the competitiveness of various countries. Low per capita income corresponds to low wages and is likely to favor competitiveness in labor-intensive industries. Low labor costs are the basis for the export advantage of some East Asian countries in manufactured products like apparel, toys, cell phones, etc. The higher-income countries tend to produce more technologically advanced products that do not depend as much on cheap labor.

Remarkably, economies that were once heavily agricultural are now overwhelmingly industrial (Figure 4.3). The figure shows the share of agriculture, industry, and services in GDP in 1990 and in 2001. The countries are shown in order of their

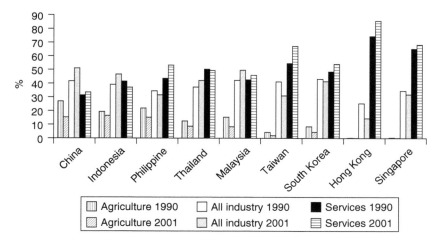

Figure 4.3 Sectoral composition of GDP, 1990–2001.

purchasing power parity (PPP) income, going from the left, the lowest-income countries, to the right, the highest. The declining role of agriculture with economic development is apparent. Agriculture accounts for a smaller share in 2001 than in 1990. Moreover, agriculture becomes less and less important as living standards rise. The urban centers of Hong Kong and Singapore have no local agriculture at all.

East Asia is clearly becoming industrialized. Some of these countries such as Taiwan, Korea, and Singapore are well along the way to becoming modern high-tech economies. Because of its sheer size and growing export industry, China has become a center, if not quite yet *the center*, of the world's manufacturing industry. Other countries, like Indonesia, remain for the most part agricultural or resource-based, though here, too, industry and services are growing rapidly. The industries of East Asia are first of all export oriented, though, as incomes have risen, the domestic market is taking larger shares of their production of consumer goods and equipment. Hong Kong and Singapore and, to a lesser extent, Taiwan and South Korea, have become important centers of service activity. This includes trading activities, management of local and foreign operations, finance and insurance, and some tourism.

Growth and competitiveness

An attempt to evaluate the growth potential of various countries is made in the Growth Competitiveness Rankings produced by the World Economic Forum (WEF). The idea is to produce a rough measure of sustainable growth prospects for many countries.[21] The actual numerical scores obtained do not have much meaning, since they are averages of real data (sometimes called by WEF "hard data") and of opinion surveys ("soft data"). Consequently, the WEF prefers to rank countries giving some indication of their relative position among the 104 developed and developing countries recorded. Table 4.7 shows the growth

Table 4.7 WEF Growth Competitiveness Index 2004 rankings (104 countries)

	Overall	*Technology*	*Public institutions*	*Macroeconomic environment*
China	46	62	55	24
Hong Kong	21	34	9	13
Indonesia	69	73	68	63
Malaysia	31	27	38	20
Philippines	76	61	99	69
Singapore	7	11	10	1
South Korea	29	9	41	35
Taiwan	4	2	27	9
Thailand	34	43	45	23
Vietnam	77	92	82	58
United States	2	1	21	15
Japan	9	5	16	29

Source: WEF (2004) Rankings over 104 countries.

competitiveness rankings for East Asian countries and, for comparison, for Japan and the United States. The results are quite suggestive.

The low per capita income countries are ranked low in terms of overall growth competitiveness. Vietnam, Indonesia, and the Philippines are, respectively, seventy-seventh, sixty-ninth, and seventy-sixth. They are consistently low in their standing on technology, public institutions, and macroeconomic environment. It is interesting to note that WEF ranks China somewhat higher than the other countries with similar incomes, forty-sixth, apparently a result largely of a much more positive evaluation of China's macroeconomic environment. On the other extreme, ranked high, comparably to developed countries like the United States and Japan, are Taiwan and Singapore, fourth and seventh respectively. Taiwan is very high in technology, second, and Singapore is number 1, worldwide, in the appraisal of its macroeconomic environment. The other East Asian countries are ranked somewhat below the leaders, but they still rank well in the top half of the 104 countries considered.

Another insight on the diversity of the East Asian countries looks at technological advancement, one of the factors already considered. In this respect, the lower and mid-income East Asian countries do not do as well as the more advanced ones, so that even China and Thailand rank in the lower half of the countries considered. (We will look further into the basis for this technological ranking in Chapter 7, which considers the digital divide.)

Introducing some content into these figures, Hobday (1995) presents a table of technological stages attained by various Southeast Asian countries. We have expanded this approach to include some additional East Asian countries (Table 4.8).

The ranking of the activities in terms of advancement on a scale of technical development is:

1   assembly
2   process engineering
3   product development
4   management and finance
5   R&D.

The first stage, assembly activities, is labor intensive and takes advantage of low wage rates. Subsequent stages call for more capital or education-intensive activities like engineering, product development, R&D, and management and finance. Only Singapore and Taiwan are at the most advanced level. Singapore is a "headquarters" economy, offering management and financial services to the region. Taiwan is turning increasingly to investing and managing production operations in China. Other East Asian countries still lag, though most of them are advancing rapidly toward more sophisticated operations.

The diversity between the countries with respect to technology and IT potential also shows up in an evaluation of the WEF group (Table 4.9). The scores represent rankings with regard to technology, innovations, and the status of the information communications technology and (ICT) industries.

Table 4.8 Technological stages in Southeast Asia

	Singapore	Taiwan	South Korea	Malaysia	Thailand	China	Indonesia	Vietnam
1960s	Assembly	Assembly	Assembly					
1970s	Process engineering	Assembly	Assembly	Assembly	Assembly			
1980s	Product development	Process engineering	Process engineering	Process engineering	Assembly	Assembly	Assembly	Assembly
1990s	R&D	Product development	Product development	Product development	Process engineering	Process engineering	Process engineering, assembly	Assembly
2000s	Management/ finance, R&D	Product development, Management/ finance	Product development, R&D	Product development	Process engineering, assembly	Product development, assembly	Process engineering, assembly	Assembly

Table 4.9 WEF rankings with respect to technology and innovation 2004

	Technology	Innovations	ICT	Tech transfer
China	62	70	62	37
Hong Kong	34	33	8	n.a.
Indonesia	73	71	74	53
Malaysia	27	41	35	6
Philippines	61	48	72	23
Singapore	11	13	4	n.a.
South Korea	9	7	18	n.a.
Taiwan	2	2	9	n.a.
Thailand	43	37	55	4
Vietnam	92	79	86	66
United States	1	1	7	n.a.
Japan	5	4	15	n.a.

Source: WEF *Global Competitiveness Report 2004–5* (2004). Rankings over 104 countries.

Note
n.a. not available.

Some of the rankings, too, are based on hard numbers, like the availability of cell phones and internet connections whereas others are based on judgmental evaluations in surveys. Note that many of the East Asian countries including China remain far down in worldwide rankings in technology and innovations and the status of ICT industries. On the other hand, Taiwan is in the number 2 position, worldwide, with respect to technology and ICT, and Singapore, Taiwan, and Hong Kong get relatively high rankings in the ICT sector. Technological transfer measures the ease of "in-transfers" of technology and are, consequently, not shown for countries like Singapore that are already exporters of technology. Rankings can, and do, change very quickly as some of the East Asian countries achieve some peaks of technological development.

Intra-country regional disparities

There are also substantial differences in living standards and industries within countries. With the exception of city states like Singapore and Hong Kong, there is great diversity within the countries in the living standards of the countryside, where a good deal of agricultural production remains on a near subsistence basis, and the urban centers that have relatively high income, high consumption economies. Thailand, for example, still has 80 percent of its population in the rural sector and has only one truly large modern city, Bangkok. The case of China is also particularly interesting (Map 2).

> Sharp territorial disparities in China are a long standing phenomenon that date(s) back to the 19th century. The dichotomy of a coastal China, geared towards exports, and an inland China, a supplier of labor and raw materials,

Map 2 The high and low income provinces of China (high income = white, low income = dark).

was to a large extent the result of the "open ports" policy. Forced upon the Qing dynasty by the European powers, it was the consequence of the Opium war and of unequal treaties.

(OECD Territorial
Development Service 2001: 1)

This discrepancy between the East and the West in China persists. The provinces in the East of China, shown in white (Map 1) are the areas that are most heavily industrialized, most involved in export trade, and most closely linked to the world economy. Per capita incomes in the West average one half of those in the Eastern provinces. West of the dividing line, the larger inland part of China, is still far behind. This is the reason for the "Go West" development plan started by the Chinese government in 1999. Perhaps even more important are the discrepancies between life in the modern Chinese city and in the countryside. These remain very large.[22] These discrepancies have their root in the development process that has favored urban development and industry over agriculture. The difference between urban and rural living standards has been a principal factor in the massive migration from rural areas to the cities in China creating a rootless population that may number in the tens, if not hundreds, of millions. Similar discrepancies between life in the country and in the city and migration trends have been a feature of development in most East Asian countries.

Cultural considerations in East Asian development

Social scientists have long debated whether culture is an important, or, indeed, *the important* common factor in East Asian development. In this section, we consider the cultural considerations that may have influenced East Asian growth, in general and in specific East Asian communities.

There is substantial cultural diversity in East Asia. Some of the East Asian countries follow a Confucian/Buddhist tradition. Others, like Malaysia and Indonesia, are Muslim and others may still retain the remnants of a Communist state-led ideology. However, many East Asian countries share an overlay of business carried on by overseas Chinese who have substantial cultural homogeneity and cohesion. This group has played an important role in pushing forward the development of Malaysia, Thailand, and even Indonesia. Taiwan, of course, has significant business financed and organized by Chinese businessmen who migrated in 1947 from mainland China. In turn, these experienced free-market managers have played a very important role in mainland China. Chinese from Hong Kong and overseas Chinese from East Asian countries as well as from the United States are behind many of the new export enterprises concentrated in Eastern China, in Guangdong and Fujian Provinces. In addition to capital and technology, they have brought experience in business management and worldwide contacts that would not have been available to Chinese brought up under the managed economy system.

The old theme of cultural or religious considerations as a factor in economic development has been revived to explain the spectacular growth of East Asia (Harrison and Huntington 2000). Values related to Confucian and Buddhist traditions—a collectivist view in which the group takes precedence over the individual and in which harmony, respect, and top-down relationships prevail— are said to lie behind the success of East Asian business. We will term this view the "Asian values, Asian success" (AVAS) paradigm. There is no agreement, however, on the precise cultural traits that foster rapid development. It has been argued that thrift and hard work lead to capitalist growth. That was Max Weber's (Weber 1904–5) original view with respect to the impact of the Calvinist reformation on European development. The AVAS argument would have it that East Asian development is a result of Asian cultural characteristics such as group cohesion, respect for family, and work ethic. Landes (2000) argues that "Culture makes almost all the difference" (Harrison and Huntington 2000: 2).

How such ideas can be extended to economic development in East Asia has been subject to dispute. There is no doubt that businesses relying more on established personal relationships than on formal governance and legal procedures have operated widely in East Asia. Many of these have been family-owned enterprises. Much of the entrepreneurial activity in the region has been fostered by the overseas Chinese community, even in countries like Indonesia and Malaysia where the Chinese ethnic group represents a minority. At the early stage of development, the family-based relationship system led to "economically efficient use of limited entrepreneurial abilities, internal financing, and effective monitoring" (Khan 1999). Relationship networking, *guanxi*, helps to explain the rapid expansion of Chinese investments in the coastal areas of China (Perkins 2000).[23] Whether this is a matter of cultural values, of traditional relationship patterns, or of family-based firms is not certain.

On one hand, it is true that the East Asian countries typically have high savings and investment rates. Confucian values also put strong weight on group cohesiveness and self-development, qualities that can be said to play a part in organizational strength and expansion of human capital and a long-term perspective. As Fukuyama has pointed out (Fukuyama 1995), relationship-based connections are useful in fostering interaction among Chinese ethnic group members in a small-scale regional setting, but they may not be a good basis for operating large firms in a global environment. Fukuyama is concerned with the increasing difficulty of "trust" as the scope of business operations widens. In the same vein, Khan (1999) questions the effectiveness of the family-based system at a more advanced stage of development in view of the need for outside financing and independent monitoring. For this reason, a number of economists have argued that the relationship-based financial system, sometimes referred to derisively as "crony capitalism," may have contributed to the 1997 crisis. "[T]here was for a time much talk about an Asian model of economic development. But then, even more suddenly in the late 1990s, there came crises and collapses...A decade of hype about superior 'Asian values' was tellingly deflated." (Pye 2000: 244)

Fortunately, another strain of thinking suggests that while cultural values between East and West and among the East Asian countries may differ, there is likely to be increasing convergence: "What we are witnessing, in many ways, is the emergence of the core of an international economic culture that cuts across traditional cultural divides and will increasingly be shared" (Porter 2000: 27).[24] Increasing communication and globalization may contribute to this convergence process.

There is little doubt that the entrepreneurialism of the East Asian Chinese community has contributed to East Asian growth and is continuing to do so. But, even if one were to support an "Asian values, Asian success" explanation for East Asian growth in the past, one may be more skeptical about its use to project the future IT/e-business economy. Perkins says it well:

> Organizational forms that were effective in exploiting one state of technology can turn out to be liabilities with newer technologies. This having been said, it is true that several of the East Asian economies have recovered more rapidly than many expected, and the recovery doubtlessly reflects in part the same cultural factors that contributed to the rapid growth of recent decades.
> (2000: 255)

Institutions and government

> A clear lesson that emerged from the Asian crisis is that strong "market economy fundamentals"—including institutions, regulatory frameworks, and business practices—are essential for sustaining rapid growth, and increasing resilience to shocks in countries that are rapidly integrating into the world economy.
> (Kato 2004: 3)

The evidence of the 1997 crisis suggests that many difficulties could have been avoided if government policies and public regulatory institutions had maintained a more stable economic pace and had assured the soundness of the credit system. Some economists have argued that solid institutions concerned with macro-economic and exchange rate policy are often more important than the specific choice of policy and exchange rate regime (Calvo and Mishkin 2003). The same can be said, perhaps even more forcefully, of institutions involved in micro-economic issues. A well-developed sound financial sector is a primary require-ment for maintaining stable growth. Banks play an important role in financing the East Asian economies, but they must avoid crony capitalism and/or unrealistic credit expansion. The corporate sector must be sound, competitive and, preferably, open. Finally, legal institutions must be supportive of contractual relationships and must permit expeditious bankruptcy proceedings, when these are needed.

The East Asian countries differ markedly in the maturity of their institutions. Moreover, they differ greatly with respect to public sector regulatory supervision of the banking system as well as of business enterprise in general. On the other hand, there is a narrow line to tread. Regulatory restraints and intervention have often been a constraint on growth and entrepreneurship, but some policies are essential to maintaining a stable macro environment.

Some countries are politically and economically stable; others have lacked stability, as the 1997 crisis demonstrated so clearly. There is little doubt that stability is important for rapid development and that political problems contribute to economic difficulties. The frequent problems of the Philippines point in that direction as do the recent difficulties in Indonesia. Strong governments seem to be able to better control economic policy. In East Asia, strong governments have not been inimical to economic success as they have in some other parts of the world.

There is considerable controversy with respect to the role of government in East Asian development. (For a detailed discussion, see Chapter 8.) The literature on the relationship between government and economic success remains inconclu-sive. In addition to the question of interventionists versus laissez-faire policies, there is the related issue of autocratic versus democratic government. East Asia has some powerful examples of countries where more or less autocratic govern-ments have intervened to advance economic development and have done so with great success. Singapore is an important example. Other countries like Thailand have achieved rapid growth with much less interventionist policies. And we must not forget that China in transition from socialist economy to a market economy has shown remarkable entrepreneurship.[25]

In any case, a market economy is not always congruent with Western style political democracy. Democratic governments in the American or Western European mold are relatively new in East Asia. It is not possible to establish a firm link between political democracy and the effective operation of free markets.

There are big differences among the East Asian countries with regard to indus-trial structure and market intervention. Some countries encouraged industrial combines and intervened in their operations—Korea, for example. Others relied

Firm size

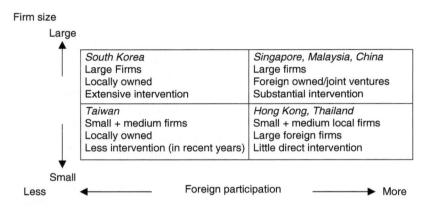

Figure 4.4 Diversity of foreign participation and size of firms.

more on competitive markets with small or medium size firms. China, with its history of state-owned and provincially owned large-scale manufacturing firms and banks, is a special case. The links between the characteristics of industrial organization and economic progress are not clear.

The East Asian countries used to differ substantially with regard to the degree they were open to foreign investment although today many barriers have been taken down. Figure 4.4 illustrates this diversity with respect to firm scale and to foreign participation. The figure focuses on a long-term period, although it would do well to remember that significant changes occurred in these countries in various phases of their development. Differences in the scale of enterprises are noted in the vertical direction. In the horizontal direction, we follow a perspective of foreign participation from relatively small participation by foreign direct investors or managers (closed) on the left to wide involvement by foreign investors and managers (open) on the right. In the upper left quadrant, South Korea, following closely on the Japanese model, was a country with large industrial groups (chaebols). There were strict limits on foreign investment, although these have been relaxed in recent years. Taiwan relied more heavily on the actions of smaller entrepreneurial enterprises and Thailand sought, successfully, to attract foreign investment.

Socio/political considerations that may influence development have been different among the countries in the region. The WEF group makes an appraisal of political conditions as part of its growth competitiveness index. The country rankings for the political component are shown in Table 4.10. The essentials of this WEF ranking focus on the quality of institutions as measured from the perspective of contracts and laws and as seen from the perspective of corruption. With the striking exception of Singapore and Hong Kong, who are ranked higher than the United States and Japan, the WEF evaluations place most of the East Asian countries substantially down the list. Note particularly Indonesia and the Philippines that are sixty-eight and ninety-ninth, respectively, in the overall

Table 4.10 WEF evaluation of institutions

	WEF Public Institutions Index 2004		
	Overall	*Contracts/law*	*Corruption*
China	55	54	60
Hong Kong	9	13	4
Indonesia	68	59	73
Malaysia	38	33	44
Philippines	99	79	100
Singapore	10	10	7
South Korea	41	43	50
Taiwan	27	31	24
Thailand	45	45	52
Vietnam	82	55	97
United States	21	19	21
Japan	16	20	11

Source: WEF *Global Competitiveness Report 2004–5* (2004). Rankings among 104 countries.

ranking for institutions and seventy-third and one hundredth (out of 104) with respect to corruption.

It is probably wise not to take such evaluations too seriously. Clearly, this has not proved a barrier to foreign enterprise entry into China, a country that is way down the list. But it may account for the fact that few Western enterprises "go it alone" and that most of them form joint ventures with Chinese partners. We will consider the role of government in promoting economic development in connection with promoting IT at greater length in Chapter 8.

Conclusion

The surge of East Asia from poor largely agricultural producers to industrial leaders is visible throughout the region. One is tempted to ask what it is that these countries have in common that explains their rapid development. Besides their geographic proximity, the countries of the East Asian region have many things in common but not all of them would appear to be conducive to rapid development. There is a common cultural overlay that some experts see as an important factor. Emphasis on education, on family relationships and teamwork and on commercial success (on the part of the overseas Chinese) are widespread in the region. Governments have put high priority on development, though not all have used the same mechanisms. Export promotion (EP) has been a general theme, particularly since it is consistent with the comparative advantage of low labor costs. On the other hand, many of these countries were ravaged by war, they have little in the way of resources (with the exception of Indonesia), and they were originally poor not only in terms of income but also in terms of infrastructure and technology.

We have shown in this chapter that there has been and still is considerable diversity between the countries of the region. Some countries have pioneered development, achieving a high level of per capita output and income and sophisticated technology. Others have lagged. Some countries had very small domestic markets, but others offer huge market potential. Some have relied heavily on foreign direct investment (FDI), as others have sought to develop productive abilities on their own. Public sector interventions have been very different. Indeed, some countries still have some vestiges of their communist past.

In Chapter 5, we will argue that diversity has been an essential ingredient in the growth of the East Asian economies. East Asian growth has been a process taking advantage of the competitive advantage of one country after another, allowing them in turn to reach higher and higher stages of development.

5 Development economics, the ITC revolution, and East Asian growth

The rapid economic development of East Asia has changed many preconceived notions about the development process. The decline in transport and communication costs and the new mix of products associated with globalization and the ITC revolution have sharply changed the development perspective. This experience and the resulting views about what it takes to improve living standards has also had a significant impact on development policy.

Development economics

Traditional development economists were quite pessimistic. Since the middle of the nineteenth-century, economics has been known as the "dismal science."[26] This is because economists used to think that prospects for economic development were, well, dismal: that poor countries would not be able on their own to increase their living standards. A number of vicious circles seemed to block economic development:

- Malthusian (Malthus 1798) view saw growing population and limited resources as barriers to economic improvement. If living standards rose above bare subsistence, more children would survive. A larger population would have an increasingly hard time raising enough food from the limited available land resources. There would be a decline in living standards back to a subsistence level.
- Low income permitted only low rates of saving and, in turn, only low rates of investment and capital accumulation. A poor country was thought to be forever short of capital.
- Low-income societies had inadequate education and would not support the high technology that is required for economic progress.

But East Asia proved the economists wrong. East Asia's phenomenal growth experience shows how far from reality the pessimists were. East Asian growth reflects virtuous circles rather than vicious ones. What are these virtuous circles?

- As per capita income levels rise, population growth declines. What Malthus had not anticipated was that with rising incomes, people tend to have fewer children. This is because with progress has come urbanization and in an urban environment, children are harder to bring up and are not useful tending the fields or milking the cows. China, of course, supplemented such natural tendencies with its "one child per family" policy, although enforcement of this approach has not been strict in recent years. Thailand claims to be a leader in promoting birth control practices among rural women. Certainly, as income and educational levels rise, there are increasing incentives and means to limit the size of families. Once living standards have begun to rise, population does not "outrun subsistence."

- As income levels grow, the economy's stock of capital increases. The Malthusian assumption of a fixed or slowly increasing resource base is no longer appropriate. Quite the contrary. Rising incomes cause people to save more. (Adams and Prazmowski 2003; Modigliani and Cao 2004). High rates of domestic saving are characteristic of the East Asian economies. Some people have argued that this is a cultural trait (Harrison and Huntington 2000) but most economists are not so sure. High saving rates in turn have made possible high rates of investment. The stock of capital is growing rapidly. Moreover, domestic saving has been supplemented by foreign capital inflows, as foreign investors recognize the opportunities in East Asia.

- As income levels grow, more money can be allocated to education. Education levels rise rapidly enabling improved technology and management. In East Asia, educational standards have been increasing rapidly. Compulsory education has been extended to a minimum of nine years in most countries, though the rules are frequently not enforced. Increasing numbers of people are attending universities and technical schools. However, lags in technological capability still represent a serious barrier to progress in some countries of East Asia. (We discuss the "digital divide" in Chapter 7.)

- Technology, too, creates virtuous circles. As technology improves there are increasing potentials for applying new techniques. In the past few years, we have observed a faster pace of technological change and innovation, what we have termed the ICT/e-business revolution. New technology is based on or derived from a base of existing technology. The greater the technological and educational base, the greater the potential for technological advancement. Today's emerging countries have available to them a vast body of knowledge already being used in more advanced economies. For them, technical change is not so much a matter of "reinventing the wheel" as it is applying more advanced, often more capital intensive and technologically sophisticated, production and management techniques that are already available. Below the "technological frontier" at which we find only the most advanced countries, the more sophisticated the economy, the greater its potential for further progress. Technical change has been taking place with increasing rapidity in East Asia.

- Improved communications and transportation technology facilitate trade and financial links between the advanced countries and the developing economies. This enables greater international specialization and competition, further advancing economic development.

Rather than being kept permanently in check by vicious circles, the East Asian countries have found themselves in a world of virtuous circles favoring rapid economic development. Whether this favorable situation is the result of policy, of appropriate institutions, or of culture is still a subject of vigorous debate. There is little question, though, that globalization and the IT/e-business revolution offer many new opportunities for further advancement.

Output, inputs, and technological change

We turn toward another perspective on growth: how economists explain economic growth and, specifically, what lies behind the rapid growth of East Asian countries.

Economists usually divide discussions of growth of the economy's output—its Gross Domestic Product (GDP)—into two parts, that attributable to inputs and that attributable to technological change.

$$\text{Total growth of output} = \text{Growth attributable to growth of inputs} + \text{Growth attributable to "technical change"}$$
(5.1)

This is a simple, some people would say simplistic, statement. Inputs consist of capital and labor (and land). In practice, the effect of "technical change" is measured as a residual:

$$\text{Total growth of output} - \text{Growth attributable to growth of inputs} = \text{Growth attributable to "technical change"}$$
(5.2)

so that "technical change" represents the residual, the gain in productivity, output per unit of input. It is defined to include all the factors that might account for the growth of output other than increases in inputs. This means that category may include not just technical change but also the effects of economies of scale, improvements in management, the shift from low productivity to high productivity activities, and, negatively, the cost of pollution abatement.

We can describe the production relationship in two dimensional terms by holding constant for labor input; we measure growth in terms of the percent change per year of output per person. The contribution of input of capital is measured as the capital intensity of production, capital stock per person.

$$\text{GDP}/L = a \times K/L + b \times \text{Technology}$$
(5.3)

Output per capita (GDP/L), labor productivity, depends on capital per capita (K/L), capital intensity, and technology. The coefficient a declines as K/L increases. As we have noted, the other element accounting for gains in productivity is usually referred to as technology, although most economists will use that term broadly including improved management and resource allocation.

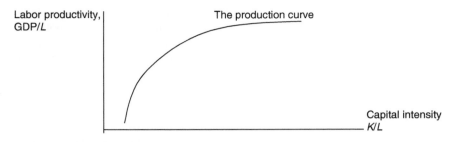

Figure 5.1 A simple production curve.

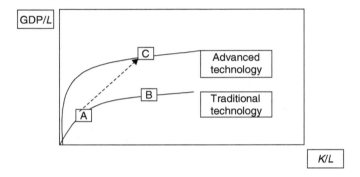

Figure 5.2 Production possibilities with technological change.

We show the relationship between output and increased quantities of capital in Figure 5.1. To allow for two-dimensional presentation, the chart holds labor inputs constant and tracks output only in relationship to increased inputs of capital. In the vertical direction, we show productivity, output per worker. In the horizontal direction, we show the capital intensity of production, capital per worker. The line shows the relationship between productivity and the capital intensity of production. Technology is assumed fixed. Note that as each worker has more machinery, that is, as capital intensity increases, output increases rapidly at first but then the line flattens, that is, each additional unit of capital input produces a smaller increase in output, what economists call *diminishing returns*. If a country continues to use its traditional technology, the addition of more capital will do less and less to increase living standards. Indeed, eventually productivity fails to increase with additions of capital, when the production curve flattens.

In Figure 5.2, we introduce technical change to shift the production curve upward. The lower line shows what a country can do using its traditional technology. The upper line shows what can be achieved by using the technology of the most advanced countries. The difference between the two lines represents the effect of adopting new technology. Supposing a country starts at point A, it can improve its performance by using more capital along the traditional technology production function line to position B. But ultimately, the addition of still more capital with the traditional technology adds little to output.

At first neoclassical growth theorists introduced technological change simply as an exogenously determined input into the growth process. More advanced endogenous growth theories (Arrow 1962; Romer 1986, 1990) have made technical progress part of the theory itself, arguing that knowledge capital has externalities and does not incur diminishing returns and that there is learning-by-doing.[27]

How can a country avoid diminishing returns? It must move from one production function to a higher one. That calls for using new technology. As we have noted above, the term *technology* must be interpreted very broadly here. It is not just a matter of using more technically advanced production processes. It can simply mean producing manufactures rather than agricultural products, doing a better job of management, etc. If a country introduces new technology in that sense, it has the potential to go from A to C, a gain in productivity taking advantage of new knowledge and technology. Though this remains a matter of some disagreement as we see in the next paragraph, it appears to be what is going on in East Asia. Improvements in production and management methods have enabled the East Asian economies to move rapidly to higher and higher production functions. Typically, this has meant shifting to more sophisticated production methods and more technologically advanced industries. The introduction of IT-based products and e-business will enable further technological shifts.

Lack of flexibility with regard to new technology was an important factor in explaining why increasingly capital-intensive state-owned industries in the Soviet Union and China failed to make progress in the 1970s and 1980s. Diminishing returns to capital were the basis for theoretical arguments that capital accumulation would soon run out of impact and that technological change was necessary for long-run growth. Some economists have taken the unlikely position that there was little technical change in some parts of East Asia. "The assertion that 'perspiration' rather than 'innovation' explained the Asian miracle caused some consternation in the region" (Kato 2004: 3).[28] Indeed, during the years of rapid growth in Singapore, the growth of inputs into production was staggeringly high; investment represented 30 and 50 percent of GDP. (Figure 5.3, horizontal axis). Referring to Singapore, in a classic article entitled "The Myth of the Asian

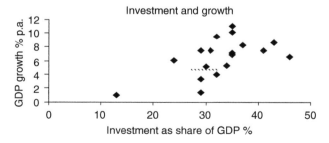

Figure 5.3 Investment and economic growth.

Miracle," Paul Krugman (1994b) wrote that there was no miracle; it was all "input-based" growth. Inevitably, as production becomes more capital-intensive, growth would slow—diminishing returns, once again. Others have argued that if we also take account in our calculations the contribution of the growth of knowledge and the interaction between investment and knowledge there would be nothing left over to call a "miracle" (Young 1995; Lau 1998). But that approach throws the baby out with the bathwater. If you account separately for the contribution of knowledge, there is little left to call technological change.

The above discussions notwithstanding, technological change is an important ingredient in the East Asian growth. This is all the more so as production turns from traditional manufactures to IT products and services. Technical progress in East Asia is both of external and internal origin. Foreign entrepreneurs, some from other parts of East Asia, particularly from Taiwan, and some foreign multinational companies have set up production operations in China and elsewhere in the region, contributing knowledge of production operations as well as capital. But endogenous technical change resulting from "learning-by-doing," from changes in the structure of production, improvements in the scale of output, shifts between various types of products, etc. has also taken place.

Investment and growth

Investment can play a dual role in increasing labor productivity. First, investment increases the stock of capital causing production to move to the right on the production curve in Figure 5.1. Second, in accord with endogenous growth theories, new investment often implies the use of new more advanced technology. Investment often represents a move to a new higher technology production function, that is, the fancy new machine usually takes advantage of the most advanced technology. Modern growth economics focuses on the interaction between capital accumulation and technological improvement. The substitution of robotics for electro-mechanically controlled weaving machines is an example. In East Asia, increasing investment has been closely linked to the use of more advanced techniques, particularly among foreign-owned firms who first introduced their home technologies along with new machinery.

The relationship between investment and East Asian growth is clearly apparent in Figure 5.3. This graph shows the relationship between growth and investment in East Asia covering a number of countries over a period of 20 years, 1980–90 and 1990–7. Each dot represents a country and a time period. In the vertical direction, we measure the growth rate and in the horizontal direction we measure investment as a share of GDP. For example, the highest point on Figure 5.3 represents the performance of China in the 1990s. The scatter diagram shows a broad positive relationship: as anticipated, growth is more rapid the greater investment share. Since numerous other factors also influence the rate of GDP growth, the fit is not very precise.

The persistently high level of investment in China, amounting to 40–50 percent of GDP is illustrated in Figure 5.4. Other East Asian countries have also had high rates of investment, certainly compared to the advanced countries in Europe and

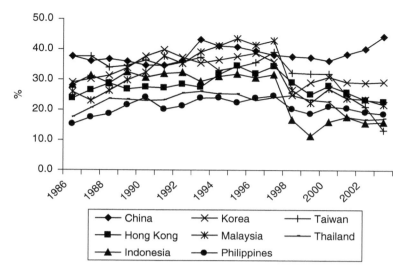

Figure 5.4 Gross domestic fixed investment as percentage of GDP.

North America, but the share of investment shows a more cyclical pattern and has been significantly lower than in China in recent years. There are likely to be significant implications for the growth rates of the various East Asian countries.

Exports and growth

Exports have been a critical factor in East Asian growth. Traditionally countries have favored exports because they earn foreign exchange and they create employment in the exporting industries. Exports exploit a country's comparative advantage—low labor cost in the early stages of East Asian development. But perhaps the most important linkage of exports to East Asian development has been the need to produce quality products to world market specification, meeting the competition of other world producers. This has forced firms to improve quality and performance. Export production has important externalities. Once firms in a country learn to produce goods competitively for the export markets, firms supplying the domestic market typically follow suit. Export production has consequently been an important force for development and, specifically, for product and productivity improvement.

The linkage between exports and growth is apparent in Figure 5.5, growth in GDP related to growth of exports. Each point refers to a country during the periods 1980–90 and 1990–7. We have omitted later data because of the effect of the East Asian crisis. The faster the growth of exports, the faster the growth of the economy as a whole. The highest point is, again, China in 1990–7. The laggards in the lower left of the diagram are Indonesia and the Philippines.

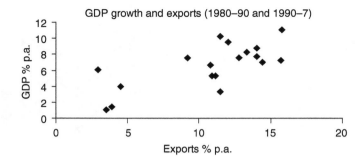

Figure 5.5 Exports and economic growth.

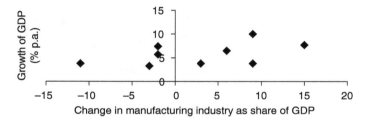

Figure 5.6 Industrialization and growth in East Asia, 1990–2001.

Industrialization and growth

Finally, a very important factor that is often neglected or misunderstood is simply the shift in the structure of output with economic development that shows up as an improvement in productivity. Clearly as countries increase the role of industry—in poor countries this means a shift from subsistence—agriculture to manufacturing, there is an improvement in measured aggregate productivity. This could occur even if there is no productivity improvement within sectors themselves, though often there is intra-industry improvement in productivity as well. Figure 5.6 shows growth of GDP in the vertical direction and the change in the share of manufacturing on the horizontal axis during the 1990–2001 period. The point farthest to the right is Vietnam, a poor country at the beginning of the industrialization process. China shows the highest growth rate. The countries that were growing slowly are Hong Kong, that was shifting industry to neighboring provinces of China, and countries that were hard hit by the 1997 crisis or by political instability like Thailand, Indonesia, and the Philippines. The share of manufacturing industry in GDP is declining modestly in South Korea and Singapore since these were already relatively advanced countries that were shifting into services and sophisticated IT products. The underlying data treat industry as one class. As a result switches between industries, from low-productivity to high-productivity industries, are not considered. These kinds of changes may be the most important ones for the countries that lead East Asian development.

It is apparent from the scatter of the points in the chart that industrialization is not the only factor influencing growth. Indeed, as countries become more advanced, industry tends again to take a back seat to growing services production.[29]

Technical change and new economy

In spite of the disputes among experts that we have noted above, we can be quite sure that technical change plays an important role in the development of East Asia. Most of the countries in the region are not yet at the technological frontier and still have much room to absorb modern technology. The new economy has a vital impact, not so much directly as in the changes that lower communication and transportation costs have made possible. In some countries, the new economy is changing the structure of production, for example in Taiwan, where many PCs and high-tech electronic consumer products are being built. But many of the East Asian countries are not quite yet at the point where the "new economy" has had major direct impact on the products they produce. We can be sure, though, that sophisticated infrastructure like computer networks, broadband connections, and wireless is being installed in this region as in others. These play an important role in linking East Asian producers to each other and to the world economy.

Acquisition of knowledge is an essential ingredient for IT-based development. Advanced engineering technology is central. But modern manufacturing and e-business also depend on less technical aspects of knowledge, for example, advanced management techniques such as inventory controls, "six sigma" quality programs, supply chain optimization, etc. How the factory floor is organized— whether the site is kept clean and neat, whether production is located sequentially, and how parts and supplies are handled—may make the difference between whether or not products are competitive and meet world market specifications. The application of new technologies and, especially, new economy management and e-business may take a while to achieve widespread application.

The requisite information may be acquired by *assimilation* or by *invention*.[30,31] Enterprises not yet operating at the world technological frontier can improve total factor productivity quickly by adopting or adapting techniques already in use in more advanced countries elsewhere. There are a number of ways of acquiring foreign technology. Advanced capital goods frequently embody the latest technological wrinkles. Alliances or licensing agreements may provide patented technology, and managers and engineers may be sent for training abroad. As we have noted, technology transfer is one of the signal advantages of foreign direct investment (FDI) or joint venture enterprises. The foreign investor sets up a production facility and transfers to it technical and management knowledge as in his home country.[32]

Technological skills are also not yet sufficiently developed in some countries to make high-tech manufacturing competitive, or, even, possible. There is widespread fear that a high-tech approach will create foreign-owned enclaves, using techniques that are not transferred to local operations. For this reason, some countries have preferred to develop their own new technologies through R&D, experimentation, and experience. But this may pose difficult, if not insurmountable, challenges. The farther a country's technology is from the technological frontier, the greater the difficulty of inventing its own production processes and the greater the advantage of technological assimilation.

The East Asian development process

As we have noted, East Asian development has turned on its head the notion that developing countries cannot grow. East Asian development is not unique in the context of world history. After all, even the most advanced countries started out poor countries a couple of hundred years ago. What has been unique about East Asian development has been its spectacular speed. In the course of two generations some of these countries have risen to advanced country living standards. Others are well on the way. How can we explain this spectacular growth process?

The S-Curve of East Asian development

There are a number of ways to describe the East Asian growth process. One approach is to see it as the "takeoff" of a jet airplane, in this case from low-income traditional production to high-income advanced technology (Rostow 1960). Rostow saw five development stages:

- the traditional society
- the preconditions for a take-off
- the take-off
- the drive to maturity
- the high mass consumption economy.

Such a path is described, on the basis of real country data, in Figure 5.7.

On the vertical, axis we show for each country GDP per capita in the mid-1990s, before the 1997 crisis, in thousands of dollars, purchasing power parity (PPP) adjusted. The horizontal axis is harder to explain. We show for each country *the number of years since the start of rapid growth*. That means, for Japan, for example the 50 years since the Second World War. Other countries began their growth spurt somewhat later. Singapore began after separation from Malaysia in the early 1960s. China started in the late 1970s when its leaders opened toward the West and turned toward building a market economy.

The points lie fairly neatly along an S-curve. At the beginning when growth has just started, it seems to be relatively slow—Vietnam, Cambodia. Then in the mid-period, some 20–30 years, growth is extremely rapid—China, Thailand, Malaysia. During this time, the growing countries can acquire industries and make use of technologies that have already been developed by countries that are

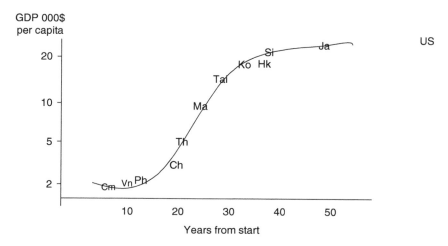

Figure 5.7 The S-Curve of East Asian development.

ahead of them along the development process. And finally, when countries mature, growth seems to go more slowly—Singapore. The most advanced countries are, presumably, the ones putting into place the most technically sophisticated systems, many of which they have to develop for themselves.

This picture, that seems to describe East Asian growth quite well, lacks an underlying theoretical rationale. Why should growth take this path? What causes growth to be initiated? Is there a dynamic that will cause the growth path to continue? And we must be aware of the fact that some developing countries have run into difficulties along the way. The 1997 East Asian financial crisis is an example.

The flying geese pattern of development

The flying geese pattern (Akamatsu 1962; Kojima 2000) is another figurative way to describe the development process and to give it a rationale (Figure 5.8). Have you ever been up early on a spring morning to see the geese flying in formation on their migration northward? There is a lead goose and the others follow. The idea here is exactly the same. There is a lead country and the others follow using the same strategy and same policies. Japan might have been the leader showing the way. Then, we might see Korea and Taiwan, and further behind, Malaysia and Thailand, etc. The idea is that all of them must follow the same trail, using similar policies, as they advance along the development path from underdevelopment to a modern economy. Is that really fact?

There is a little something to this analogy. Some countries did indeed follow the leaders. The focus on export markets was a common pattern. South Korean development policies were very similar to those of Japan, as we see in Chapter 8. There was a great deal of industrial planning, an emphasis on large industrial

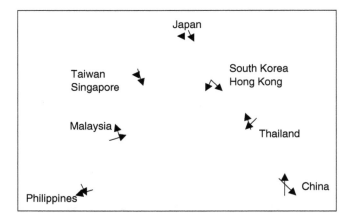

Figure 5.8 The flying geese pattern.

conglomerates (called *chaebols*) in Korea, building of heavy industry, and focus on export markets. But other countries did it somewhat differently. Taiwan had much more emphasis on small- and medium-size enterprises, though at early stages it also relied heavily on government/business cooperation and planning (Wade 1990). In contrast, Hong Kong, under British rule, minimized direct government intervention, taking a liberal free market approach and eschewing infant industry protection. Singapore relied much more than the others on foreign direct investment (FDI). Thailand provided investment incentives through its Board of Investment. Malaysia promoted specific industries and technological infrastructure, its indigenous automobile industry and high technology cities linked by fiber optic information systems. Geographic proximity and cultural affinity no doubt had much to do with the common elements of development strategy in East Asian countries.

The flying geese pattern is an interesting analogy, but it also does not provide a solid explanation for the East Asian growth phenomenon. In particular, it misses the movement of one country after another toward greater sophistication in its industries, observed in East Asia. We need to look at this phenomenon to find out what motivates the connection between growth in the more advanced countries and the ones that are following behind.

The development ladder

Akamatsu's early work already pointed to a rationale for East Asian development based on changing patterns of comparative advantage as countries advance. The basic idea that changing patterns of comparative advantage cause industries to shift from advancing countries to those behind them in terms of economic development fits in well with Vernon's classic product cycle (Vernon 1966, 1975).

Table 5.1 The stages of the development ladder

Stage 1	Primary products	Abundant cheap land and labor
Stage 2	Labor intensive manufactures	Low-cost labor
Stage 3	High-tech manufactures	Capital intensive, technically sophisticated products
Stage 4	Servies (high level)	Educated labor force

East Asian growth can be described as a growth ladder, a hierarchical process leading countries stepwise from primary production to ever more sophisticated production sectors. (Balassa 1979; Chenery and Syrquin 1989; Adams 1998). Beginning in the post–Second World War years, as primary product producers, largely in agriculture, these countries have moved, one after another, up the manufacturing technology scale, from simple labor-intensive assembly, clothing, and shoes to more advanced mechanical products such as automobiles, electronics, and high-tech capital goods. Behind these steps lie profound changes in competitiveness related to rising labor costs, appreciating exchange rates, and growing availability of capital and advanced technology in the leading countries (Table 5.1). As a country advances, living standards rise, and labor cost increases. Even though there are often large gains in productivity, labor-intensive industries lose competitiveness. For many products, it is cheaper to produce elsewhere where labor cost is lower. Industries migrate to the lower labor cost countries that are also, of course, at lower rungs of the development ladder.

Where does the IT/e-business economy belong on this scale? Principally in Stages 3 and 4 of Table 5.1, although assembly of consumer electronics is already an important Stage 2 activity. Manufacturing of advanced electronic equipment for computation and communication—chips, routers—are sophisticated Stage 3 activities. Financial and communications centers, computer programming, and the establishment of e-businesses fall into Stage 4, requiring computer network facilities, highly qualified labor, and, particularly, a cluster of related high-tech firms such as network support and programming enterprises. These innovative activities have advanced most rapidly in an entrepreneurial environment where venture capital supports bright young technologists.

Historically, the results of such a process in East Asia are summarized in Table 5.2. The table shows the changing situation of the East Asian countries from 1965 until the current 15-year period ending in 2010. The groupings are intended to describe the principal emphasis of each economy. No country's activities fall exclusively into one category. We mean to give a broad description of the nature of the production processes that are being carried on, although, at any time, a country may have some industries at higher stages and also some at lower ones.

In the earliest period, 1950–65, only Japan and Hong Kong were manufacturing economies. These countries were pioneers in what has been termed export-led growth. Other countries of East Asia were still primarily agricultural. In the next

Table 5.2 East Asia and the production cycle

	The stages of the product cycle process			
	1950–65	*1965–80*	*1980–95*	*1995–2010*
Stage 1	China Korea Taiwan Phillippines Malaysia Indonesia Thailand Singpore	Thailand Malaysia China Indonesia Philippines	Indonesia Philippines Vietnam	Laos Cambodia Myanmar
Stage 2	Japan Hong Kong	Taiwan Singapore Hong Kong South Korea Japan	Thailand Malaysia China	Indonesia Philippines Vietnam Thailand China Malaysia
Stage 3			Taiwan Singapore Hong Kong South Korea Japan	Taiwan South Korea Japan
Stage 4				Singapore Hong Kong

15 years, Taiwan, Singapore, and South Korea developed important labor-intensive manufacturing industries such as apparel, toys, athletic shoes, consumer electronics, etc. Beginning in the 1980s, Japan, Taiwan, Singapore, Hong Kong, and South Korea also became producers of high-tech products, Japan, particularly in the advanced machinery and equipment area, while the others became producers of chips, computer peripherals, and telecom gear.

A still more advanced stage of development involves primarily high-tech services. These include financial services, technical services, communications, and, importantly, regional headquarters and management of FDIs. But note that only small centrally located regions or city-states like Singapore and Hong Kong (now of course a part of China) have moved on to become principally regional financial and communications centers. Along with Taiwan, they have also become owners and managers of sizable direct investments in neighboring countries.

A relay race

The process of shifting the locus of production to where goods can be produced most competitively is illustrated in Figure 5.9. Garments are among the simplest and most labor-intensive industries. These industries have been moving from South Korea, to China, and most recently to Vietnam. Some have moved still farther afield to Bangladesh, Mauritius, Sri Lanka, and India, for example. Although basic steel is capital intensive, many countries seek to develop the steel industry

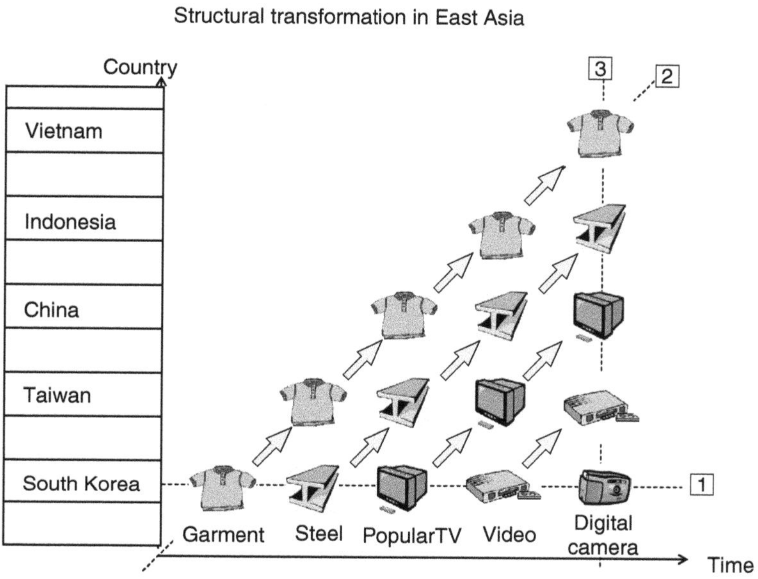

Structural transformation in East Asia

Figure 5.9 Transfers of production along the development ladder.

as a springboard to further industrialization. Assembly of electronic products like TVs and video recorders has become another focus of more sophisticated production. Most recently, digital cameras are being produced in quantity in South Korea and Taiwan. As countries advance, industries become more sophisticated, producing more capital- and technology-intensive products.

Today, Singapore and Hong Kong are largely advanced service economies, communications and financial centers with heavy emphasis on information technology and networking. Korea and Taiwan and, of course, Japan, are powerhouses in the production of high-tech hardware such as chips, disk drives, cellular phones, and advanced equipment. Other East Asian countries like Malaysia, China, and Thailand are at the edges of the IT revolution with substantial production of consumer electronic equipment although their most competitive industries still call for labor-intensive processes. Much of their high-tech production activity is the result of FDI, some from Japan, the US, and Europe and some from Taiwan and Korea. Much of the technology originates in the parent companies abroad. One should not underestimate the importance of the technological transfers, often a result of FDI, that make possible advancement on the development ladder.

This process also reflects the technological capabilities of the various countries that we considered in Table 4.9. The first stage represents assembly activities, work that is labor intensive and takes advantage of low wage rates. Subsequent stages call for more capital- or education-intensive activities like engineering,

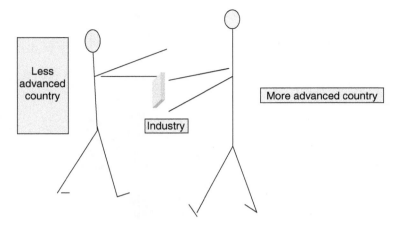

Figure 5.10 The relay race among East Asian countries.

product development, R&D, and management and finance. Only Singapore and Taiwan are at the most advanced level, in both cases managing many operations elsewhere in the region. Other Southeast Asian countries still lag, although most of them are advancing rapidly toward more sophisticated operations.

A figurative way to think about this development process is as a relay race (Figure 5.10). In this picture, the runners are the countries following each other along the development ladder. The more advanced country hands off the baton—the industry—to the less advanced country. Such transfers of an industry from the more advanced country to a less advanced one are motivated by the relevant cost pressures, largely the cost of labor. As a country makes progress, wage levels rise (and usually exchange rates appreciate). It no longer pays to produce labor-intensive products in such a country. Entrepreneurs set up production in neighboring countries where labor costs are lower. Some examples of this phenomenon are the movement of production out of Hong Kong into neighboring Shenzhen province of China and, as we have noted, from Taiwan to Guangdong province in China. In both cases the investors have a special advantage since they know the local culture and speak the local language, Cantonese and Mandarin, respectively. Because of the advantages of cultural and geographic proximity, it is much less likely that East Asian producers will soon shift production sites to far off areas like South Africa, even if labor costs there were advantageous. On the other hand, new ideas summarized in the term, *global production chain*, suggest that eventually the inputs into many complex products will come from many diverse parts of the world, each production phase being carried on where it is most economic.

A classic illustration of this process is the shift of athletic shoe production, originally from the United States to Korea, from there to Taiwan, and then on to Thailand, China, and more recently Vietnam (Adams 1998). Only the most complex shoe designs are still being manufactured in South Korea. Today, athletic shoe production is largely carried out in Asia under contract with local firms. Plants were organized and the workers trained by Korean technicians and, frequently, Taiwanese entrepreneurs. This approach makes it possible to overcome local shortages of technology and capital. Production processes are labor-intensive and they may not be at the technological frontier. If labor costs rise, more sophisticated machinery from abroad may be imported, or production may be shifted toward a location where labor costs remain low. Company headquarters remain largely in the developed countries, the United States and Germany. The American and European companies do not own or run the production shops. Trademarks and the management, distribution, financing, and marketing functions are, however, still sited in the advanced countries, the United States and Western Europe.

The new economy and the development ladder

The IT/e-business revolution represents a further step in world technological and economic progress. It offers new opportunities for the development ladder process. Many entrepreneurs are taking advantage of the new technological developments to advance themselves and their businesses. This is taking place in East Asia as well as in Europe and the United States.

The underlying economic considerations may be different than they used to be, but they are not eliminated in the new economy. Competitive advantage still depends on the ability to produce products more cheaply and with higher quality than elsewhere. If the product calls for high level skills or high quality, it will be produced in the most advanced countries. On the other hand, if it calls for cheap labor, manufacturing or assembly, then some of the East Asian developing countries are ideal low-cost sources.

Some countries have proposed to "leapfrog" into the twenty-first century. Advancing technology is an important objective, but it is a vain hope to push production into high-tech products when the technological basis for them is not sufficiently developed. Many such ventures have not panned out, incurring high costs without producing viable products. This means that the production of the most sophisticated IT products will still be carried on in the most advanced countries. On the other hand, even sophisticated products often require low-tech low-wage services. A good example is the business of mounting and encapsulating electronic chips on their bases and inserting and connecting their numerous wire leads, a task that is carried out economically in the Philippines. Increasingly, businesses are producing products in a transnational production chain, carrying out each segment of the production process where it can be done most economically. The international supply chain and the relocation of production are integral to the new economy.

6   From miracle to meltdown and beyond

From the perspective of economic development, among the important events of the late twentieth century was the 1997 financial crisis that interrupted the "miracle" economic growth in East Asia. Some countries crashed in 1997–8—Indonesia, Thailand, South Korea, the Philippines, Malaysia—whereas others such as China and Taiwan passed through the turbulent period of the late 1990s largely unscathed. In the meantime, rapid growth has resumed in the region, but some East Asian countries are still feeling the effects of diminished competitiveness and financial disarray. Technical change has continued to sweep rapidly across the world. Today, we can again ask: "Will this 'new economy' be the basis for renewed and sustainable growth in East Asia?"

We look at the East Asian experience in four phases (Figure 6.1):

- the period of rapid growth (that we have already described in Chapters 4 and 5);
- the 1997 meltdown generally known as the East Asian financial crisis (this Chapter);
- the recovery period (discussed in this Chapter);
- prospects for the "new economy" (to be discussed in Part IV).

Economists are seldom certain about the future. Perspectives can be optimistic or pessimistic, as we suggest with the arrows in Figure 6.1. The question is where the future points and will economic opportunities generated by new technologies, what we have termed the "new economy," put East Asia on the optimistic growth track?

The East Asian crisis: what happened?

The East Asian boom came to an abrupt stop in 1997 (Figure 6.2). For some East Asian countries it was a violent turnaround causing serious disruption—high rates of unemployment, bank and other business failures, and thousands of unfinished construction projects. Note particularly the sharp decline of Gross Domestic Product (GDP) in Thailand and Indonesia in 1997 and 1998. On the other hand, Taiwan and China were less affected.

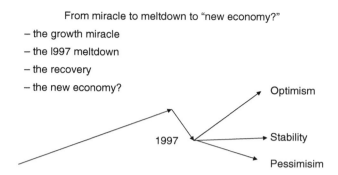

Figure 6.1 Optimism and pessimism about East Asia.

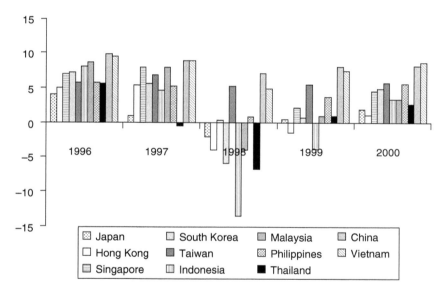

Figure 6.2 Change in GDP over the East Asian crisis.

Source: Asian Development Bank.

Since 1999, there has been widespread evidence of recovery in the East Asian countries. Thailand and South Korea were able quite quickly to pay back their borrowings from the IMF and claim that "they are out of the woods." The export performance of the East Asian countries was boosted by economic recovery in the United States and by the staggering boom in China, a country that buys almost as much abroad as it sells abroad. The medium-term regional outlook is optimistic. For the longer-term perspective, the question is how the East Asian region can take advantage of the "new economy" to sustain its progress.

The developing crisis

The 1997 East Asian crisis[33] followed from:

- the internal and external business cycle disequilibria associated with the rapid growth of the region in the first half of the 1990s;
- the failure of monetary and exchange rate policies to take account of liberalization of international financial flows that had served as a catalyst for the boom.

The crisis began in 1997 in Thailand. International financial contagion combined with domestic financial and business cycle problems, similar though perhaps less intense than those in Thailand, soon extended the difficulty to other East Asian countries, particularly Indonesia, South Korea, and Malaysia.

Thailand was one of the leaders of the rapidly growing economies in East Asia. It was also the first country in the region in trouble. At least in hindsight, the evidence that the country's boom faced some serious challenges was already apparent a year or two earlier. The seeds for the collapse were sowed as early as 1993 (Adams and Vernon 1998). At that time, Thailand sought to expand its role as a financier in South East Asia by creating the Bangkok International Banking facility (BIBF), a vehicle for offshore banking services. It was also a step toward liberalizing international capital flows, as had long been favored by the IMF. Thai officials thought that foreign funds would be brought in from outside and that, in turn, they would be lent by Thai banks to borrowers in other countries in the region, creating a regional financial center. These were to be "out–out" transactions. But, in fact, funds were borrowed by Thai finance companies and banks abroad at hugely favorable rates of interest and lent at home, "out–in" transactions. The opening to foreign capital markets became a way for Thai firms to borrow capital at more favorable rates than could be obtained from purely local sources. The inflow of capital, fed by a 7 percentage point differential between interest rates in the world and Thailand (7% and 14% respectively) was enormous. Most of the investments were financed indirectly through finance companies borrowing from foreign banks. Since the foreign loans were denominated in US dollars, they were sound only so long as it could be assumed by the borrowers that the exchange rate would remain at its traditional (since 1984) 25 baht to the dollar rate. Moreover, there was a substantial maturity mismatch. Much of the money coming in was borrowed short-term, six months, though the ultimate investments were clearly long-term in nature. The capital inflow was the basis for an unsustainable investment boom, building far more office buildings, hotels, apartment houses, and even golf courses than would be needed for a long time to come. Demand pressures strained capacity and shortages of skilled labor, managers, and engineers increased labor turnover and cost. In short, the inflow of short-term foreign currency financed a domestic boom that contained the seeds of the subsequent downturn.

Second, also in 1993, China combined its various controlled exchange rates at the market rate, in effect a devaluation. At the same time, Chinese industry learned how to manufacture goods to world market specifications. We cannot be sure whether it was the Chinese devaluation or the improvement in Chinese product that was responsible for the ensuing trade problems of other East Asian countries. Thai firms as well as other East Asian manufacturers lost competitiveness, particularly with respect to China. In 1996, when the US dollar to which the baht exchange rate was tied, appreciated, the baht appeared to be substantially overvalued from a commercial perspective. Business people in Thailand and Indonesia complained that they could no longer sell their goods in export markets. As Figure 4.3 shows, after rapid increase earlier in the 1990s, there was a zero increase in exports in 1996. Booming consumption of imported consumer goods, capital goods, and industrial inputs sharply increased imports causing the trade deficit to reach 8 percent of GDP. For a while this deficit was offset by inflows of foreign capital. But when confidence in the financial system and in the domestic economy collapsed, a reversal of capital flows became inevitable.

As the boom neared its end and confidence declined, there were runs on smaller banks. Two-thirds of the finance companies were closed and some banks were nationalized and/or consolidated. Knowing that obligations in dollars could not otherwise be met, the Bank of Thailand (BoT) made a valiant and, perhaps, foolish intervention effort to maintain the exchange rate peg. Yet, after the expenditure of $23 billion in the exchange futures market, the BoT ran out of foreign exchange reserves and was forced to float the baht in mid-1997. The baht collapsed with a depreciation of some 50 percent from 25 baht to the dollar to 50 baht to the dollar at year end 1997 (Figure 6.3).

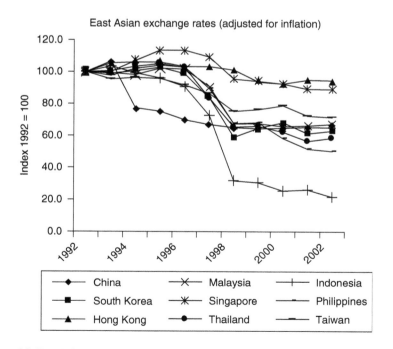

Figure 6.3 East Asian exchange rates, 1992–2002.

The resulting drop in investment and consumption demand led to a serious recession. Economic growth slowed in 1996 and collapsed in 1997 and 1998 (Figure 6.3). In the second half of 1997, auto sales were running less than a quarter their rate of the previous year. Many firms lacked working capital. At one point, there were 400 unfinished buildings in Bangkok. Unemployment rose sharply among white collar managers as well as production workers, causing serious social problems. To make matters worse, many financial intermediaries had borrowed in dollar terms, what Calvo *et al.* (2004) term Domestic Liability Dollarization (DLD). When the baht depreciated, liabilities quickly exceeded the value of the underlying assets. Many loans were not repaid. Many finance companies and banks failed. The government was forced to turn to the IMF for assistance. In August 1997, the IMF provided a rescue package of loans amounting to $17.2 billion.

The foreign exchange crisis spread quickly to other East Asian countries. By the end of 1997, Indonesia, Malaysia, and Korea had been affected. Many of the explanations of the crisis emphasize the collapse of confidence and the movement of exchange rates, thinking of these developments as a case of contagion, sort of like the spread of an infectious disease. There are also other channels of contagion through trade links, capital markets, and lending banks (Kaminsky and Reinhart 1999). When investors lost confidence in one country, they became fearful about others as well. There is a degree of truth to the contagion theory. Contagion certainly made things worse for many countries. Many of them, like Thailand, were also in overextended situation. Indonesia and South Korea, for example, had also seen booms though their economies were not as threatened as Thailand's. Some politicians have argued that the spread of the crisis was largely the result of contagion, that Malaysia, for example, was not overextended and was "attacked" by hedge fund speculators. Other major East Asian countries with large foreign exchange holdings, like Taiwan and China, were not severely affected.

By December, the crisis had hit South Korea, forcing the United States and Japan to provide credits, in addition to those from the IMF. The following year, we were to see serious difficulties in Brazil and in Russia, leading to fears that the entire world financial system would break down.

A number of factors stood in the way of a quick recovery. Most of the East Asian countries took a long time restructuring their financial systems. Lack of appropriate bankruptcy laws stood in the way of a quick resolution of the non-performing loan problem and the presence of large numbers of non-performing loans made resumption of credit expansion difficult. There were also substantial political problems. In Indonesia, the political situation was in turmoil. There were also political threats in the Philippines and in Malaysia. There was serious concern about whether the growth miracle would resume.

The data (Table 4.2 and Figure 6.2) indicate that there has been a substantial turnaround, some of it related to the cyclical recovery of the world economy. At the time, there were real doubts about whether the growth miracle that propelled East Asia so rapidly for 30 years would resume and become the basis for sustained rapid growth.

The role of the IMF

The IMF had warned Thai officials in 1996 about the country's excessive domestic budget deficit, its overvalued currency, and its large trade deficit and enormous capital inflow that was financing a speculative construction and real estate boom.

After the crisis developed, the IMF stepped in quickly to provide credits and to help stabilize the exchange rate. In accord with its standard operating procedures, the IMF imposed conditions as a price for providing aid. There is disagreement about whether these conditions did or did not make economic sense, but there is no question that they made the social consequences of the crisis more damaging than they might have been, particularly to the poor. For example, in dealing with the crisis in Thailand in 1997, the IMF at first called for higher interest rates and insisted that the government budget be balanced, calling for substantial cuts in spending and increases in taxes. The problem was that Thai businesses could ill afford to pay higher interest rates—they could not afford to meet the obligations they already had. Increases in taxes and cuts in spending to meet the budget targets would lead to more personal suffering. After a few months, responding to popular pressure and criticism by policy experts the IMF had second thoughts and permitted Thailand to run a deficit in order to aid the unemployed and to provide some stimulus to economic activity. As a consequence of such misunderstandings and perhaps also for political reasons, economic problems in the developing countries have often been blamed on the IMF. Few countries have been willing to accept the fact that the crisis may reflect some of their own actions.

Many politicians and some economists, Stiglitz (2002), have argued that the IMF did its job badly. "How IMF policies brought the world to the verge of a global meltdown."[34] The IMF did not prevent the crisis. Stiglitz argues that "After the 1997 Asian crisis, IMF policies exacerbated the crisis in Indonesia and Thailand" (2002: 18).

> The IMF typically provides funds only if countries engage in policies like cutting deficits, raising taxes, or raising interest rates that lead to a contraction of the economy. Keynes would be rolling over in his grave were he to see what has happened to his child.
>
> (2002: 12–13)

> The IMF is pursuing not just the objectives of its original mandate, of enhancing global stability and ensuring that there are funds for countries facing a threat of recession to pursue expansionary policies. It is also pursuing the interests of the financial community.
>
> (2002: 206)

Is it really true that the IMF did its job badly in East Asia? Obviously, Stiglitz thinks so. But the reality may be quite different. Kenneth Rogoff, chief economist of the IMF argues: "Regrettably, many of the charges frequently leveled against the Fund reveal deep confusions regarding its policies and intentions.

Other criticisms, however, do hit at potentially fundamental weak spots in concurrent IMF practices" (Rogoff 2003).

The most common criticism has been about the "cookie-cutter" conditionality aspect of the IMF's assistance programs. When the IMF provides emergency assistance to cash-starved countries, it customarily makes its loans conditional on restrictive fiscal and monetary policies, often much the same program regardless of the particular circumstances. Some would say the IMF calls for "harsh fiscal austerity" whether it is appropriate or not. Rogoff argues that in the absence of IMF intervention the outcome for Thailand, and for South Korea, would have been much more damaging. In Rogoff's words: "the institution provides a convenient whipping boy when politicians confront their populations with a less profligate budget. 'The IMF forced us to do it' " In the end, the IMF compromised and permitted Thailand to run a budget deficit of 3 percent of GDP.

Thailand, South Korea, and Indonesia worked with the IMF to resolve the crisis, in some cases only on and off. On the other hand, Malaysia, whose government claimed steadfastly that it was not overextended and suffered only from exchange rate contagion, refused the IMF's help. Malaysia turned temporarily to exchange controls, but in the end Malaysia, too, instituted many of the restrictive policies that would have been imposed had they sought IMF assistance.

Explanations of the 1997 crisis: a result of globalization and the IT revolution?

There have been numerous attempts to explain the 1997 crisis. A challenging question is whether the crisis was related to the changes in the world economy associated with the IT revolution.

The many alternative explanations for the crisis that have been presented and that appear in our account of the crisis can be summarized concisely as follows:

- macroeconomic vulnerabilities;
- excessive and volatile financial flows;
- inappropriate exchange rate policies;
- Domestic Liability Dollarization (DLD);
- banking sector problems;
- international contagion;
- political uncertainties;
- IT and communications boom.

Most writers rightly emphasize the confluence of several causes. It is not possible simply to associate one explanatory factor with the crisis. It was undoubtedly the result of the combination of several related forces. Were the changes related to IT and e-business one of the major factors? Did the East Asian crisis have anything to do with the New Economy? The answer must be "Perhaps, but only in part." The changes under way in trade patterns, industrial structure, and especially, globalization and worldwide communication may have contributed, at least indirectly.

The East Asian development process is closely linked with the international-ization of world markets. That trend has been under way for a long time. We have seen that increasing flows of manufactured goods from East Asia to the advanced countries are part of the miracle of East Asian growth. A slowdown in these exports can be very damaging to the producer countries. The East Asian countries are increasingly more closely linked to the fluctuations of demand in the advanced countries. But, the collapse in 1997 did not stem from a collapse in demand in the advanced countries.

In the 1990s, few of the East Asian countries were yet seriously involved in new economy IT products. The trade flows of manufactures from East to West were not, by and large, related directly to the "new economy," though some of them represented the early stages of the production of consumer electronic products in East Asia. Only Taiwan and Singapore/Malaysia were deeply involved in advanced electronics, though South Korea was already mass producing TVs and other consumer electronics. Taiwan pretty much escaped the crisis altogether, having large reserves of currency, though South Korea was seriously affected. Singapore had a slowdown, as did Malaysia. It is relevant to note that these coun-tries were at the upper end of the East Asian advancement scale and were not, like Thailand and Indonesia, competing with China and other low-income countries with labor-intensive manufactures. It is evident therefore that the crisis was not about "new economy" products. The slowdown associated with these products was to come later in 2001 after the dot-com boom collapsed.

On the other hand, the crisis clearly reflected a new sensitivity in the relation-ships between East Asian countries and the advanced world. In this case, it was largely a matter of open capital markets and improved communication relation-ships. Where once financial flows to East Asia were relatively modest and focused toward long maturities and direct investments, in the 1990s East Asia was a target of volatile short-term capital flows seeking the highest yield. What has been added in the 1990s are highly volatile international capital flows. Appropriately, Blustein (2001) refers to the stampeding speculators as "the electronic herd." Now there was an opening of financial markets to flows of for-eign short-term funds in place of fairly stable long-term international capital movements. One may blame the borrowers in the Asian countries. But remem-ber foreign banks were willing lenders. Again one cannot simply relate this phenomenon to the new economy, but there is no doubt that improvements in computer and communications technology greatly facilitated the links to far dis-tant financial markets. Before the advent of internationally networked computers, movements of short-term capital were not feasible at the speed and quantity in which they have been occurring recently. One would have hoped that increased knowledge would also make decision-making more rational, that there would not be irrational bubbles in investors' thinking. Unfortunately, that does not seem to be the case. In spite of the availability of so much information so quickly, investors' expectations have often been out of line with reality. That was true during the boom; it appears to be true during the collapse as well—excessive enthusiasm on the way up and then excessive pessimism on the way down. It is as if the swings of emotion are passed from one market participant to another electronically.

Where is East Asia now?

Today, most of the East Asian countries have overcome the crisis period. In 2004–5, most of East Asia has been close to its pre-crisis growth rates, particularly China, Thailand, and South Korea. This recovery largely reflects the high level of economic activity in China and the cyclical recovery in the United States, Australia, and Japan. For the near term future, East Asian growth must still be considered cyclical.

Finally, from a longer-term perspective, it is important to return to the globalization of production, the shift of production from West to East. Although we have just dismissed this sea change in the world economy as an immediate cause of the 1997 crisis, we note how much the rapid growth of East Asia in recent decades has been tied to increases in manufacturing for export and for their domestic markets. (See also a discussion of this process in Chapters 5 and 10.)

7 The digital divide

Conditions in East Asia are changing rapidly as labor costs in many parts of the region are rising and as increasingly sophisticated technologies must be applied. That raises the question of whether the East Asian growth process can be expected to continue, smoothly and simply, in the new world of IT and e-business. Do the technological and business aspects of the new economy pose special requirements that must first be overcome? What is the "digital divide" and can it be crossed?

Table 7.1 contrasts the significant elements of old economy industries with those of the new economy activities. As the East Asian countries advanced, they have been producing increasingly complex products like consumer electronics and autos. Many of these resemble traditional manufacturing in their need for repetitive labor-intensive work, so that East Asia has continued to be able to take advantage of its competitive advantage of abundant cheap labor. In contrast, many, but not all, IT/e-business activities have altogether different resource and technology requirements. They call for sophisticated advanced technology and engineering, for highly skilled workers, for fast broadband communication facilities, and, in some cases, for a good knowledge of the English language.

The new fields cover a broad range, from sophisticated technical products like chips to relatively much simpler assembly of cell phones. They also include services, ranging from call centers to computer programming. Importantly, the IT/e-business opportunities include many products and services that do not require transportation, that can be delivered by wire, even wireless.

The implications of these differences are best described in terms of examples. We have described in Chapter 5 how the athletic shoe industry was one of the first to be largely globalized. The geographic transfer of shoe production from one country to another was relatively straightforward. The international transfer of IT/e-business products is a much more complex matter. It depends greatly on the kind of product. Let us begin with DRAM chips. These are technologically complex. Even the standardized DRAM that has become a "commodity," calls for highly complex "clean room" production processes. The machinery may be imported, but the plant management and engineering are largely local. Some countries, like South Korea and Taiwan, have become masters at producing DRAMs and related electronic circuits. In these countries, the industry is nearing maturity. But in

Table 7.1 Differences between conventional and IT/e-business
products

Conventional goods— manufactures	IT/e-business products— hardware, software, e = business
Manufactured goods	*Complex high-tech products*
Labor intensive Transportable Standardized	Knowledge intensive Sophisticated capital and communications Customized Electronically transmissible Depend on intellectual property rights English language

other East Asian countries, high-tech products like chips are still beyond the
prevailing technological frontier. Production technology can be a serious challenge,
particularly, if there is a lack of experience. IT and e-business operations call
for specialized trained personnel. They also require suppliers of critical raw
materials (gases), experienced maintenance operators, and engineering consultants
that may not be adequately available in many East Asian locations. Similar
limitations apply to other high-tech products, like high end computers, although
standard model PCs are being built widely.

Many high-tech products require assembly. Once the basic parts are available,
either domestically or imported, assembly or the soldering of wire terminals is a
task that is labor-intensive and usually performed in developing countries like the
Philippines where labor costs are low. The advent of locally integrated production
systems in regional "clusters" is a step in the direction of optimizing production
sites on the basis of local comparative advantage. They are also a way to provide
and utilize specific support skills, like machine maintenance, that high-tech
operations require.

Programming of software is an altogether different aspect of IT/e-business
activity. The pioneering and development stages of programs were dominated by
American firms (and some European and Israeli ones), many of them originally
small entrepreneurial efforts. New computer programs often represented radical
innovations, a new computer language, operating system, or application. These
endeavors called for a culture of innovation and entrepreneurship. They required
interaction between developers, many of them young and not yet affiliated with
large organizations. They depended on advanced education. Some developers
were graduate students at major universities. Perhaps, most importantly, the
programming pioneers needed familiarity with computers and what can be done
with them. They also required venture capital, albeit, often on a modest scale.

Today, the pioneering stage is long past for much of the programming field.
This has become a mature industry using standardized software components to
perform various tasks of business management. This field is now dominated by

large business programming and management consulting companies like SAP, IBM, Peoplesoft, Microsoft, and Oracle, mostly North American or European. The bulk of their business is "systems integration" and customization, where they tie together existing programs to meet their customers' specific needs. The requirements of the mature stage of the programming business are very different than they were at the beginning, calling for large organizations that can provide their own communications infrastructure and can train specialists. Later, we also elaborate on the important issue of protecting intellectual property from unauthorized use.

E-business between businesses or between businesses and consumers is an altogether different activity. It hangs critically on the widespread availability of broadband networks and use of computers by most businesses and a large share of the population. The critical requirement is not so much expertise as availability. It also depends on being able to handle the delivery of the product and payment in ways that are very different from traditional commercial activities.

The digital divide

The East Asian countries differ greatly with respect to IT/e-business readiness. Most still have a long way to go before they cross the digital divide to rely on these new activities as a basis for development.

The term "digital divide" usually refers to the fact that in some countries most people have access to computers and in others they do not. Meaningful access to computers and related technology takes in much more than the availability of PCs and Internet connections. Many considerations influence whether the new technologies can be used widely and effectively. While these include physical infrastructure and computer connectivity, they also relate to literacy and education, technical training and experience, and even language. Moreover, computer availability and literacy are not a matter of black and white. There are degree differences in access to communication, differences in computer knowledge and skills, differences in command of specific languages, and differences due to government restrictions. "Compare for example, a professor at UCLA with a high-speed connection in her office, a student at Bangkok who occasionally uses a cyber-café, and a rural activist in Indonesia who has no computer or phone line, but whose colleagues in her women's group download and print out information for her" (Warschauer 2002: 5). Countries differ widely in computer availability and computer literacy. Similar divisions affect computer users within countries. Note, for example, the difference between urban and rural users in China.

As is apparent in Table 7.2, much of East Asia, but not all, remains on the shady side of the digital divide. In comparison to the advanced countries of Europe and North America, computer ownership and use are still very limited in some East Asian countries, as is the availability of rapid broadband network service. The case of China is a good illustration. In view of China's huge population, the absolute number of Internet users is substantial (some 20 million or so, and growing rapidly), but these represent a very small fraction of the potential population of

Table 7.2 Computer/Internet statistics of East Asia

	Computers per 1,000 people (2001)	Internet hosts per 10,000 people (2000)	Internet users per 10,000 people (2000)
China	19	0.6	176
Hong Kong (China)	386	336.9	3,359
Indonesia	11	1.3	68
Malaysia	126	29.3	1,505
Philippines	22	2.6	266
Singapore	506	492.3	2,987
South Korea	256	84.1	4,025
Taiwan	n.a.	n.a.	2,813
Thailand	28	10.5	266
Vietnam	12	0.0	13
Japan	349	365.6	3,044
United States	625	2928.3	3,466

Source: World Bank, ADB.

users and few of them have high-speed broadband service. In China, the Internet café is still the most popular way to access the worldwide web. In contrast, Singapore and Hong Kong are leaders with high computer density and have developed Internet host sites comparable in numbers to many Western countries. South Korea has the world's highest level of computer penetration and is also a world leader in cellular telephones. On the other hand, some populous countries in East Asia, including Indonesia and Thailand, are not as far along in IT development. Popular awareness of the computer and of its potentials is still limited to an urban elite. Among most of the population, computer literacy is low. Except in Singapore and South Korea and elsewhere in the biggest cities, Internet access remains difficult. But that is changing very rapidly.

Recent empirical studies (Dasgupta *et al.* 2001; Chin and Fairlie 2004) suggest that the digital divide is mainly, but not entirely, accounted for by income differences. Human capital, telecommunications infrastructure, and the nature of the regulatory system also have important explanatory effects. Chin and Fairlie suggest that public investment in human capital, telecommunications infrastructure, and regulatory reform can reduce the discrepancies in PC and Internet use.

A similar result is apparent with respect to information and communication technology (ICT) spending (Table 7.3). These statistics include spending on communication infrastructure as well as computers and related equipment. Only Singapore and Hong Kong (and probably Taiwan) come close to the advanced countries, both in terms of IT and communications expenditures as a percent of Gross Domestic Product (GDP) and in per capita expenditures. For the low-income countries like Vietnam, even a relatively high share of GDP going into advanced technologies amounts to very little spending per capita. In China also the figures are very low, though there are undoubtedly great disparities among the regions of China and between the cities and the countryside. The comparison

Table 7.3 ICT spending in East Asia (2001)

	% of GDP	*$ per capita*
China	5.7	53
Hong Kong (China)	8.7	2,110
Indonesia	2.2	17
Malaysia	6.6	262
Philippines	4.2	41
Singapore	9.9	2,110
South Korea	7.4	676
Thailand	3.7	76
Vietnam	6.7	26
Japan	9.6	3,25
United States	7.9	2,924

Source: World Bank, ADB.

Table 7.4 Rankings of the WEF Networked Readiness Index (NRI) 2003, 2004

	NRI 2004	*NRI 2003*	*Environment 2003*	*Readiness 2003*	*Usage 2003*
China	41	51	63	54	43
Hong Kong	7	18	11	28	15
Indonesia	51	73	68	69	81
Malaysia	27	25	26	29	26
Philippines	67	69	82	72	50
Singapore	1	2	2	4	2
South Korea	24	20	20	19	17
Taiwan	15	17	8	17	22
Thailand	36	38	41	37	40
Vietnam	68	68	74	67	56
United States	5	1	1	3	1
Japan	8	12	19	11	11

Source: WEF Global Information Technology Report (2004, 2005) figures for 2004 include 104 countries. Figures for 2003 are based on 102 countries.

between the East Asian countries and the United States (about $3,000 per capita in the United States and Japan and $53 per capita in China) gives an indication of the enormous effort, relative to GDP, the poor countries would have to make to build information and communications systems comparable to those prevailing in the high-income countries.

The World Economic Forum (WEF) Networked Readiness Index (NRI) (Tables 7.4 and 7.5) takes a somewhat different approach. The NRI is an attempt to compare countries with respect to their "degree of preparation ... to participate in and benefit from ICT developments" (WEF 2002–3: 10). Based on data for 64 variables, the index tries to separate the dimensions of Environment, Readiness, and Usage.

Table 7.5 Components WEF Networked Readiness Index (NRI) 2003

	Environment			Readiness			Usage		
	Market	Political regulatory	Infrastructure	Individual	Business	Government	Individual	Business	Government
China	44	68	72	62	59	47	55	69	21
Hong Kong	23	2	16	24	31	27	22	14	4
Indonesia	50	71	80	71	62	72	84	89	60
Malaysia	26	31	27	47	38	6	31	22	7
Philippines	78	63	94	65	80	56	72	59	29
Singapore	1	5	5	22	4	1	18	2	1
South Korea	19	25	9	21	23	9	13	18	10
Taiwan	6	16	10	17	19	12	27	21	6
Thailand	28	38	54	44	44	22	65	33	24
Vietnam	38	78	92	73	74	52	79	53	50
United States	2	8	2	5	3	3	8	1	2
Japan	7	37	21	14	6	17	12	10	14

Source: WEF Global Information Technology Report (2004). Figures are based on 102 countries.

The challenge is to measure not only the actual use of IT services but also the readiness for expanding that use and its ultimate potential. The wide range and variety of variables underlying the indexes is a reflection of the varied potentials for IT application by consumers, business, and government. The variation between the data recorded is great so that indexes are difficult to compile and standardize. At best, the WEF rankings of the different countries are an approximate measure of how far along a country is on the scale of IT development. (Note, high rankings are low numbers, number 1, and low rankings are high numbers, number 102.)

With respect to the environment for the IT and communications industries, information is assembled on various relevant elements:

- the market assessment evaluates human resources and business relationships in relation to their ability "to support a knowledge based society"—issues such as venture capital availability, competition in telecommunications, spending on education and information technology, etc.;
- the political regulatory environment involves the nature of the legal system and regulations and their application in connection to fostering IT development— legal framework, government restrictions on internet control, etc.;
- infrastructure availability and quality to support adoption and use of IT technologies—number of telephone lines, switch capacity, local availability of specialized IT services, etc.;

With respect to readiness, the underlying data measure:

- consumer readiness to adopt and utilize IT—availability of Internet access and broadband, literacy and education, cost of communications, etc.;
- business readiness to make use of IT methods in management, supply chain operations, and marketing—capacity for innovation, business Internet sophistications, quality of IT training programs;
- government readiness to use IT in its various operations—government prioritization of IT, competence of government officials, government online services.

In terms of usage, the focus is on the following:

- consumer use that is measured in terms of the level of adoption and usage of various types of consumer IT—use of online payment systems, use of various types of consumer electronic equipment, household spending on electronics, number of broadband subscriber lines;
- business usage that is concerned with the adoption, utilization, and range of business uses of IT measured by percent of businesses using e-commerce, use of Internet for business coordination, and use of e-mail;
- government usage that is concerned with the level of IT use in government operations and relations to its citizens—use of Internet-based transactions with government, government online services, and government success with IT promotion.

The wide range of IT development in East Asia is readily apparent. Some East Asian countries such as Singapore, Taiwan, South Korea are seen to be far in advance—leading even some of the most mature countries. In some respects, Singapore is number 1. Others like Vietnam, Indonesia, and the Philippines are very much at the tail end of the readiness scale. In most cases, high income corresponds to a high ranking in IT readiness. High rankings in readiness also typically correspond to high rankings for the component indexes such as infrastructure and usage. It is most interesting consequently to note the discrepancies:

- Among developed countries, Japan is not as highly ranked as the United States and other countries with approximately equivalent income. This may reflect lags in the policy/regulatory index and in IT usage by government.
- In East Asia, Singapore is a leader in all categories, though government is especially highly ranked, number 1 in market environment, and government readiness and usage. Singapore appears to benefit from the strong government push on IT to develop a "wired island."
- Korea and Taiwan have a relatively high ranking with respect to individual usage, probably reflecting their high rates of consumer connectivity and infrastructure.
- China has considerably higher standing in government usage than in consumer and business use. That is consistent with its relatively low readiness index, suggesting that consumers and businesses lag behind. On the other hand, China is a large heterogeneous country and computer readiness in major urban centers like Shanghai is much further along and rural areas may be much further behind than the national average figures indicate.
- Not surprisingly, Vietnam, with low income and low readiness, ranks ninety-second in infrastructure and seventy-ninth in consumer usage.

The disparity in IT development between various countries depends greatly on their incomes and stage of development. Even in the advanced world, the spread of IT equipment and practice to business and to consumers has been uneven and recent. To some extent, improvement may be largely a matter of time. Eventually some of the laggards may catch up with the leaders, but that may well be a matter of much effort and many years. Developing countries, where technology is less far along and labor is relatively inexpensive, have been followers. In time, as part of the development process, many, but not all, aspects of IT are likely to progress in East Asia as elsewhere. Indeed, as we have noted, some countries have made tremendous steps in that direction. Existing systems have sometimes been inadequate, the case of land-based telephones, and, as a result, there have been some spectacular examples of *leapfrogging*, the overwhelmingly rapid development of cellular phone service throughout East Asia, for example.

But the arguments in the opposite direction, that in some countries development of IT activities may be difficult and/or slow, are at least equally compelling. IT calls for skills and resources that are not available in some developing countries. Much technical progress proceeds step by step: you must learn to walk before you can run. Some experts have suggested that introducing IT into developing countries is easy because there are no existing infrastructure or business practices to displace. Lau (2000), for example, has argued that conversion to high-tech and e-business management systems will be easier in Asia than in Western countries since there is not a legacy of existing electronic systems. He calls it "creation without destruction."[35] But in general that is not true. There are usually traditional systems of doing business that are well suited to local business culture. These may not be easily displaced by new technology. For example, *guanxi*, the network relationships that underlie Chinese business practice may persist because they are more "bonding" than the impersonality of e-business communication.

A knowledge divide?

As we have noted, acquisition of knowledge is an essential ingredient for IT-based development. Is there a similar divide with respect to knowledge?

Data on knowledge *per se* and its application are not available or meaningful. The issue is how widely information is available and how effectively it can be used. It is not possible to put a numerical dimension on the availability of knowledge in different East Asian countries, other than the surveys provided by WEF that we have discussed earlier. In principle, knowledge, except for protected intellectual property can be moved readily from one country to another. These days much information is available on the Internet. But, in practice, transfers of technology are very difficult and much information is gathered through practical experience rather than through formal teaching or reading. There is no doubt, that some countries are much ahead of others in their abilities to use advanced technologies and, probably, in management information and its application as well. Differences in knowledge are, of course, particularly important in the IT fields where the latest in engineering and information technology is central.

The involvement of foreign companies, either in the form of fully owned subsidiaries or joint ventures is an important means for transmitting knowledge relevant to business and technical practice. Often local managers go abroad for training or foreign management has introduced advanced techniques. Traditionally, this has been the role of Western multinational enterprises including firms from Japan that have set up subsidiaries in East Asia. In recent years, a similar role has been assumed by entrepreneurs, technicians, and managers from Taiwan and Korea.

Technological clusters, geographic centers where there are lots of high-tech enterprises, technicians, and suppliers with upward and downward linkages, like Silicon Valley in California or Austin, Texas make the transmission and application of technological knowledge much easier. Some similar clusters have grown in developing countries, like Bangalore in India, and some are being fostered in industrial and research parks in Malaysia, Taiwan, and China (Suzhou). In the end, they are a result, as well as the source, of successful learning and innovation in the IT field. Interaction and networking among high-tech experts are important ingredient of IT advancement and a way to overcome the knowledge divide.

Educational attainment

The prevailing level of educational attainment is obviously an important issue. There might also be an educational divide. Some countries lack the educated labor force that is required to run IT operations. Scarce IT educated staff is often costly, even in a low-wage economy.

IT development and computer use require high-tech programmers and network operators. Less intensive consumer computer applications may not call for the same high level of technical expertise, but they still require familiarity with the potentials of computers and, in many cases, an elementary knowledge of English. These can be acquired through training or through experience.

Significant educational progress has been made in recent years. At the university level, in South Korea, 72 percent of the college age population attends universities or technical institutes. However, in the most populous East Asian countries, the share of the college age population that gets tertiary education remains small. In China, for example, only 7.5 percent of college age persons are attending universities (Table 7.6). On the other hand, the total number of graduates is large. Moreover, a large fraction of Chinese students are in engineering where they may be gaining IT-relevant training.

The experience with setting up the Microsoft research center in Beijing in 1998 is a striking example of how quality and numbers matter in China, regardless of the relatively small share of potential students attending college. Microsoft sent teams to China to administer IQ tests to top engineering graduates. Out of 2000 students tested, Microsoft hired 20. Today, the research group in China is reputed to be the most productive at Microsoft (Friedman 2005).

Table 7.6 Tertiary education in East Asia

	Education in East Asia
	Tertiary education rate (% of age group) 1999
China	7.5
Hong Kong (China)	23.3
Indonesia	11.3
Malaysia	23.3
Philippines	29.5
Singapore	43.8
South Korea	71.7
Thailand	31.9
Japan	46.0
United States	71.6

Source: World Bank.

Outside engineering and specialized institutions, few public university curricula in East Asia have, yet, been widely adapted to computer applications. But some institutions focused on management and engineering with emphasis on computers like Shinawatra University in Bangkok, founded in 1996 by the then business magnate, more recently, Prime Minister Thaksin Shinawatra, focusing on IT management, are a good example of the new trend.

At lower levels of education, computer use is limited or just starting in many locations. However, private profit-making technical institutes are growing rapidly in China and other East Asian countries to teach programming and computer related practice.

The digital divide and technical progress in East Asia

We can conclude that there is, indeed, a digital divide in much of East Asia. It is not that all countries in East Asia are behind the more advanced Western world. Some of them, like Singapore, Taiwan, and South Korea, are about as far along as Japan, Europe and the United States. But others do still lag behind. Also, there are substantial differences in the level of technological and IT advancement even within the East Asian countries. China with its differences between East and West and between city and country is a particularly good example of this phenomenon.

Yet the digital divide is surely a moving target. Every year, the statistics show an improvement in computer literacy and computer availability. Every year, educational levels, particularly those related to computer use and training, are increasing. In most countries advancement is occurring very rapidly. Even so, a high level of technology and e-business sufficient to provide competitive advantage in the IT/e-business fields is still out of reach in some of the larger East Asian countries.

Part III
Policy and development

8 The role of government in East Asian development

Governments have played a considerable role in promoting East Asian growth. What is not so clear is what aspects of government initiatives were effective in promoting growth and what government development policies should be in the future. These questions have been the source of considerable controversy among economists and government officials. In this chapter we ask:

- Did government policy cause the East Asian countries to "take-off" on such a spectacular growth path?
- Can government policy explain the pattern of growth, an industrializing East Asia feeding manufactures to markets in the advanced economies?
- And, specifically, in the context of this book, how do government policies relate to the IT/e-business revolution? Can government policy sustain the application of the new technologies to advance East Asian growth?

The "East Asian miracle"?

By the scale of economic history, East Asia's rapid growth is astonishing, as we have noted, but there is a question of whether it was miraculous. Arguments have been made *pro* and *con*. While few conclude that it was just a plain miracle, rapid growth has frequently been attributed to unexplained considerations, the "residual factor in economic growth" (Solow 1957), or broad imperfectly defined factors such as culture (Harrison and Huntington 2000). As we have concluded in Chapter 5, East Asian growth reflects increases in inputs of capital, shifts toward more advanced industries, and use of more sophisticated technology. It follows from globalization of trading patterns. Moreover, it reflects globalization that has allowed local and foreign entrepreneurs to exploit low labor costs and to participate in a sequential development process in a world economic setting.

Was government policy responsible?

A decade after the publication of the World Bank's seminal volume on *The East Asian Miracle* (World Bank 1993), the role of public policy in economic development remains controversial.

Free market proponents like Helen Hughes (1995), formerly with the World Bank, take a neoclassical position, opposing government intervention. "Just get prices right," presumably in line with free market prices. "Growth would have been even faster if reforms had enabled intervention to be reduced." Most economists from the developed countries would support a free-market view, although many would also recognize an important role for government actions.

Robert Wade (1990), on the other hand, has argued that, in the successful East Asian countries, government policy *leads* development. Focusing on Taiwan, Wade pushes his version of the "The Developmental State," one that guides sectoral investment into the most promising fields. Lall concludes "The evidence of the most successful industrializing countries in the world, the NIEs of East Asia, supports the case for government intervention, albeit of a very different form from that practiced earlier" (1996: x).

Disputing the judgment of many Western economists that market forces were largely, if not wholly, responsible for East Asian growth, the Japanese government financed the elaborate World Bank studies of East Asian development on which the "East Asian Miracle" book was based. The book concluded with a mixed message:

> Fundamentally sound development policy was a major ingredient in achieving rapid growth: macro management, saving promotion policies, education, agricultural productivity, ... But these fundamental policies do not tell the whole story. Government intervened, targeting selected industries, promoting exports, low interest rates, protecting certain industries, ... rapid growth has at times benefited from careful policy intervention.
>
> (1996: 5)

The World Bank book went on to say "the promotion of specific industries generally did not work (1996: 24) ... the fact that interventions were an element of some East Asian economies' success does not mean that they should be attempted everywhere" (1996: 26). In effect, the World Bank is making a grand compromise: general industrialization incentives are OK, particularly ones that operate in a stable macro policy setting, but industry-specific or selective industrial policy is often not a good idea.

In the intervening years, public policies in the East Asian region, as elsewhere, have become somewhat less narrowly interventionist than they used to be. Instead of promoting specific industries such as steel or autos or imposing government regulations or building state-owned enterprises most but not all policy makers have turned to greater reliance on private initiative and market forces to advance development. The dispute between neoclassical economists, whose strategy can best be summarized as letting free markets do the job, and the industrial strategists, as Pack and Westphal (1986) call them, who favor selective industrial promotion, has become somewhat muted. This is because high technology IT/e-business activities pose special challenges that call for public intervention in some respects and that hinder it in others. Some important considerations, like physical infra-structure, education, and intellectual property protection fall naturally into the domain of government. But others such as decisions about high-tech projects, what industries to build, and what technologies to use are probably better handled by profit-seeking risk-taking entrepreneurs.

Public policies for development

In this section we consider the nature of policies that have influenced economic development in East Asia. (Policies that are narrowly directed at promoting IT and e-business are discussed in Chapter 9.)

There is an important distinction among policies dealing with basic government functions, macroeconomic stabilization, and promotion of economic development. Another distinction is between broad functional targets, such as the promotion of investment and exports, and sector or industry-specific interventions. These differences can be made in conceptually focused terms, as we do in our discussion here, even though many policies are aimed at more than one objective.

While there are important common elements between East Asian countries in development policy, strategies and institutions for development do differ among the various countries. We consider these policies in greater detail here.

Traditional government services

For political reasons or for economic reasons many services have traditionally been provided by the public sector rather than left to private enterprise. Government institutions play an important role in all countries providing public services such as police, military, roads, sewers, postal services, bank regulation, and public health. Governments have traditionally been responsible for infrastructure like roads, dams, waterways, and communications. In many developing countries, the scope of activities taken on by government authorities is somewhat broader than in the developed world, presumably because the private sector was thought to lack incentives to provide transportation, petroleum refining and distribution, and banking, for example.

In recent years, in East Asia as in other parts of the world, there have been moves toward privatizing some public sector activities. In part, this reflects the widespread recognition that private sector enterprises can be more efficient and more flexible than bureaucratic public sector business. It also reflects the influence of technological changes that have broadened the scope of competition. Telecommunications is a good example, where initial impetus has almost always come from the public sector, publicly-owned telephone companies. In recent years, wireless telecommunications and satellite services are being provided by privately-owned companies. Such a business is the Shin Corporation that dominates the market for cellular telephony and satellite communications in Thailand.

Institution building

Development experts are increasingly realizing the importance (and the difficulty) of building efficient domestic institutions. This applies to public as well as to private organizations. In the public sector, some East Asian countries still need to establish transparent legal institutions and systems of laws that are enforceable. One of the advantages of Hong Kong and Singapore has been the tradition of the legal systems these cities inherited from their British colonial rulers. Foreign direct investment (FDI) depends greatly on the legal system. Such laws must include ways to handle bankruptcy. They must also include enforceable legal protection for intellectual property. After the 1997 East Asian financial crisis, it was widely recognized that inadequate financial sector regulation (and perhaps political favoritism) had allowed banks and credit companies and the businesses they financed to take on extremely risky exposures. In some countries, like Thailand and Indonesia, these problems have not yet been fully resolved. Efficient banking and financial institutions guided by market signals and supervised by honest and conservative regulators are an important ingredient of economic progress.

China, in particular, continues to face important problems of institution building. Free-market forces more or less influence business decision making as the traditional state-owned industries have been phased out or revamped. Thus, businesses no longer need to provide social assistance and housing or to plan on the basis of political priorities, although many of them remain with substantial public ownership interests, often by local and regional governments. The financial and banking system remains a big problem in China. Financial exchanges are still rudimentary, hardly serving as a source of corporate finance. The four principal banks are still majority publicly owned and continue to extend credit liberally (except for recent government restrictions) despite an enormous pile of "non-performing" loans.

In some countries, large-scale companies have been the vehicle for development. But encouragement of small- and medium-size business is particularly important since these types of ventures have served as the beginnings of IT and e-business in many parts of the world.

Education

Education has been a fundamental task of government in most countries. Improvement of educational attainment with focus on activities that are requisites for participating in the new economy and in related IT activities is seen as an objective in almost all countries. As we have seen in Chapter 7, there is a vast chasm between countries that have provided advanced education to a majority of their citizens and those that are still far behind.

The difficulty lies in the facts that mass education is expensive, takes many years, and is a sequential process. Creating a population of trained, or even trainable, people is a process that takes enormous resources. It requires schools, teachers, books, computers, etc. It diverts young people who would otherwise be working. The sequential nature of education is illustrated by the fact that one has to learn to read and to do elementary mathematics before one can proceed into applied fields such as computer programming.

The problems are not only the gross educational attainment of the population, the share of the secondary school age population attending school, for example.

The problem goes deeper in a number of respects—how to select the most promising students and to advance them into appropriate training? What are the disciplines of the education to be provided: whether to improve proficiency of computer use or technical practice as compared to focusing on more traditional fields like history and law? Is it necessary to emphasize competence in English? A populous country with many people in traditional agriculture, like China, sees these issues quite differently from a small middle class city-state like Singapore. In any case, although there is scope for private schools and training, throughout the East Asian region, education is seen primarily as a public responsibility. However, public universities have found it difficult to adapt to the requirements of the new technology. Some specialized private institutions are now being developed.

Basic and applied science

The development of scientific expertise and the support of science and technology accompanies educational attainment. The world of science is international but it goes almost without saying that most scientific work is concentrated in the advanced countries. In most countries, support for basic science comes in large part from public sources. Applied science is left to a much greater degree to private profit-making effort. In the applied technology area, intellectual property protection like patents is an important role of government, a topic that is discussed at greater length later in the text.

East Asia has some high points of scientific attainment, particularly in applied science and technology in Singapore, Taiwan, and South Korea. These have been the basis for high-tech industries in these countries. Support for scientific institutions is a strategy that becomes increasingly important as countries shift their industries toward high-tech fields. (We consider the role of public policy with respect to scientific applications in the IT fields in Chapter 9.)

Stabilization policies

Stabilizing the economy's business cycle swings and balance of payments have long been important policy objectives in advanced and developing countries, alike. The experience of cyclical ups and downs and balance of payments and debt crises has been widespread in developing economies. East Asia has had a number of such problems though many countries have been able to maintain extended periods of growth. We were reminded of the difficulty of avoiding recessions and financial difficulties by the 1997 East Asian financial crisis and by the relatively precarious situation of some of the East Asian countries more recently.[36] It takes careful fiscal, monetary, and balance of payments policy management to maintain macroeconomic stability in developing countries.

The temptation is to use government policy to force development with high levels of government spending, much of it justified as investment in productive infrastructure or as job-creating expenditure. Excessive government deficits and growing money supply cause inflationary pressure. In 2004, for example, rapid growth of China, in large part financed by bank credit expansion resulting from government deficit and loans to business by nationally owned banks, raised fears of inflation. Policy also frequently aims to stabilize the exchange rate, often at an undervalued exchange rate in order to make exports more competitive and to discourage imports.

In recent years, volatile international capital flows have introduced additional elements of instability. Capital flows have greatly increased as capital controls have been relaxed in many countries. Computer networks have facilitated the integration of many developing countries into the world's financial system. But, as is amply demonstrated by East Asian experience during the 1990s, the volatility of capital flows has added a dimension of difficulty to the task of stabilization. Fiscal and monetary policies must act not only to offset domestic recession or inflation but also to maintain equilibrium in international trade and capital flows. This has proved to be a difficult challenge in some East Asian countries, not surprisingly since theorists have argued that free capital movements, control of interest rates, *and* control of the exchange rate are an impossible combination.[37] As we have noted, issues of domestic and international stabilization have also been a source of conflict between the IMF and the countries that find themselves in balance of payments difficulties.

Development strategy

Development strategy is a central concern of policy-makers in developing countries. Discussions of development strategy range from aggregate policies concerned with trade and investment to narrowly specific measures promoting particular industries and, even, particular projects.

Import substitution and export promotion

The rapid growth of the East Asian economies is closely linked to the swing from policies of import substitution (IS) to policies of export promotion (EP). A couple of generations ago, traditional economic development policy was inward-oriented, promoting industrialization by IS, developing and protecting domestic industries to take the place of imports. This appeared to be a way to save foreign exchange and to build employment in more advanced industries.[38] Another rationalization for such an approach was the "infant industry argument," the position that new advanced industries were frequently not yet ready to meet competition and would require temporary protection until they had reached a degree of maturity and scale.

Such policies frequently resulted in inefficient production at low volume, given the limited size of the home market and the fact that domestic producers were protected from effective competition. And, frequently, products sold in protected domestic markets fell behind the equivalent product sold in the more competitive world market. While IS policies have been widely viewed by development and trade economists as a failure, a variety of limitations of imports, intended to develop local industries like automobiles, still apply.

East Asian countries like Japan and Hong Kong that did not initially have strong home markets pioneered by promoting exports into world markets. The examples of Japanese cars, East Asian garments, and South Korean and Taiwanese electronics come to mind. The turn toward EP was a fundamental switch in policy that appears to lie behind the growth of East Asian industrialization. Participation in export markets helped the East Asian countries to build new industries and participate in world markets. The development ladder process created opportunities to take advantage of the producing country's stage of development. Low-income countries would export labor-intensive products; higher-income countries would be most effective in exporting technologically more advanced goods.

EP and, in some cases, domestic industry protection as well has played a central role in various East Asian countries.[39] The issue is not whether a variety of such policies have been implemented, since they have been used widely to a greater or lesser degree. The question is whether they will yield continued advantage in a more globalized and more technically dynamic world economy.

Growth and dynamic resource allocation policies

The issue of promoting growth, sometimes seen as dynamic resource allocation, is central to economic development in East Asia. All governments want to see faster growth to advance a country's living standards. A country seeks to utilize available resources, domestic and foreign, shifting them if possible to take advantage of upcoming opportunities. In many cases, this has meant promotion of broad activities like investment and exports. In others, it has meant industrial policy, promotion of specific industries or, even, construction and public ownership of plants such as steel, autos, chemicals, shipbuilding, energy, etc.

Looking over the range of the East Asian development experience, the East Asian governments differ quite considerably in the degree to which they intervene in the market.

Wade (1990) classifies the various approaches to dynamic resource allocation into three categories:

- free market (FM)
- simulated free market (SM)
- governed market (GM).

The FM approach is the predominant view of Western-educated economists and, it is not unfair to say, of the international economic institutions, the World Bank, and the IMF. FM calls for maximum reliance on markets and for minimum government intervention. To apply such an approach broadly to explain East Asia's rapid growth, one would have to argue that these countries have been significantly more open to free-market operations than other developing countries and that they have seen a much greater reduction in government intervention than other parts of the world. In some cases, Hong Kong, for example, there is substantial support that such a policy perspective has been a factor in rapid development. In most East Asian countries, the pure FM policy approach did not apply. In many countries, substantial intervention was maintained, at least until very recently.

The SM approach is somewhat more sympathetic to the role of government, arguing that government intervention, modulated by cooperation with business groups, accomplishes more quickly and efficiently what market forces would have achieved eventually anyway. Proponents of SM argue that markets are frequently slow and inefficient and that there are many cases of market failure. Incentives should be provided, for exports or foreign investment inflows, when there are structural or policy biases against these activities, or when market forces alone would not get a sufficient and dynamic response to a country's needs. Such a view can be applied selectively to explain many aspects of East Asia's growth particularly in Singapore, Taiwan, and Malaysia. It also applies in countries like Thailand, where public sector intervention to advance economic development has been less industry-specific, though still substantial. But, it is easy to say that government bureaucrats along with their business associates in the successful East Asian economies simulate what would have happened in a properly operating free-market. It is far more difficult to demonstrate that the decisions and the outcomes of government policy were indeed consistent with free-market outcomes, particularly if the correspondences are noted on a selective basis and ex-post!

Wade's GM view of the forces that molded the spectacular growth of Japan, Korea, and Taiwan, is linked to, but goes beyond, the older "developmental state" tradition (Johnson 1982; Wade 1990). The latter saw governments actively promoting growth by pushing investment and exports, regulating the financial system, advancing the acquisition of modern technology, and in a few cases, helping the development of particular industries. Supportive of such broad policies, Wade argues that the GM approach "enabled the government to guide—or govern—market processes of resource allocation so as to produce different production and investment outcomes than would have occurred" (Wade 1990: 6). In his thinking, the overall results were better than the free-market outcome might have been. In addition to other broader measures, government officials stimulated investment in "key" industries, those that would be competitive in world markets and would use new technologies. Thurow writes:

> The importance of creating man-made sources of comparative advantage can be seen in South Korea and Taiwan. Both first sought to acquire and exploit technologies that would allow them to compete in world markets. They did not centrally plan their economies, but each had a national technological strategy for economic development that involved around becoming the masters of particular technologies.
>
> (2003: 281)

But Thurow also notes that the strategies were different, "One size does not fit all," as we will see in more detail later.

Sectoral and industrial development policies

The distinction between industry-specific policies and more general activity- or function-specific policies involves the degree to which public sector officials intervene in economic decision-making. Activity- or function-specific industrial policies mean that government provides broad incentives for business activities thought to be important for economic development, investment, FDI, or R&D, for example, but does not intervene directly in a particular decision (Adams and Klein 1983). Industry-specific or even project-specific interventions mean that bureaucrats make business decisions to create industries, to build plants, or otherwise to intervene in the business world.

In contrast, more general promotion policies, leave the basic decision making to business forces, though they may provide incentives to advance certain kinds of activities. The objective ultimately is to create industries that are strategic for industrial development, like steel, or that advance the state of the art. Quoting Pack

> Proponents of an active industrial policy place considerable emphasis on the potential of such activity for encouraging a shift to newer and more modern sectors—sectors that are characterized by industry-wide external economies and by learning-by-doing on the part of individual firms.
>
> (2000: 48)

Many countries have engaged in focused programs to develop industrial output and productivity. South Korea and Taiwan closely followed the pattern of Japan's MITI, building specific industries that were considered basic to the early stages of industrialization. (A more detailed discussion of policies in the East Asian "tigers" is provided in Appendix 1 to this chapter.) Referring to South Korea and Taiwan, Wade writes "Cotton textiles, synthetic fibers, plastics, other petrochemicals, basic metals, shipbuilding, machine tools, automobiles and industrial electronics show that the government has frequently initiated new capacities in important industries" (1990: 303). In retrospect, it is not clear how effective the efforts to build specific industries were.[40] Since considerations of political or social benefits broader than those encountered in normal business practice are taken into account, it is not certain that economically optimal judgments will be made. In the 1990s, Malaysia promoted the construction of its Proton car as a public sector effort to build the industry. Indonesia tried to develop an aircraft industry. Such practices have not been unique to East Asia, but they have been part of development strategy in many of the countries in the region. Many such government-sponsored firms did not survive in a free market economy. But that does not prove that their existence might not have played an important role, in the absence of private entrepreneurship, at the beginning of industrial development.

In more recent years, though there is still occasional government intervention, industrial development in private hands accounts for the remarkable success of the East Asian economies.

China is an interesting example. In the years 1958–66 and again after the Cultural Revolution in the mid-1970s, China followed the Soviet pattern of economic planning and industrialization, building large-scale industrial complexes run by the national government. Since 1978, industrial decision-making has been largely on a free enterprise basis, though many firms still have substantial central or provincial government ownership and are being financed by state-owned banks.

Industrial promotion programs may also be quite general, offering tax incentives for investment like the Bureau of Investment in Thailand.

The critical issues with respect to industrial policies are:

• whether the policies are broadly general, or whether they are narrowly specific focusing on particular projects or firms;
• whether the policies are consistent with market forces;
• whether, instead, they are intended to direct development into particular paths that might not otherwise have been the result of private decision-making.

The argument for industry-specific development policies rests principally on the assumption that market forces on their own would not produce an optimal development result. A simple statement to support such a view might be that businesses, particularly small local ones, are likely to be short-sighted. But a stronger case can be made on the basis of market failures which may involve various considerations:

• The externalities of the accumulation of knowledge and skills are well known. The inability of the individual investor to capture the gains from investments in R&D is the classic argument for public support for basic research. The externality benefits are considerably more widespread when we consider education and the accumulation of skills in developing countries. Lack of an educated and skilled labor force represents a serious barrier, yet it is frequently not worthwhile for businesses to invest in training and learning-by-doing. During the 1990s boom in Thailand, a freshly minted engineer would quickly skip from one employer to another as soon as the required skills and a minimum of experience had been acquired. No wonder that few Thai firms invested in engineering training!
• Failures of coordination are particularly widespread in developing economies and involve far more than small technical inconsistencies. The issue is that some parts of such an economy may be behind others. For technology, this means that the knowledge of advanced manufacturing techniques may be available, but their application is limited by the lack of appropriate infrastructure—high speed communication, for example—or by the lack of supporting specialized suppliers. This is one reason why industrial "clusters" or even just location in industrial parks may make the process of industrial innovation more accessible. Technological relationships may also be improperly coordinated. An advanced production process may not fit well with the

technology employed elsewhere in the economy. In the development literature, this question is often considered under the term, *appropriate technology*. Other failures fall into the same classification. For example, it is widely assumed that financial capital is difficult to obtain in developing countries, other than from family sources or "friendly" banks. Admittedly, there are often shortages of information and transparency, but the critical lack may be the absence of a developed financial market and banking system that would meet the needs of business. The argument for public selection and support of strategic industries, for example the development of a local steel or chemical industry, may have a similar basis, though frequently such industrial development has been seen as a cornerstone of an industrial development policy based on leading sectors or leapfrogging.

• Economies of scale tend to reduce the competitiveness of smaller newcomer firms relative to larger competitors. Even if a firm would be competitive once its scale of operation is sufficiently high, many firms never reach economic size and competitiveness. This has been seen as a basis for infant industry protection. Most economists, going as far back as Alexander Hamilton (1791) and John Stuart Mill (1848) recognize the validity of the infant industry argument, but most also are aware of the dangers of prolonged protection for inefficient industry. The issue of economies of scale is also related to first mover advantages. If a foreign firm develops a production line to economic scale, it is very difficult for local latecomers to compete successfully, often even if the underlying comparative advantage is in their favor.

• Network interdependence is closely related to scale and coordination. The issue is often discussed as a "chicken and egg" question. A networked computer has many advantages that an individual unconnected computer does not. To be useful, e-mail requires that many users be connected by the network. Yet, how does one persuade people to acquire a network connection if there are no other users? Some assurance must be provided that the network will develop and that the individual's investment in a connection will pay off.

Before one subscribes to the arguments favoring selective government intervention, it is also important to remember the many cases when public sector sponsored projects have gone wrong. It has often been argued that government officials are not sufficiently informed or experienced to make business decisions; that they have very different incentives from business people; that they are inflexible—making decisions too slowly and hanging on to failing projects too long—that they are influenced by political considerations; and, sometimes, that they are corrupt.

Trends in the role of government in business in East Asia

The role played by government in influencing the development process and the business sector varies greatly among the East Asian countries. In recent years,

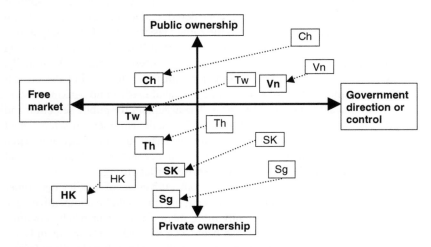

Figure 8.1 Government versus private ownership and control.

Notes
Ordinary type font—1980s.
Bold type font—2005.

that role has been changing and will change further as the focus of development shifts from manufacturing mass-produced products to more sophisticated and complex goods and in the direction of software and e-business.

Figure 8.1 illustrates broadly the trends in government regulation versus free markets (measured from East to West) and in government ownership versus private ownership (measured from North to South) in East Asia.

In each case, the country designation in ordinary type font represents the early 1980s, and the designation in bold print stands for the situation in 2005. For example, we show the shift of China from a state-owned and state-directed economy at the beginning of the 1980s, to a market-driven economy, albeit with substantial state ownership, even today. Vietnam is going along a similar path but is not as far along. On the other hand, Korea and Taiwan have been market-oriented economies, largely with private ownership, all along, but the government has exercised substantial control. Direct government intervention appears to have lessened though decisions still involve substantial consensus between government officials and private business. For Hong Kong, there is only a small shift since the basic free market and private enterprise orientation has not changed despite the move from British to Chinese sovereignty.

The important thing to note in Figure 8.1 is the consistent movement from northeast (government ownership and control) toward the southwest—private ownership and market orientation—that is apparent in all of the East Asian developing countries. The details differ by industry and by country.

Government intervention and IT

The advent of the IT revolution with its emphasis on technological change and advanced skills poses some special problems to government policy makers in these countries, as we will see in Chapter 9. The development of e-business may pose still more complex issues.

The issues related to government interventions apply even more intensively to the IT/e-business sectors than to traditional industry. On one hand, market failures are a hallmark of the high-tech knowledge-intensive fields. The more sophisticated the technology, the more important the informational content, and the more likely it is that a simple market-based solution will not produce optimal results. On the other hand, one must also recognize that decision making in the high-tech fields requires a high level of specialized expertise that is frequently not available in the public sector.

It is doubtful, however, that publicly owned or controlled industries, even those designed to leapfrog the economy into the industrial age, are an efficient way to take part in modern industry. In an age of high tech, where technologies are still evolving, a narrow focus on promoting or building particular industries is a risky proposition. For this reason, advancement of high-tech industry calls for broader, less specific, schemes to promote technology. This involves upgrading the relevant transport and communications infrastructure, promoting advanced education in science and technology, facilitating technological transfers, provision for venture capital, etc. We discuss IT and science policies in Chapter 9.

Appendix 1

Policy and industrial development: the East Asian Tigers

Government policies played an important role in the success story of economic development of the East Asian Tigers—South Korea, Hong Kong, Taiwan, and Singapore. Many politicians have espoused the "East Asian Development Model" as the optimal strategy to advance their countries. Yet, on closer examinations, although these countries had much in common, in many respects their objectives and their policies were different. Today, although they are leaders in many aspects of IT, their potentials in the industrial and high-tech fields differ greatly. In this section, we expand on the introductory discussion in Chapter 4 and provide more detail on the development of the Tigers and the implications for IT-based development.

Many aspects of the East Asian development are common to the Tigers and to other East Asian countries. The East Asian Tigers are undoubtedly the leaders on the East Asian development ladder. The East Asian countries followed policies of EP and some protection for their domestic industries, though most stopped short of explicit IS policies. They provided tax incentives for investment, and many, but not all, have encouraged FDI. They have high rates of savings and domestic investment. But diversity in size and resources, industrial structures, economic management, and, in some respects, differences in policies between some of these countries belie the notion that there is a simple common recipe for economic development. This is true for the Tigers as for the rest of the region.

The Tigers represent an interesting case study of parallel but not identical development. The years from 1960 to 1990 witnessed a transformation to modern industrial economies, competing effectively in the world economy. They have a number of features in common:

- relatively small size—Hong Kong and Singapore are city states, Taiwan and South Korea are relatively small countries.
- *semi-periphery* status (Dent 2002). On one hand, they are still very dependent on the advanced country suppliers of investment, technology, and markets. On the other hand, they are advanced compared to the neighbors: high incomes and costs, high-technology industries, sophisticated management and legal institutions.
- a history of foreign domination, that may have set the framework for later development through education, capital flows, and land redistribution.
- non-democratic or imperfectly democratic governments that put high priorities on advancement in education and development.
- focus on export orientation over domestic market development, reflecting their small size and international links.

Despite these common elements, their policies were different in many essentials. Figure 8.2 shows the four countries on a scale from low government intervention and free markets, on the right, to active government intervention at the micro-level, on the left. It should not be surprising that Hong Kong occupies the right position, while South Korea is furthest to the left, though, importantly, this scale does not imply traditional right wing or left wing political or social views.

Hong Kong

Hong Kong has clearly been at the non-interventionist side of the range, minimizing government intervention and emphasizing free trade and incoming FDI.

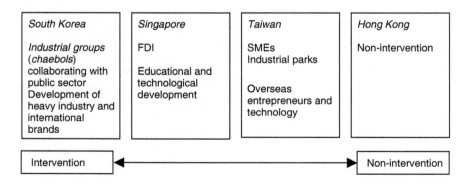

Figure 8.2 Non-intervention to intervention among the East Asian Tigers.

This reflected Hong Kong's unique position as an *entrepot* and its period as a British enclave. As a result, Hong Kong started the race with a developed infrastructure, an effective system of banking and finance, and the presence of many multinational firms. In the early postwar years, Hong Kong attracted an inflow of skilled and, often, wealthy people from China with an entrepreneurial tradition. With its continued linkage to the West, Hong Kong proved to be in an advantageous position for channeling business from the outside world into China and from China to the rest of the world.

It is not surprising that Hong Kong provided a free-market setting with bias toward free trade. Aside from provision for infrastructure and housing (land is owned by the Hong Kong government and there was much public housing), there were no selective industrial policies designed to support particular industries. Lall (1996) argues that for this reason "Hong Kong started and stayed with light labor intensive industry. ... there was little industrial or technological deepening" as in some other East Asian countries. In the late 1980s and 1990s, Hong Kong entrepreneurs began to shift production to adjacent areas of China where labor and land costs were much lower. Hong Kong, itself, underwent deindustrialization with sharp declines in industrial output and employment. Hong Kong's entrepreneurs provide headquarters, management, and capital for production activities moved to neighboring mainland China. It also serves as a channel for foreign business seeking to operate in China.

Hong Kong lacked an explicit technological development policy and lags behind Singapore, Taiwan, and Korea in technical sophistication (Thurow 2003).

Despite its political integration with China, Hong Kong remains a management and financial center but one that appears to be increasingly competing with Shanghai and other Chinese centers.

Singapore

As a city state, Singapore has many similarities with Hong Kong, though smaller and clearly more distant from and less integrated with mainland China. Singapore started as an *entrepot* for trading, ship servicing, and oil refining, taking advantage of its strategic location along the central shipping routes of Southeast Asia. After merger with Malaysia fell through in the early 1960s, to create a world-class international city economy, Singapore needed to extend its reach toward the region and the outside world.[41] Initial development took the form of export-oriented production in the apparel and light technology industries, some to be based in adjacent areas of the Singapore "Growth Triangle" in Malaysia and Indonesia. Since there was little tradition of locally-based entrepreneurship, Singapore's long time Prime Minister Lee Kuan Yew turned to attracting foreign multinationals and their FDI. "Singapore's governmental Economic Development Board (EDB) aggressively fights for foreign direct investment and the technology that goes with it" (Thurow 2003: 293). Priorities were placed on technological upgrading and on higher technical education. The government tried to guide business into higher value-added activities focusing on specialized products that were well integrated into the world economy.

The government remains a shareholder of some important high-tech enterprises. More recently, efforts have been made to further upgrade specialized technology by attracting high technology centers, developing technical education and creating a "wired" island.

More than the other countries studied, Singapore has been able to maintain its highly controlled political system and use it as a basis for directive development policies (Rodan 1989). Singapore's bureaucrats take a paternalistic state-centered approach focused on a distant strategic horizon. Massive foreign investment in petroleum refining, of course, reflected Singapore's strategic location. The initial developments of low-wage export industries in apparel and electrical equipment were upgraded repeatedly by public policies raising wages and by encouraging foreign investment ventures in higher value-added products like electronic equipment, precision engineering, telecommunications, and instruments. Singapore also put considerable emphasis on services, particularly as a regional financial and telecommunications center.

Lall (1996) argues that the fact that Singapore has not been "hollowed out" and has developed a higher level of technical sophistication than Hong Kong demonstrates the importance of policies of selective guidance. It is not clear, however, whether such an example can be generalized from the special case of Singapore, with its small size and all-controlling government, to larger economies with less qualified bureaucratic elites and under less top-down public sector control.

Taiwan

Taiwan is substantially larger than the city states discussed earlier. But like them, it was the recipient of substantial inflows of qualified Chinese workers and entrepreneurs. From early on, the Taiwanese government practiced policies of sector-specific and sometimes enterprise-specific industrial policy. Taiwan sought to attract FDI particularly into priority industries and sought to transfer information from the foreign multinationals to local enterprises. In some cases, the government took a direct stake in developing industries, steel and chemicals for example, or used joint ventures to obtain high-tech endeavors. The efforts at government industry were not always successful. Yet, some of the largest Taiwanese companies were once government owned.

The special aspect of Taiwanese industry is its reliance on small- and medium-sized firms, in contrast to the large companies and company groups encouraged in South Korea. Many families had links to the towns and villages in China from which they had emigrated. Family-owned firms were promoted and large corporations were limited with respect to vertical or horizontal integration. Economic policy has tended toward liberalization and internationalization. The link between government and business has been through business associations that have sometimes directly administered economic policy regulations. These were promoted by government policy with special incentives and industrial parks, especially with the aim of introducing high technology.[42]

Hsueh *et al.* summarize industrial policy developments in the 1980s and 1990s in Taiwan as follows:

> Only when the electronics industry rose to be the primary industry in Taiwan and the second oil crisis occurred did the government consciously try to foster this industry and provide it with the resources it lacked. What was unique in this intervention was that it was mainly focused on the provision of capital for research and development. The government chose not to interfere in the actual production and sales of goods, unlike the government's decision in the case of the petrochemicals and textile industries.
>
> (2001: 291)

Taiwan's entrepreneurs have built Southeast Asia's most advanced and broad-based electronics industry. They control the supply chain for cameras, PCs, computer screens, laptops, scanners, and many other state-of-the-art electronic computer products. Basic electronic assembly operations have been moved to lower-income countries. Taiwan has become a dominant producer of high-tech chips, cameras, instruments, etc. Taiwan has encouraged investments from abroad, in recent years, particularly from Taiwanese expatriates who have been encouraged to return home after doing their studies and, often, making their fortunes in the United States. Taiwanese entrepreneurs have increasingly directed their activities into China, where they own and operate labor-intensive production facilities directed at export markets leaving only the more advanced production processes in Taiwan.

Taiwan has in recent years developed a more society-centered and, presumably, less business-centered approach that is expected to deepen as a result of the change in political control in 2000. Mainland China remains a primary factor influencing Taiwan's policy. The ever-present threat of Chinese takeover is an important element in policies intended to maintain political independence and economic security. However, as we have noted, increasingly Taiwanese business has found outlets for capital and entrepreneurship on the mainland, making for closer economic links between China and Taiwan.

South Korea

South Korea began with a lower level of per capita income and got a late start in creating its economic bureaucracy and financial system (Wade 1990). Korea and Taiwan shared a Japanese colonial background during the first half of the twentieth century. The Japanese colonial rulers encouraged education and strict governance, a fact that may help to explain the high level of educational attainment and effective government administration (also in Taiwan). Establishing and maintaining national identity has been important.

> As a late industrialiser, Korea's success has been founded on its ability to acquire and develop foreign technologies at different stages of its economic development. Throughout the country's economic history, Korean firms have

used a variety of methods—informal learning, turnkey plants, capital importation, licensing, joint ventures, and alliances—to acquire and develop technological competencies. Their success in steel, automobiles, consumer electronics and—quite lately—semiconductors is a testament to their abilities to learn and develop technological competencies faster than many competitors.

(Ungson *et al.* 1997: 134)

Following the Japanese model, the *keiretsu*, the government of Korea encouraged the formation of large industrial conglomerates, *chaebol*.[43] A small number of these huge groups, clustered around their own bank, account for a dominant share of Korea's industrial output. The aim was to put production in the hands of a few large groups that would attain economies of scope as well as of scale. The result has been the creation of large companies with international reputations like Samsung and Hyundai. This structure has meant a focus on large-scale industries, autos, TVs, DRAM chips, etc. that are increasingly competing effectively in world markets. There is considerable debate about the extent to which Korean government officials determine industrial development strategy of the major *chaebols*. But there is little doubt about the important role of government in the development of Korea's heavy steel and chemical industries (Stern *et al.* 1995). Government agencies played an "orchestral role" (Kim's words, Kim 1997) in directing the industrial groups and providing financial support. Stern *et al.* (1995) note that some of the efforts at heavy industrial targeting, such as aluminum smelting, were ultimately failures. Others like shipbuilding and autos showed mixed success though even here some firms have established a worldwide reputation. Other industrial targeting efforts have been hugely successful. Posco steel has turned into a competitive world leader. Public sector organizations also financed and directed efforts to develop technology and to build a semiconductor industry that was expected to be, and probably was, strategically important.

Today, South Korea may be seen as a deconstructing developmental state, an advanced economy and a member of the OECD in which political uncertainties have undermined the directive power of public economic policies (Lall 1996). Nevertheless, South Korea's large-scale industries continue to face a large measure of governmental intervention. Government influence was surely much different at the beginning of the development drive than it has been recently when needs to reorganize some industrial groups have been paramount (Ungson *et al.* 1997). Large, powerful labor unions have also influenced industrial restructuring and control.

There is still a high degree of economic nationalism and neo-mercantilism reflecting the history of South Korea's struggle to establish an independent state. Since the 1997 crisis, which affected South Korea much more than other comparable countries, significant changes are occurring in the direction of an open trading nation, but a wholesale transformation cannot be expected too soon.

The Korean approach has also been largely consistent with a strategy of self-sufficiency, keeping out foreign investors from Japan and the United States. Only in recent years, after the crisis, have foreign firms been able to stake a sizeable foothold in Korean business.

Table 8.1 Industrial focus in the Tigers

	HongKong	Singapore	Taiwan	South Korea
Petrochemicals and oil refining	Limited	Priority industries, relying on strategic location	Some public enterprises beginning in 1970s	For local use
Steel	None	None	National firm	Pohang Steel (world's biggest)
Automobiles	None	None	Largely for local use	For domestic use and export Hyundai, Kia, Daewoo
Semiconductors	Little	Priority sector	Advanced chips and electronics	DRAMs, advanced chips, electronics
Electronics	Little	Disk drives and components, subsidiaries of MNEs	Acer Pcs, cameras, flat screens	PCs, TVs, screens, Samsung
Finance	Financial center	Financial and regional management center	—	—
Entrepreneurship in neighboring countries	In neighboring China	In Malaysia	In China	Limited

Source: The approach follows Hobday (1995).

Summary

In the Tigers, with the exception of Hong Kong, government has worked closely with the business community to "lead the market." Even a staunch believer in free markets would find it difficult to disagree with Robert Wade's perception that these countries, along with Japan, had "in common an intense and unequivocal commitment on the part of government to build up the international competitiveness of domestic industry and thereby raise living standards" (Wade 1990: 5).

Table 8.1 compares the way in which the Tiger countries have managed some important industries.

As the East Asian Tigers have developed, the role of the public sector in building basic industries like steel, chemicals, and petroleum refining has diminished. Today, some have become strong producers of mass produced industrial products. In South Korea, we note the emphasis on consumer-oriented mass production industries such as autos and televisions, with local supplier industries and significant international distribution. Taiwan plays a similar role but with smaller electronic products like cameras and computer screens. On the other hand, Hong Kong and Singapore have been reducing their role as manufacturers. They serve to a large extent as a location for regional management headquarters and financial institutions. Hong Kong has been cutting back industrial employment in favor of neighboring areas of China, and Taiwan has been heavily involved in the development of export industries in Guangdong, China.

9 Science, IT, and communications policies for East Asian growth

The direction of IT and e-business development in East Asian countries will be greatly influenced by government policies. That is the concern of this chapter.

Science, IT, and communications policies

As we have noted in Chapter 8, even in a free-market economy, there is theory-based support for government policy intervention in the IT fields. Individual profit-based initiatives may not allocate sufficient effort and investment to high-tech development. With regard to IT and e-business, *public good* considerations are especially important. New technology has spillover effects; innovations introduced by one individual may also be useful to many more. Networks provide linkages and communications, choices that are not available to separate operators. Externalities and network effects imply that the sum of benefits is bigger than would be the total value of the individual parts. In other words, technical knowledge, that is so central to applications of IT, benefits the society beyond the gains to the initial investor.

There are important initial barriers to new industries. Large risky investments in communications infrastructure may not be justified at the start when there are few users. The advantages of the network come when it is fully operational, not when the first users get online. Moreover, there is the learning curve: as IT techniques become familiar, they become easier to apply.

Unless initial inertia is overcome, market forces may not lead to the development of certain IT operations. Economic theory would suggest that private markets will not invest sufficiently in IT facilities, R&D, and education and will not employ socially optimal amounts of IT on the basis of individual private profit expectations. Thus, a variety of arguments suggest that public initiatives to promote IT in the private as well as the public sector are necessary stimulants for rapid IT innovation and adoption.

On the other hand, public sector planning and decision making may not deal well with the complexity of high-tech and e-business endeavors. There have been many examples of publicly promoted projects in developing countries that have gone wrong, that were not consistent with a country's comparative advantage even if one takes a forward-looking view. This could happen because they were beyond the country's technological capabilities or they could not be justified by profit and loss considerations, even in the long run. The complexity of the IT industries and the rapid technological changes in this field have frequently been a barrier to successful public sector intervention. Public IT plans tend to be more rigid than the efforts of competitive private firms and are often guided by political considerations. As a result they may lag behind the newest technology and may continue to support entrenched technical standards longer than is desirable.[44]

The advantage of private sector initiatives is that they "let many flowers bloom" and that the failure of individual projects in the evolutionary selection process does not typically impose heavy and persistent burdens on the economy.

Some scholars (Wade 1990; Westphal 2002) place great emphasis on the role of government planning and intervention in South Korea and Taiwan not only in connection with traditional industries but, more specifically, in connection with industries that offer opportunities for technological advancement. These countries combined technology promoting measures with traditional export promotion (EP) with import protection.

> In essence, technological learning was subsidized largely through import protection and disciplined through export incentives and planning... Import protection made possible the creation of export industries in advance of the point at which they would otherwise have become established, thus leading to precocious initiation of learning and accelerating the rate at which new export industries were established.
>
> (Westphal 2002: 39)

Most of the East Asian countries are putting into place plans to advance IT. In this section, we briefly summarize some of the IT-policy efforts at the country level and their background. These policies range widely and appear to be greatly dependent on the economic, cultural, and political setting.

Singapore

Singapore has had a long tradition of such development intervention. Technology policy has been one of repeated upgrading, using selective interventions to move sequentially toward more capital- and skill-intensive activities. Singapore has long sought to attract foreign direct investment (FDI) as a means of advancing and deepening technology. Westphal (2002) refers to it as "MNC-mediated industrialization." This approach has enabled Singapore to specialize in particular intermediate products, like disk drives, gaining the advantages of establishing a technology cluster that fits into the worldwide production system of multinational corporations. Important links have also been established with production sites in neighboring countries, Indonesia and Malaysia, where more land and labor are available. To supplement the limited number of local entrepreneurs, the public sector has frequently initiated or promoted activities that were seen as important for development. Some promoted domestic enterprises rely on substantial government ownership and control using holding companies like Temasek.

The Singapore government has greatly encouraged local R&D. It has extensively supported private research efforts covering up to 50 percent of their cost under an Innovation Development Scheme (Lall 1999). Much research is being done at the publicly supported National University of Singapore (NUS).

Singapore is probably the most advanced East Asian country in the promotion and implementation of the e-conomy. It is providing high speed Internet access to its entire population under Singapore's IT2000 plan. Public authorities have also played a significant role in providing network services, forging alliances with international industry leaders and establishing an appropriate policy and legal framework for free market competition. "Government intervention in the market has been successful because it has been accompanied by a unique civil service policy" (ITU 2001: 32).

Singapore is particularly distinguished in its IT educational programs at its many universities and other higher educational institutions including new schools of management. Singapore is a leader in employee industrial training. The Singaporean Ministry of Education operates a unique primary and secondary education program, connecting all schools, offering computer training to teachers, and providing IT accounts to all students above third grade.

Realizing the limits to production of electronic products, particularly in view of Singapore's relatively high wages, the Singaporean government is seeking to move the economy upward into higher value-added activities. This involves, for example, deregulation of high value-added services. It is also reflected in the National Biomedical Sciences Strategy to promote research, teaching, and, presumably, entrepreneurship in the biomedical fields. Singapore hospitals serve as a medical center for the entire region.

South Korea

South Korea's export production is in the hands of highly concentrated horizontally and vertically integrated *chaebols*, privately-owned though with substantial government collaboration and support. Many of them have been able to gain international recognition for their products and brand names. South Korean firms are organizing collaborations with Chinese enterprises for labor-intensive aspects of the IT production chain.

Korea has sought to develop indigenous technological capability since the 1970s. However, it has clearly been a latecomer. As such, it has been able to take advantage of technology already developed elsewhere in more advanced countries. Once, the largest industrial groupings—Samsumg, Hyundai, and LG Group—saw semiconductors as one of their principal priorities, they developed extensive licensing agreements with major producers in the United States and Japan and acquired "packaged" foreign technology to produce already developed products (Ungson *et al.* 1997). Korean industry has largely acquired technology by importing capital goods, technology licensing, reverse engineering, and domestic R&D.

It then proceeded to develop homegrown process improvements and refinements. Government policy that, at first, discouraged foreign investment in favor of control by domestic enterprises, has played a catalytic role and has provided extensive incentives and support for these developments. Under government and industry sponsorship, several largescale cooperative development projects have been set up for high-tech technology development and for improving electronic industry capabilities.

With respect to communications, Korea has one of the highest rates of mobile phone use in the world, extensive broadband connections, and a high level of education. However, this may not yet translate directly to business or consumer Internet applications. Surveys indicate that Korea's industries are still behind the world leaders. "Since they started as final assemblers of imported parts and components, many Korean industries are weak in terms of forward and backward linkage. This discourages innovation by user-producer interactions" (Lee 2001). Many public policy decisions, for example, by the National Assembly's Science, Technology, Information and Telecommunication (STIT) Committee were long pending without resolution (Choung *et al.* 2002).

Recently, Korea has placed great emphasis on development of science and technology allocating as much as 3 percent of its GDP to science and technology investment. The forward-looking range of this work and its practicality is suggested by the ten fields selected for priority: digital television and broadcasting, digital displays, intelligent robots, future-type automobiles, intelligent home networking, digital contents and software solutions, next-generation batteries, new biomedicines and organs.[45]

Taiwan

Taiwanese policy has emphasized incentives and support for small- and medium-size private enterprises located in technology parks. A mix of policies has spawned geographic clusters of IT-related activities.

Early on, Taiwanese electronics producers were still at the stage of assembly production. Small- and medium-size entrepreneurs were reluctant to take on high risk capital-intensive high-tech projects. So the Taiwan government needed to initiate a tradition of facilitating the acquisition of technology through cooperation between government officials and industrial leaders. Subsidies were provided to establish a public–private enterprise, United Microelectronics Corporation (UMC). This group spread new technology and research results and worked closely with the Electronics Research and Service Organization (ERSO) to provide training. This was the basis for a tradition of government encouragement and facilitation of acquiring new skills and transferring them to industry (Hsueh *et al.* 2001).

Policies toward FDI were designed to increase local benefits. The government sought to maximize the technological and skill linkages of foreign investments and encouraged local sourcing. Taiwan has made important efforts to assimilate technology, to make the technology indigenous, supported and developed by local firms, even by firms under the direction of Taiwanese entrepreneurs returning from abroad. Taiwan's government-sponsored science parks, the Hsinchu science-based industrial park, for example, were intended to attract foreign and domestic capital and technology. The parks are located near universities with the intent of drawing on the skills of high-level university scientists and technicians. The science parks have played an important part in forming technological "clusters."

In some cases, government organizations took direct responsibility for developing process technologies for high-tech electronics. The government also made investments to help start new corporations like the Taiwan Semiconductor Manufacturing Corporation (TSMC), one of the biggest success stories. Taiwanese contract manufacturers have grown rapidly relying on the growth of a local components supply industry, in the Taipei–Hsinchu technology corridor. They have become world leaders in bringing personal computers to market quickly (Yusuf and Evenett 2002). As in Hong Kong and Singapore, local investors have gone on to move production of labor intensive and price sensitive products like desktop computers to China, in this way providing a transfer of technology in the outward direction.

Statistics on computers and Internet use in Taiwan are more difficult to obtain than for other East Asian countries. The data available suggest that use of mobile phones and number of Internet users (per 10,000 population) falls only a little short of the highest in the East Asian region.

Hong Kong

Hong Kong has been very much a special case in East Asia. It has always followed free trade policies, with little or no technology strategy. As we have noted, after the Communist takeover in China, Hong Kong's growth as a manufacturing and trading center was initiated by textile workers and entrepreneurs from other parts of China As a result, Hong Kong became the home of small- to medium-size businesses specializing in relatively simple labor intensive products like clothing, toys, and simple consumer electronics. As local labor costs rose, manufacturing activity was shifted to Special Economic Zones (SEZ) in China, where low wages encourage labor intensive assembly operations. Hong Kong became a trading, finance, and transportation center.

There was little need to develop advanced manufacturing technology. Most of what was needed came with the imported capital goods that enabled some upgrading of technology but did not require complex research. The government of Hong Kong has given limited support to exports and export-related technology, especially in textiles but did not engage in selective industrial policies and public support for IT. Hong Kong has lagged behind other East Asian countries in advanced technological development. We cannot be sure that is a consequence of Hong Kong's special economic situation relative to China, or, as Lall (1996)[46] argues, because of its lack of technology-promoting policy.

To offset the deindustrialization that has been taking place in Hong Kong, the local government has provided support to an Industrial Technology Center and efforts are being made to encourage Chinese firms to develop high technology products in Hong Kong research centers (Lall 1999).

Public sector and private entrepreneurs have provided a high level of communications infrastructure that made possible the establishment of a financial and communications center. Whether such a center can continue to prosper in competition with other Chinese cities, now that Hong Kong is officially part of China, remains an unanswered question.

China

China is not nearly as far along technologically as many other East Asian countries taking an overall average view, though the high points of Chinese technology may be quite advanced. A transition economy, China used a parallel system to continue (and gradually phase out) its state enterprises along with turning its collective firms, still largely publicly owned, into market-oriented enterprises. Foreign-owned and joint venture businesses dominate the export market and have been a source of great gains in productivity. An undervalued exchange rate and low wage rates have assured competitiveness in the world market. (This topic is considered in more detail in Chapter 10.)

China's comparative advantage remains in labor cost where it is competitive not only with the more advanced East Asian countries but also with some more traditional exporters like Thailand and the Philippines. This has meant that most Chinese exports are textile and leather goods, toys, etc., though there is a rapidly increasing output of consumer electronics. These products were intended first for export to the West but are increasingly being directed to the home market and to other parts of East Asia. With a huge domestic market potential and as a low-cost producer, China offers great opportunities for electronic assembly operations for cellular phones, computers, etc. China is, however, a very heterogeneous country with divisions of authority between provincial governments and the central administration that may stand in the way of effective technology policy. Highly sophisticated products in large volumes are for the future, though perhaps not the far off future.

China has its "Golden Development Plan" which aims to achieve advances in science, technology, education, and public administration. As part of this broad scheme, the Golden Bridge/Information Superhighway Project, Tsinghua University and a consortium of US Middle Western universities are setting up programs to train as many as 30,000 Chinese engineers, 100,000 computer professionals, and many more government officials.

Malaysia

Malaysia has followed a strategy similar to Singapore. It has been able to attract high technology multinationals beginning with electronics companies relocating their labor-intensive activities from their base in Singapore. Once established there, these firms have been persuaded to upgrade technologically, a strategy the Malaysian government has encouraged. The result has been the formation of high-tech electronics industry centers in Penang, for example, though much of the country is still technologically less advanced.

Malaysia faces great disparities within the country between regions and between its Chinese, Malay, and Indian ethnic groups. It seeks to accommodate advanced high-tech operations at the same time as it wants to create industrial employment and build up rural areas. The Malaysian government has organized and protected some highly sector-selective heavy industry projects.

In recent years, the government has become more activist with respect to high-tech and is creating a Multimedia Super Corridor and Cyberjaya as an intellectual industry city. The idea is to create a geographic cluster of high-tech companies and their headquarters, research centers, and a multimedia university. Direct financial incentives and tax exemptions are provided for companies in the area that attain special status employing knowledge workers and transferring foreign technologies. The aims of these policies is clearly to advance, if not leapfrog, Malaysia's technical competence in the IT fields. Though Malaysia has had a series educational development plans, it is not clear that, outside the technological "clusters," Malaysia yet has sufficient skilled technicians to support an IT-based development strategy (Anuwar 1992).

Thailand

Thailand has had a long history of investment promotion through its Board of Investment (BOI). The Eastern Seaboard has been a preferenced site for manufacturing and technology firms, though in recent years the BOI has sought to disperse such operations throughout the country. Industrial development has expanded manufacturing. There is hope that Thailand may become a center for auto parts production, serving the Southeast Asian region.

A number of scientific development efforts have sought to stimulate science and its applications, for example, Thailand's National Technology Framework, 2004–11, that plans the development of Thailand's biotech industries, hoping to turn Thailand into the "kitchen of the world." In 2004, the Thai Ministry of ICT announced its ICT Master Plan 2010 with a key objective "to exploit the benefits of ICT to transition Thailand to a knowledge-based society and economy." (From an advertisement by the BOI in *The Economist*, October 15–21, 2005) It is important to note that, so far, Thailand's principal ICT export activities are in manufacture of disk drives and in packaging and testing integrated circuits, activities that are more labor- than technology-intensive.

Despite the fact that the National Information Technology Committee (NITC) has been operational since 1992, public policy toward Internet and technology development and educational development has lagged. Policies have been less aggressive and less focused than in the leading countries. Thailand continues to face a mismatch between demand and supply of qualified manpower. The shortage of high-level skilled technical workers and managers is discouraging investment in consumer industries and high-tech. Even with rapid expansion, the educational system may not be sufficient to meet needs for technical manpower.

The State Communications Authority of Thailand (CAT) has maintained considerable control of Internet operations. Limited high-speed access, lack of competence in the English language, and cultural factors have been a barrier to the development of e-commerce.

Philippines

The Philippines ranks among the lower-income countries in the region and has continued to focus its activities on labor-intensive activities, some like assembly and wiring of chips, related to high-tech but calling for ample supplies of low-cost labor.

One of the first countries to allow private telephone service, the Philippines has numerous internet service providers, but most are simply resellers. While there is much interest on the part of the government to promote IT, the private Philippine telecom market limits the government's ability to develop IT infrastructure. The Philippines still lags far behind in terms of computer literacy and use.

Indonesia

Indonesia faces the prospect of losing some of its labor-intensive production to countries that have still lower wages. Political uncertainties, also, have stood in the way of FDI. And a low level of technological development prevents expansion of the more sophisticated high-tech industries.

In an effort to advance technology, Indonesia was planning an aircraft industry, a field inconsistent with its technological capabilities.[47] Government support for this project ended as did the domestic car project (Iqbal and James 2002). Indonesia has lagged behind in Internet development as a result of low income and economic and political turmoil. The telecommunication/Internet sector in Indonesia remains dominated by government controlled telephone providers. More than half of Indonesian users access through internet cafes, locally known as Warnets.

Vietnam, Myanmar, Laos, and Cambodia

Vietnam, Myanmar, Laos, and Cambodia are at a far lower stage of development than the other countries in the region. Vietnam has been a beneficiary of shifting production of labor-intensive activities from elsewhere in the region, particularly the production of athletic shoes.

Vietnam's Internet penetration is growing but remains far behind other East Asian countries. The field continues to be state-dominated and access remains tightly controlled. Myanmar, Laos, and Cambodia, similarly, are latecomers hindered by tight political control, low income, and limited infrastructure.

Intellectual property protection and the problem of piracy

Intellectual property issues are a particularly important policy consideration for the IT industries. Firms are reluctant to provide their computer code and technical secrets to areas of the world where intellectual property protection is likely to be inadequate. As an American entrepreneur said to me recently: "Do I dare take my procedures to the Far East? I have heard that in that part of the world they will dispense with you as soon as they have acquired the information they are seeking."

The issue of protection of rights to software is particularly important in East Asia, and specifically in China, since this vast market has been expanding with astonishing rapidity. From the perspective of the software producers, this region of the world represents the future. But copied software is a revenue loss of major proportions. Moreover, software distribution carries the danger that unlicensed program content will be used as a stepping stone to more advanced developments that may represent a threat to the original intellectual property producer. Firms may seek to block the importation, legal or otherwise, of their software into countries that do not provide adequate intellectual property protection. And, perhaps most importantly, they may hesitate to set up programming centers or to use advanced technology in countries where intellectual property is not secure.

"Pirates are not just characters in the movies. In the global economy, software piracy will cost these countries [the reference is to Vietnam, China, and Russia] dearly in terms of trust" (Kumasaka 2003a). In this case, the term piracy refers to unauthorized, and consequently, unpaid-for use of computer software. The Business Software Alliance, a group seeking to protect worldwide intellectual property rights for software producers, has been carrying on an annual survey of software piracy. The approach is to compare the installations of software applications (demand) with software applications legally shipped (supply). The difference between these two figures, on a country-by-country basis, equals an estimate of piracy (a figure usually shown as a percentage of total software installed in each country). The statistics are quite tenuous. Only a rough estimate is possible since guesstimates of the installed PC base and shipments as well as of the number of software applications on each PC are required. It is not, after all, possible to count pirated installations directly. But the numbers may not be an underestimate, since they exclude home computer use where unlicensed programs may be most prevalent. These calculations (Table 9.1) find that, worldwide, 2 out

Table 9.1 Rate of software piracy, 2001

Vietnam	94
China	92
Indonesia	88
Philippines	63
Thailand	77
Malaysia	70
South Korea	48
Taiwan	53
Singapore	51
Hong Kong	53
United States	25
Japan	37

Source: BSA Piracy Study (2002).

of 5 business software applications were illegally installed with a revenue loss to the software industry of approximately $10 billion.

With respect to some countries in East Asia, the problem has been particularly severe. As compared to a piracy rate in advanced countries in the 20–40 percent range, the piracy rate in China is 92 percent, that is, 9 out of 10 program installations are outside of license. The more advanced East Asian countries, Taiwan, South Korea, Singapore, and Hong Kong, do better with piracy rates about 50 percent. With the admission of China into the WTO, the Chinese government has promised to protect intellectual property rights, but it is not at all clear how the improvement will be effected. In the meantime, programming firms must rely on secrecy and copy protection devices to assure that their intellectual property is not violated. Recently a large number of US and European firms have announced the creation of programming centers in East Asia (and India) where workers are far cheaper than in the advanced countries. It is not clear how serious a barrier inadequate intellectual property protection will be to the expansion of programming operations in the region.

10 Trends in East Asian high-tech export performance and competitiveness

The headline reads: "High Tech in China: Is It a Threat to Silicon Valley?" (*Newsweek*, October 18, 2002) Note the question mark!

In the past decades, the export performance of the East Asian economies has been phenomenal. The issue of East Asian competitiveness has expanded in force as more and more products manufactured in East Asia displace goods that had been produced in the advanced countries. Recently, as China has become a powerhouse of mass production, the issue has turned from "Why is East Asia so competitive in Western markets?", to a more focused question "Why is China so competitive in all markets?" (Western markets and those of other East Asian countries.)

Some economists, but by no means all of them, have been worried about the growing centralization of the world's manufacturing production—not just of traditional products but also of high-tech goods. In East Asia, China is being seen as an important contributor to shifts in production and foreign investment that have affected growth of other countries in the region. In the advanced Western countries and Japan, where a large fraction of East Asian exports are directed, many people are concerned about the implications for inflation (deflation?) and manufacturing employment (unemployment). Such worry is being registered in Japan.

> A situation, largely without precedent in the industrialization of other nations, is thus unfolding in China where there has been long-term economic growth without rising wages. Judging from the large surplus [of] labor in the hinterland, this situation could continue for about another decade. If so, the deflationary pressure on the global economy from China will continue.
>
> (Kojima 2002: 22)

In the United States, too, China's exchange rate and its implications for (unfair?) competition have become a political issue as the US trade deficit toward China has risen to over $100 billion. It is not altogether surprising that new trade restrictions are being proposed.

These issues are of particular importance as one looks ahead to an increasingly integrated global economy with growing emphasis on trade in high-tech and e-business. An important dimension of this question is to what extent the East

Asian manufacturing and export prowess is simply an extension of the "old" economy or whether it already represents a first stage of the "new." Will East Asia, and perhaps simply China, take over the world's IT and e-business markets?

This chapter considers why East Asia and, in particular, China has become so competitive.[48] Does East Asian competitiveness reflect the "new economy?"

East Asia's IT export performance

The composition of East Asian exports is an important consideration in a discussion of East Asian competitiveness. As we note in Chapter 5, advancement on the East Asian development ladder implies systematic change in a country's cost structure and in its production potentials from primary and simple labor-intensive products to sophisticated high technology. We are concerned here with the last stage, the introduction of high technology exports. Where does East Asia stand with respect to these advanced products?

Table 10.1 shows a breakdown of East Asian exports into six categories that correspond to products at different stages of advancement from simple agricultural production, through labor intensive activities, to high technology.[49] The high-tech and capital goods category accounts for half or more of exports in all the listed countries, except Indonesia. While food and agricultural category exports have been increasing slowly, fuels, industrial materials, and mass production manufactures are increasing in line with world market growth. The high-tech and capital goods category is generally the fastest growing, particularly in China where annual growth was at 15 percent. However, in China the high-tech category probably includes a large share of relatively simple products, like PCs and cell phones as well as parts, rather than highly sophisticated complex capital goods and chips.[50] Some of these exports represent a shift of production from neighboring countries, especially Taiwan and South Korea where costs of simple components and of assembly operations have been rising.

Looking more closely at the composition of East Asian exports, Table 10.2 records the growth of exports in important two-digit SITC (Standard Industrial Trade Classification) categories. Dividing the major categories into high-tech and low-tech groups, it is apparent that exports of high-tech products have been growing much more rapidly than the low-tech products.

In China, the growth of high-tech product groups is in a range of 17–25 percent annually, whereas exports of traditional products grew only 5–7 percent annually in the 1995–2001 period. These sectors have also shown rapid growth in other countries, for example, telecom in Hong Kong and Korea, office machines in Indonesia and Malaysia, and electrical machinery and parts in the Philippines. It should be noted, however, that the high-tech sectors in these countries are still small and largely represent processing and assembly operations on high-tech components that are imported from neighboring countries. Chinese enterprises have plans to promote their own advanced technology, but the economics still favor labor-intensive rather than capital-intensive activities in China and other

Table 10.1 Breakdown of East Asian exports by stage of manufacturing, 1995–2001

	China		Hong Kong		Indonesia		Korea	
	US$ (million)	(% p.a.)	US$ (million)	(% p.a.)	US$ (million)	(% p.a.)	US$ (million)	(% p.a.)
Raw food	12,777	4.2	2,304	−2.9	3,252	−1.6	2,204	−3.0
Processed agricultural products	5,156	−3.0	3,098	−9.5	4,595	−6.1	1,896	−0.5
Fuels	8,405	7.6	495	−20.4	14,274	3.6	8,038	19.6
Industrial materials	29,421	5.6	15,724	−2.7	4,630	7.1	22,801	2.9
Manufactured mass production	85,857	6.9	56,566	−0.2	17,164	1.8	22,003	−2.0
High-tech and capital goods	122,080	15.0	112,944	4.1	11,070	12.4	93,492	3.9
Total	263,696	9.5	191,131	1.6	54,986	3.2	148,316	3.2

	Malaysia		Philippines		Singapore		Thailand	
	US$ (million)	(% p.a.)	US$ (million)	(% p.a.)	US$ (million)	(% p.a.)	US$ (million)	(% p.a.)
Raw food	1,734	−0.6	1,302	−0.4	1,547	−49.3	9,712	−0.7
Processed agricultural products	5,571	−9.6	889	−7.8	2,093	−10.0	2,670	−4.0
Fuels	8,557	8.4	272	−0.2	9,243	2.2	1,814	24.8
Industrial materials	6,124	6.1	852	−0.9	12,296	1.8	5,757	8.2
Manufactured mass production	7,663	−0.6	3,839	9.2	4,082	−4.6	11,555	−3.0
High-tech and capital goods	58,355	4.5	24,995	13.2	91,919	0.9	33,606	5.3
Total	88,004	2.9	32,150	10.2	121,179	−3.0	62,204	2.8

Source: United Nations: Comtrade.

Table 10.2 Growth of exports in 1995–2001, selected sectors

	China		Hong Kong		Indonesia		Korea	
	US$	(% p.a.)	US$	(% p.a.)	US$	(% p.a.)	US$	(% p.a.)
High-tech sectors								
SITC 75 Office machines, ADP	23,572	26.5	17,747	10.0	2,063	23.6	28,534	−4.5
SITC 76 Telecom	16,770	14.1	7,041	46.1	27,230	−1.0	13,499	16.7
SITC 77 Electrical machinery, parts	23,759	17.3	18,697	1.8	3,354	12.0	24,187	−2.6
Low Tech Sectors								
SITC 83 Travel goods, handbags	12,170	−0.2	1,140	5.8	7,260	−9.7	15,944	9.8
SITC 84 Clothing and accessories	25,998	16.7	30,655	7.5	2,280	17.3	60,430	−3.4
SITC 85 Footwear	20,937	4.2	14,835	30.5	34,717	5.1	21,406	−4.8
SICT 89 Miscellaneous manufactures	4,378	−0.9	187	12.0	34	−2.1	19	−13.4
	Malaysia		Philippines		Singapore		Thailand	
	US$	(% p.a.)	US$	(% p.a.)	US$	(% p.a.)	US$	(% p.a.)
High-tech sectors								
SITC 75 Office machines, ADP	270	14.69	38	−8.0	233	−17.9	441	−0.4
SITC 76 Telecom	36,743	7.0	23,551	1.6	4,599	4.8	484	−2.1
SITC 77 Electrical machinery, parts	2,071	−1.5	2,423	13.3	1,632	1.8	4,320	−2.4
Low Tech Sectors								
SITC 83 Travel goods, handbags	9,676	7.2	5,575	−4.7	1,474	−5.1	29	−16.7
SITC 84 Clothing and accessories	84	−4.1	72	−12.6	112	−1.7	352	−21.1
SITC 85 Footwear	22,085	7.9	22,350	1.0	1,181	0.7	9,724	−0.8
SITC 89 Miscellaneous manufactures	2,014	1.1	514	−0.8	4,552	4.4	4,034	−0.3

Source: United Nations: Comtrade.

less developed East Asian countries. The growth of traditional East Asian exports, like clothing, is still very rapid in China.

International competitiveness and comparative advantage and IT

Competitiveness is generally meant to describe a country's or an industry's productivity (Porter 1990) and actual and potential export performance. International competitiveness is usually treated as largely, but not wholly, a matter of costs, that is, which country is able to deliver the product to the market most cheaply. It is often also a matter of quality or product specifications. Exchange rates, domestic wages and material costs, productivity and production ability, transportation and communication costs, and trade barriers and trade strategy may all play a role. Competitiveness may involve dynamic attributes in the sense that, given resource environment, countries may become more competitive as a result of learning-by-doing, assimilation of technology, capital accumulation, and policy intervention.

From a sectoral perspective, it is important to ask which industries are competitive in world markets. This calls for a cost comparison, at a prevailing exchange rate involving such factors as wages and capital costs, scale of production, and, of course, productivity. Some industries will be more suited to an economy's endowment of factors and skills than others. High-tech industries operate in more advanced countries, and labor-intensive, mass production industries in countries where labor is relatively cheap. Dynamic improvements in competitiveness, often a consequence of foreign investment or management, may mean that the competitiveness of currently exporting industries improves or that new products, perhaps technologically more advanced ones, become competitive.

Factors influencing East Asian IT competitiveness

The competitiveness of the East Asian economies relates to a number of factors. We begin by analyzing the exchange rate, and then we turn to the other elements that may well play a more important role.

The exchange rate

International competitiveness is greatly influenced by the rate at which currencies trade on foreign exchange markets. Figure 10.1 shows the path of East Asian exchange rates as compared to the US dollar adjusted for domestic price changes[51] from an assumed index value of 100 in 1992. The devaluation of the Chinese currency from 5.8 to 8.3 RMB to the US dollar in 1994 is often seen as a critical factor responsible for the extraordinary growth of Chinese exports. Note how the decline of the Chinese exchange rate preceded the depreciation of other East Asian exchange rates in 1997–8. As we have noted in Chapter 6, it has been argued that the Chinese devaluation increased the competitiveness of China as

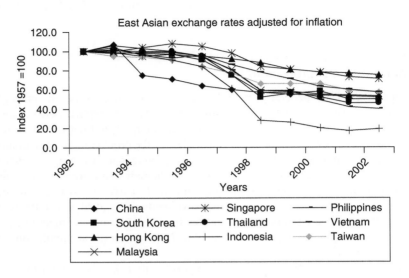

Figure 10.1 East Asian exchange rates (1992 = 100) (comparison is with the US$, after adjustment for relative inflation).

compared to other East Asian countries and precipitated the 1997 crisis. But, the 1994 devaluation was principally an alignment of official rates to market rates at which most exports were being priced anyway. The mid-1990s, when Chinese exports grew so greatly, mark the time when factories in China were being equipped to produce quality products for the world market. After the 1997 crisis, other exchange rates in East Asia adjusted downward. East Asian nominal exchange rates are now aligned with that of China approximately as before 1994, except Hong Kong and Singapore in the upward direction and Indonesia in the downward direction. The result is striking in that in China and in most other East Asian countries the real exchange rates in 2002 were one-half or little more than the level prevailing in 1992. In other words, Chinese and other East Asian exports have been supported by a substantial depreciation in East Asian currency exchange rates, the Chinese RMB yuan has been stabilized against the US dollar so that as the foreign exchange value of the US dollar declined against the Japanese yen and against European currencies the RMB yuan exchange rate depreciated despite the large surplus of Chinese balance of payments. More recently as the dollar improved, the Chinese currency has appreciated.

The discussion here deals with the changes in competitiveness over time. An important question is the level across countries, Have exchange rates favored exports from East Asia all along? In this sense, there is little disagreement that many East Asian currencies, the Chinese RMB yuan in particular, are under-valued. The question is by how much. International comparisons of purchasing power have long indicated that for many developing countries per capita GDP on a purchasing power parity (PPP) basis yields much higher figures than the corresponding comparison based on the exchange rate (Summers and Heston 1991). Though some East Asian countries have very low incomes in comparison to the United States and other advanced countries, the disparity is not as big as the translation of local currency to US dollars on an exchange rate basis indicates. For China, this discrepancy is very large—Chinese exchange rate-adjusted GNI (gross national income) per capita of $1,100 versus PPP adjusted GNI per capita of $4,990 (for 2003, World Bank) a factor of 4.5 to 1 (Table 10.3). The relationship between PPP- and exchange rate-adjusted incomes in East Asia is quite systematic. (Figure 10.2, the countries on the right are the United States and Japan, the countries on the left are Vietnam, China, Indonesia, etc.). Clearly, the higher per capita income, the less the difference between the two figures. This is an important point since international competitiveness depends on the exchange rate conversion while real purchasing power is best measured on a PPP basis.

Table 10.3 Per capita income and undervaluation in East Asian countries (US$ 2003)

	Exchange-rate basis	*PPP basis*	*Undervaluation*[a]
China	1,100	4,990	78.0
South Korea	12,020	17,930	33.0
Malaysia	3,780	8,940	57.7
Philippines	1,080	4,640	76.7
Thailand	2,180	7,430	70.7
Singapore	21,230	24,180	12.2
Indonesia	810	3,210	74.8
Vietnam	480	2,490	80.7
Cambodia	310	2,060	85.0
Laos	320	1,730	81.5
Japan	34,510	28,620	−20.6
US	37,610	37,300	−0.8

Source: World Bank.

Note

a Undervaluation is computed as $U = 1 - Y_{(x\text{-rate basis})}/Y_{(PPP\ basis)}$.

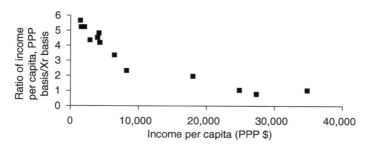

Figure 10.2 Relationship between GDI per capita and PPP income/Xr income, 2001.

Source: Based on data in Table 10.3.

Thus, the ratio of exchange rate-adjusted GNI to PPP-adjusted GNI provides a measure of undervaluation, how much the local currency is priced below its true real exchange rate. In the Chinese case, this represents an undervaluation of 78 percent (Table 10.3). In other East Asian countries undervaluation is also substantial although less in more advanced countries like South Korea. The effective exchange rate of the city-state of Singapore is almost on par with that of the United States.

Labor cost

Even the above comparison may not be appropriate to establish the competitiveness of East Asian products sold in international trade. PPP is based on price surveys covering a mix of products sold locally. The critical issue for competitiveness is not local purchasing power but rather a comparison of the delivered product cost in a world currency like the US dollar. Wages are a key cost ingredient. By world standards, wages in most East Asian countries are relatively low (Figure 10.3), and lower in China and Indonesia than other East Asian countries (though probably not than in Vietnam). For example, according to the Chinese Statistical Yearbook (2001) average wages in China in 1999 amounted to 8,346 RMB and manufacturing wages were 7,521 RMB per year—in exchange rate-adjusted terms approximately $1,000. Even though wages in some parts of China where exports originate like Shanghai, Shenzhen, and Guangdong provinces are higher,

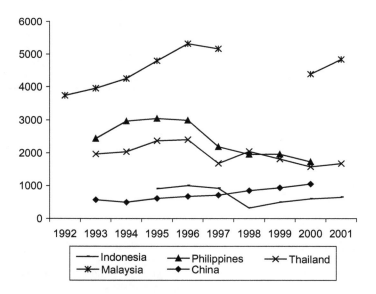

Figure 10.3 Average annual earnings in manufacturing (US$ per year, exchange rate-adjusted).

Source: ADB.

by a factor of two, and have been increasing rapidly, wage costs in China remain very low by world standards. A more *ad hoc* comparison of labor costs is as follows. Many travelers in China have noted that cost comparisons of locally supplied labor services like taxi rides often yield price comparisons that are "one to one," a 10 RMB yuan ride in Nanjing, China is roughly for the same distance as a $10 ride in Boston. When one notes that the United States' manufacturing wage averages $30,000 on an annual basis, some thirty times the exchange rate-based wages in China, it is not surprising that even with likely differences in productivity, many products can be produced in China at a much lower cost than in the United States. Similar, but not so extreme comparisons apply in other East Asian countries (Figure 10.3).

Other costs

Other cost considerations may be important but are more difficult to measure. The structure of costs is highly specific to the product and the manufacturing process, as we have already noted with regard to labor costs. With a few exceptions—energy in Indonesia, for example—the East Asian countries generally do not have cost advantages with costs other than labor. The various costs that are encountered can be summarized as follows:

- Capital costs—Capital costs in East Asia have traditionally been much higher than in Western countries, interest rates running as high as 14 percent in Thailand before the 1997 crisis, for example. Inflows of foreign capital have tended to reduce the cost of capital in recent years. Projects financed from abroad, foreign direct investment (FDI), are charged with prevailing world capital costs (long term interest rate) but they must bear a substantial risk premium.
- Material cost—Few East Asian countries supply domestic raw material inputs for their export products. Most material inputs are purchased at world market prices plus transportation. On this basis they do not offer a competitive advantage, with the exception of some locally supplied inputs like tropical lumber and some fibers and leather and tropical foods.
- Energy cost—As with materials, except for Indonesia, the East Asian countries rely heavily on the world market for energy. Many of them have developed available energy sources, natural gas in the Bay of Thailand, for example, but, on balance, energy used in East Asia should be included in costs on a world market price basis.
- Parts cost—There is substantial trade in parts, much of it between Japan, Taiwan, and South Korea and countries where electronic products are assembled like China and the Philippines. Most parts traded are sophisticated high-tech products in which only the East Asian high-tech leaders have comparative advantage (due to technology skills).
- Transportation costs—Transportation costs from East Asia to the market have been coming down for many years. Speedy container ships and air

freighters have greatly reduced costs of shipping products to the West. Internal shipping in China and in some other countries still faces many hurdles. This was a factor in the selection of Nanjing over much farther inland Chongqing as a location for the new Ford Motor Company assembly plant in China.

• Trade barriers and tariffs—Trade barriers have been reduced, though not eliminated altogether. The WTO rules now apply to most East Asian countries.

Other determinants of competitiveness

Broadly speaking, East Asia's principal cost advantage has been low labor cost. Other costs are not likely to be far enough different from world market prices in most of East Asia to serve as a basis for developing export industries. However, one may ask whether other factors affect East Asian competitiveness in world markets.

A critical consideration of competitiveness is supplying products that meet world market specifications with respect to design, quality, and technological content. Improvements in manufacturing skill represent an important step in the improving competitiveness of East Asian industry. South Korea, Taiwan, and Singapore learned early the importance of product specifications and quality. Following the example of post-Second World War Japan, they pushed their exports to high levels of technology and quality. Prior to the 1990s, China was still selling relatively low quality goods. More recently quality has improved greatly, in part as a result of the intervention of foreign investors from Hong Kong and Taiwan and, more recently, from Europe, North America, and Japan.

FDI has been a critical consideration in improving East Asia's ability to produce goods for the world market. China has been the dominant recipient of FDI in East Asia receiving almost $50 billion of FDI annually (Table 10.4).[52] As we have noted, FDI is an important factor not only for capital flows but also for inflows of technology and management skills.

Table 10.4 FDI in East Asia, 1994–2003 (net inflows, millions of US$)

	1994	1998	2000	2001	2002	2003
China	33,787	43,751	38,399	44,241	49,308	—
Hong Kong	—	−2,220	2,572	12,432	−7,781	9,791
China + Hong Kong	—	41,531	40,971	56,673	41,527	—
South Korea	−1,652	673	4,285	1,108	−224	−207
Taiwan	−1,265	−3,614	−1,773	−1,371	−3,441	−5,226
Indonesia	2,109	−356	−4,550	−3,278	−1,513	—
Malaysia	4,342	2,163	3,788	554	3,203	—
Philippines	1,591	2,287	1,345	982	1,111	—
Singapore	—	—	11,919	−2,025	2,030	5,873
Thailand	1,366	7,315	3,366	3,820	900	—

Source: ADB.

Foreign firms begin by setting up subsidiaries or joint ventures to export products to their home markets. These have to meet world specifications and quality requirements. Increasingly, they are also raising the level of technology. As a result, Chinese goods have become highly competitive in Western markets and account for a growing market share. Other East Asian countries like Malaysia and Thailand have also promoted foreign investment, hoping to gain capital and, importantly, improvements in the quality and technical advancement of their export products. China, however, offers a special advantage to investors over other East Asian countries. Many foreign producers view their entry as export producers in China only as first step, hoping ultimately also to sell in the huge and growing Chinese domestic market.

Frequently, the relationships within an industrial cluster enable East Asian domestic firms to develop products comparable to those being sold on the world market, to apply internationally-used advanced technologies, and to draw on experienced workers and suppliers. Taiwan led the way in this direction. Important knowledge externalities result from foreign investment (Liu 2002; Thompson 2003). Learning to produce and economies of scale enable East Asian producers to improve their production efficiency.

Establishing the competitiveness of the East Asian countries in the IT fields poses some special problems. These activities are diverse and some of them call for specialized skills. We will consider the prospects in these fields further in Chapter 12.

Conclusions

The issue of East Asian competitiveness does not appear to be simply a matter of exchange rate undervaluation. It is a part of a process of fundamental change in the locus of world manufacturing industries, a result of globalization, or, as we have suggested earlier, semi-globalization. Though market exchange rates adjust gradually, large differences between market exchange rates and PPP exchange rates between developing countries and advanced economies persist (Kravis *et al.* 1978). As the impediments to trade and movements of capital and knowledge are reduced, these differentials dominate competitiveness in today's world. Cost differentials between various parts of the world create incentives to shift production activity to regions where products can be produced most cheaply. These differentials also attract international movements of capital and entrepreneurship, increasing the ability of the low cost developing country exporter to compete in the world economy. "Learning to produce" is also a critical consideration in this regard, as we have noted.

The turn of East Asian production toward more advanced products with technological content is also notable. On one hand, this represents competition between the East Asian countries and with other developing countries (Mexico). On the other, it reflects a collaborative symbiotic relationship with South Korea, Singapore, and Taiwan whose cost structure has outgrown the simpler high technology goods that supported earlier phases of their industrialization. China is a good example of this phenomenon. While the Chinese industry fits well with the growing technological prowess of Taiwan and South Korea, China may not yet be sufficiently proficient with advanced technology to assume an independent leadership role in the IT fields. However, change in the range of products being produced in China is suggestive of the rapid development that is taking place. In most Asian countries, high-tech exports like office machines and telecom have been growing much more rapidly than traditional export products like clothing and footwear, though the latter remain quantitatively important.

East Asian IT export growth is, thus, more than a matter of low wages and an undervalued exchange rate. Producers have become greatly more proficient at meeting world requirements for quality and product design. The leadership of Taiwan, Korea, and Singapore in these fields has provided a channel of entry to other East Asian countries, for many years into Malaysia and, recently, in particular, to China.

A large share of the inflow of FDI to China has come from other East Asian countries and has been accompanied by corresponding flows of entrepreneurship and skills. The capital and other resource flows in turn reflect the economics of export production in China as well as the increasing possibility of serving the domestic market.

In July 2005, China signaled a change in its exchange rate regime: appreciating the value of the RMB yuan by 2.1 percent with respect of the US dollar, linking the yuan to a basket of currencies, and indicating that the Chinese would practice a managed float within narrow daily fluctuation limits. In themselves these initial steps will not seriously affect the competitiveness of Chinese goods, in view of China's great undervaluation. The critical issue, so far undisclosed, is how far China's currency will eventually be allowed to appreciate. One can be pretty sure that currency adjustments will not be allowed to interfere significantly with the competitiveness of China's export industries.

Part IV

The IT/e-business revolution in East Asia and the future

11 Presaging the future

Developing trends

Revolutionary changes are going on worldwide that will affect the future of East Asia and its relationship with the rest of the world's economies. Many of today's developments in the economy, the business world, and the IT/e-business fields already presage what is to come. The process of change is usually gradual. Many changes are introduced a small step at a time. When innovation represents a radical departure, it takes a long time before the new technology is widely diffused among potential users. Often, the new application calls for infrastructure or technical expertise that also takes time to develop. The gradual dissemination of networked computers and availability of Internet services is an example, with some countries providing widespread service and others lagging behind. Gradually most of the world's economies will move to the sunny side of the digital divide. Similarly, new technologies and programming are first introduced in some advanced countries and then gradually disseminated to the rest of the world. Consequently, we can glimpse the future by looking carefully at existing trends.

The rapid dissemination of technical knowledge that represents the information and communication technology (ICT) revolution has already been considered at length earlier. Developments that have taken place in the advanced countries of Europe, Japan, and North America and that are already a long way along in Korea, Singapore, and Taiwan, are being seen in other East Asian countries as well. However, the pace of change is more difficult to predict, since it depends on the setting and on public policy. Some of the East Asian countries like Malaysia will participate in the ICT industries and in e-business much more quickly than others. Some, like China, are so big that their participation in the "new economy" will have worldwide impact.

Much can be learned by looking closely at the innovations that are under way, some for many years and others barely over the horizon. We are going to consider the developments that are most important for the future economic role of East Asia:

- the transfer of manufacturing industry
- the evolution of international production networks
- white collar outsourcing
- development of the regional market in East Asia.

Transfer of manufacturing industry

The transfer of the manufacturing industry from the advanced countries of Europe, North America, and Japan toward East Asia is old news. While as many as 70 percent of the products in US department stores are now imported from abroad, there is still room for additional shifts of production to low-wage countries. Increasingly Japanese firms, that had lagged in this process, are also moving production to East Asia while producers in the middle-income countries like Mexico and South Korea, in turn, have been transferring operations to lower-wage countries like China and Vietnam. Such movements have been facilitated by steadily declining transportation costs and liberalization of trade and regulations affecting foreign-owned or joint-venture enterprises and affecting financial movements. The new ICT has revolutionized firms' abilities to control production at a distance and to manage the logistics of the supply chain.

The shift of the manufacturing industry into East Asia has greatly benefited the region, allowing these countries to move workers out of agriculture into more pro-ductive manufacturing operations. This process is continuing, particularly in countries like China where excess rural labor is still available and where wages are still highly competitive.

The outlook for future development raises a couple of unanswered questions: First, whether industry will eventually move to still lower-wage countries, perhaps in Africa, leaving some of the East Asian countries at a mature stage, with rela-tively high wages but lacking the technology to promote high-tech industries; Second, whether world markets for imported manufactures are sufficiently large to accept the massive production that could originate in the new manufacturing industries of East Asia and elsewhere in the developing world.

International production networks

As a result of the globalization process, we have seen the development of what are called "international production networks" (IPN) (Yusuf and Evenett 2002: 273). Definitions of an IPN vary, but the essentials of the concept can be summarized simply. A lead firm, usually but not always in a developed country, outsources many of its operations to firms located elsewhere at home or in foreign countries. "*Deverticalize* the value chain" is Yusuf's terminology. Not only does the lead firm do little or no manufacturing in-house, but it also outsources some other functions, like logistics, engineering and design, and support services. The degree to which it is integrated and where separate operations are carried out depends where and how tasks can be carried out most cheaply. The idea corresponds closely to the "virtual firm" discussed in Chapter 3. The counterparts to the lead firm in an advanced country are independent contract manufacturers and sup-pliers located in East Asia, many in Taiwan. What distinguishes this system from traditional overseas production is that the suppliers are independent firms, not subsidiaries or joint ventures, and not the result of FDI originating in the developed countries. The suppliers may be producing inputs for several lead firms, sometimes, in fact, supplying identical components, frequently under different trade names. The suppliers are frequently part of a regional network or a geographic cluster drawing on other firms in the region for inputs or engineering. Such international collaboration without vertical integration is made possible by the ICT revolution, enabling communication, coordination, and negotiation to be done electronically and greatly reducing the cost of logistical control.

The IPNs set the stage for the development of more sophisticated producers in East Asia. In the electronic components industry, overseas suppliers are being drawn into the process of design and engineering before the product design is finalized. But, so far, only a few East Asian firms have advanced from being suppliers of parts and components to introducing process and design innovations on their own.

IT industries—electronic components, office machinery, switchgear and telecommunications parts—are the major IPN operators, with primary locations in Taiwan, South Korea, and Malaysia. Increasingly manufacturing and assembly operations are being transferred to China. The motor vehicle industry is also moving to parts production supply linkages, though it is difficult for independent East Asian parts suppliers to meet standards and to reach mass production cost economies. Athletic shoes are an example of virtual enterprises, as we have noted in Chapter 3. Other mass production products like clothing and toys also benefit from cross-border production agreements, but these relationships of department store buyers to their East Asian suppliers are often less close-knit than the complex linkage between producers of components in an electronics IPN. On the other hand, the world is becoming more complex even for simple products like clothing. Increasingly large United States retailers are engaging in "lean retailing." This entails reduced inventories and current purchasing, often on a weekly cycle of products in various styles, colors, and sizes, prepackaged and labeled by the suppliers in East Asia. Relationships with suppliers are maintained on electronic databases. There is a premium on rapid delivery. Without the upgrading of delivery systems and electronic controls, East Asian suppliers lose competitiveness even to firms located in higher production cost areas closer to the market (Yusuf and Evenett 2002).

So far, with the exception of the electronics firms, the extent of international production network linkages to East Asia is still relatively limited. A World Bank survey suggests that "just under a quarter of firms surveyed in East Asia excluding China are networked with 10 percent selling both parts and final goods to foreign buyers. The comparable numbers for firms in China are considerably lower, with 15 percent being networked and 5 percent selling both parts and final products to foreign buyers" (Yusuf 2003: 295). These statistics may underestimate the extent of linkages to foreign markets since supplier firms in East Asia linked to other local suppliers at earlier stages of the market are not included. On the other hand, it is clear that the potential for further networking is great both with respect to its scope and its intensity.

Transfer of white collar jobs

The traditional distinction between blue collar work and white collar work no longer applies clearly. With the advent of the computer and cheap telecommunication, many functions that once had to be done in-house can be outsourced, indeed, they can be carried out at the other end of the earth. White collar outsourcing is a new trend that is likely to offer new opportunities to the East Asian countries and, significantly, that may have profound implications for the relative positions of the East Asian and South Asian economies. The title of a recent article "Is your job headed for Bangalore?" (Baily and Farrell 2004) gives a quick indication of some current popular fears. This paper is reassuring, but many people remain concerned and they have reason to be. In 2005, IBM announced that their workforce in the United States and in Europe would be cut back by 15,000 jobs. Only two weeks later, IBM announced that they were hiring 14,000 workers in India.

The transfer of white-collar jobs to the developing countries in East Asia is sometimes known as "offshoring." The more technical term is business process outsourcing (BPO). In increasing numbers firms are shifting back-office functions abroad and some, IBM and GE, for example, have acquired foreign firms operating in this field. The new communications technology has made it possible to provide instant contact and to allow access to a firm's financial and shipment records worldwide. Clients calling a call center no longer know whether they are speaking to a person in South Bend, Indiana, or in Bangalore, India. (Indeed, call center workers in India are trained, as much as is possible, to speak accent-less English, and are often instructed not to tell the caller where they are located.) Airline reservations databases or the telephone company's accounting data are instantly accessible wherever the inquiry originates. The effect of IT on white collar workers extends way beyond the call center phenomenon. The activities being sent abroad are not only simple tasks like data entry and order processing. Some jobs being sent abroad are high- and medium-level functions like regional managerial hubs, regulatory accounting, compliance auditing, bond pricing, and supply chain coordination. Video and audio communication enable managers in many parts of the world to work together to negotiate contracts, to plan business strategies, to discuss the mechanics of new projects, to consult on delivery problems, and do all the tasks involved in business collaboration.

The varied nature of white collar work suggests that not all tasks are equally suitable for outsourcing and doing at a distance. Levy and Murnane (2004) suggest that white collar work has various dimensions that make it more or less suitable for computer automation (Table 11.1). Routine tasks or functions that are rule based can easily by automated. Complex tasks that require judgment call for human intervention. Offshoring complicates the job because of its requirements for sophisticated high-speed communication and, in some cases, for a knowledge of English (or other appropriate languages). For certain functions the choice is between computer automation at home and manual performance by low-wage workers abroad. For others, the options are more one-sided: routine functions requiring human contact, like call centers, carried out in low-wage countries with adequate communication and language competence. Cultural differences are amplified in the artificial meeting environment of the video conference or e-mail messaging so that managerial functions are often best carried out at home with experienced staff even at higher labor cost.

Table 11.1 Characteristics of white collar activities: suitability for offshoring

Function	Task	Skill/education level	Portability	Special needs	Advantage/ disadvantage of offshoring
Research, planning, design, advanced programming	Expert thinking	High experience and education	Medium to low	English, experience	Lower wages, communications, and language problems
Management, human resources, customer–supplier relations	Complex communi-cation	High experience	Low	Need for human contact, English	Low wages more than offset by communication difficulty
Orders, logistics, accounting	Routine cognitive	Medium to low	High	High speed communi-cation	Low wages
Data entry	Routine manual	Low	High	High speed communi-cation	Low wages
Drafting, engineering, simple programming	Non routine manual	Medium	Medium	Specialized skill	Low wages
Call centers	Routine verbal	Medium	High	Verbal English	Low wages

Thus, in practice, distance working is more suitable for such routine office tasks as data entry or billing, standardized computer programming, drafting, and preparation of legal documents than for complex negotiations.

The advantage of shifting white collar operations abroad is the relatively much lower level of wages, even for college trained personnel, in many East Asian countries. Y. Kumasaka of ITEconomy Advisors, a small consulting firm, tells the following story. He says,

> Even my company has benefited from IT-generated globalization. It's expensive to hire an assistant in New York, so when I interviewed a Philippine student in Manila, I thought we were negotiating an hourly wage. But I discovered that she was talking about a daily wage. If I consider the costs of benefits such as health care, the savings grow even larger. But hiring her in the Philippines has more benefits. Her English ability is quite good. When I email her something in the evening from New York, she has finished the work by the time I begin my workday the following morning.
>
> (2003b)

A 2004 survey by A. T. Kearney, a management consulting company, produces an "Offshore Location Attractiveness Index." The survey ranks countries according to numerous criteria falling into three broad categories (the weights attached to each consideration are indicated in parentheses):

- Cost (40%)

    - compensation of employees;
    - cost of infrastructure;
    - tax and regulatory costs.

- People skills and availability (30%)

    - experience and skills in IT and telecom;
    - availability of labor and size of the work force;
    - educational attainment including language and test scores;
    - attrition rate in the BPO industry.

- Business environment (30%)

    - economic and political environment;
    - infrastructure in IT and telecom;
    - cultural adaptability;
    - security of intellectual property.

The criteria indicate that low cost labor is only one of the factors influencing whether a country is a suitable location for BPO operations. The skill and adaptability of the local labor force, especially its knowledge of English are also very important, as is the economic and political environment. In its 2004 survey, Kearney ranks the top locations as in Table 11.2.

Four East Asian countries make the top of this list, China and Malaysia are number two and three, respectively. Competence in the English language and a high level of educational attainment (often in English) are major factors sending

Table 11.2 Ranking of best locations for white collar offshoring

1	India
2	China
3	Malaysia
4	Czech Republic
5	Singapore
6	Philippines
7	Brazil
8	Canada
9	Chile
10	Poland
11	Hungary
12	New Zealand

Source: A. T. Kearney.

operations to India, by far the leader in Asian BPO. Not surprisingly, for reasons of language and culture Chinese firms encounter great difficulties in customer relationship management (CRM) and tech support center operations for the US market. The *Wall Street Journal* (April 5, 2005) comments on cultural problems as well as language problems. A Chinese respondent might say "I am deeply sorry for your inconvenience" several times in a brief e-mail. Fragmentation of the industry, lack of skilled technicians, and managerial talent are additional difficulties. A. T. Kearney staff people note that it may take 5–10 years before China can equal India in providing IT outsourcing services, at least in the English language. On the other hand, call centers for East Asia operating in Chinese have begun operations in Shanghai.[53]

As we have noted, it is not clear whether a ranking for all BPO operations together makes business sense. Some functions that require a high level of business expertise are most suited to countries where experienced workers are available and where suitable infrastructure exists—Singapore is an example. Others like call centers require low wages and good English—India. Others, like engineering and programming, may fit well with the workers available in China, though intellectual property protection issues are an important consideration in that case.

So far the flow of white collar business to Asia is important but still relatively small.[54] Estimates are some $10 billion for 2002, but the figure is expected to triple by the end of the decade. There is substantially more potential for transferring office jobs abroad, from the United States and other developed (read high wage) countries. This represents a great opportunity for East Asia though high value-added jobs that call for personal interaction are likely to remain in the West.

Growth and integration of the regional East Asian market

Another altogether different consideration is the growing scope and integration of the East Asian regional market. We have tended to emphasize the shift of production from the advanced countries and East Asia and the consequences of this still ongoing change.

As East Asia's production capabilities expand, the question of whether there will be sufficient export markets is likely to become an issue. Already a very large fraction of the world's consumer electronics are produced in East Asia. As a result, manufacturing of electronic products in Asia has become cyclical reflecting the business cycle of the market in the United States and Europe. There is still room for expansion, but as large countries like China become producers, the export market may not be sufficient. Continued expansion will need to be turned toward domestic markets in China and in other East Asian countries. Fortunately, East Asia, itself, provides large and growing market outlets.

East Asia's growth as an import market reflects East Asian consumers' growing affluence and their growing interest in foreign-type goods. An increasing share of East Asia's needs for such manufactures is being supplied by local firms. Many Western products are being produced for the local market under license, often using imported inputs. Others are being imported from other East Asian countries.

An important part of this story is that economic interaction among various East Asian countries is increasing rapidly. Intra-regional trade has been growing at twice the rate of aggregate world trade (Ng and Yeats 2003).

Intra-regional trade has long been important in East Asia, accounting for approximately one-third of total exports in the region (Table 11.3). While many observers have noted the rapid rise of intra-regional trade in East Asia, the trade statistics suggest that on average trade within the region has grown no faster than exports to the world economy. The share of intra-regional exports to total exports declined slightly between 1995 and 2003. Individual countries have differed in export trends and, once again, China is the most important and most rapidly expanding intra-regional exporter.

Until the phenomenal expansion of the huge Chinese economy, the rapid growth of the East Asian markets had slipped under the radar screen of most observers. Some East Asian countries like Singapore, Taiwan, and Korea, have achieved consumption standards close to those in the advanced Western countries and, as a result, their imports of consumer products such as motor vehicles and consumer electronics have grown rapidly. Many of these imports come from other countries in the East Asian region, although luxury consumer products are still imported from Europe, Japan, and the United States.

The composition of intra-regional exports and their growth, 1985–2001, is shown in Table 11.4. (only products that accounted for more than 1 percent of intra-regional exports are included). The most important supplier countries in 2001 are indicated.

It is apparent that much of the intra-regional trade is in electronic and telecom related products. Their share of total intra-regional trade has increased sharply and there have been phenomenal growth rates (Growth is calculated on the basis of value of shipments. In the many cases where price declined, real growth is even greater than indicated.) These products originate in Malaysia, Korea, and Taiwan.

Table 11.3 Trends in intra-regional and total East Asian export trade

	Intra-regional exports		Total exports (% change p.a.)	Intra-regional/ total exports (%)	
	2003 (US$ million)	% change p.a.		1995	2003
China	119,770	10.5	13.4	34.5	27.3
Hong Kong (China)	110,579	5.4	3.4	41.3	48.4
Indonesia	19,406	5.6	8.7	27.2	21.3
Korea	62,547	6.9	5.5	28.9	32.3
Malaysia	42,334	5.4	4.4	37.3	40.3
Philippines	13,471	14.2	9.1	24.7	37.2
Singapore	62,810	3.5	2.5	40.2	43.6
Thailand	23,262	4.6	4.4	28.5	29.0
Total	454,179	6.6	6.9	35.2	34.5

Source: United Nations Comtrade.

Table 11.4 Composition and growth of East Asian intra-regional exports

Commodity	Main supplier (share of product market %)	Share of total inter-regional trade (%)		Growth rate (% p.a.)
		1985	2001	
Electronic microcircuits	Malaysia (23)	2.3	12.4	26.7
Parts of office machinery	China (25)	0.6	5.7	31.1
Parts of telecommunications equip.	China (45)	1.3	2.5	18.6
Radio and telocom equipment	Korea (33)	—	2.1	56.3
Digital storage units	Singapore (23)	—	2.1	98.0
Petroleum	Indonesia (30)	12.1	1.6	0.4
Diodes and transistors	Malaysia (20)	0.6	1.6	21.3
Childrens' toys and games	China (95)	1.9	1.6	12.4
Other electrical machinery	China (28)	0.4	1.5	23.8
Piezo electric crystals	Taiwan (24)	0.7	1.4	19.2
Peripheral control units	China (33)	0.2	1.4	29.5
Footwear	China (93)	0.4	1.3	23.0
Other electrical power machinery	China (56)	0.3	1.1	24.9
Electrical switches and relays	China (35)	0.4	1.1	22.4
Printed circuits and Parts	Taiwan (28)	0.3	1.1	24.6
Jerseys and pullovers	China (88)	0.5	1	19.4
Polystyrene	Taiwan (44)	0.3	1	23.8

Source: Ng and Yeats (2003), table 12.1, originally derived from UN Trade Statistics (UN Comtrade).

Traditional East Asian products like toys, footwear, and textile products originate in China. Indonesia is the principal supplier of petroleum to the region.

The intra-East Asian supply chain

Perhaps most important, from the perspective of "new economy" trends, is the changing pattern of manufactures trade flows that shows increasing movements between the countries of the region of parts and partially finished products going into further processing and assembly.

A large share of intra-regional trade encompasses intermediate goods, now originating in other East Asian countries. The growth of intermediate imports into China and other countries of the East Asian region presages significant changes in world trading patterns (Ng and Yeats 2003). "Increasingly the global supply chain runs from Asian countries where high tech components are made, through China, where they are assembled, and on to their end markets" (*Wall Street Journal*, August 20, 2003, p. B-1).

An indicative fact is that very few products make up the bulk of these shipments. Table 11.5 shows the composition of the most important intra-regional trade in parts and components. Shown separately are all parts and components that account for more than one percent of parts and components trade in 2001. Parts going into office equipment (computers, largely) and telecommunications equipment, the "new" high-tech products, account for two-thirds of parts and components imports. The parts and components imports amounted to 26 percent of all intra-trade in manufactures, except chemicals, in the region.

We may conclude that intra-regional trade is growing rapidly and that an important share of it involves linkages between countries at various stages of the development ladder. Table 11.6 shows the geography of trade in parts and

Table 11.5 Parts and components intra-regional trade in East Asia

Components and parts only	*% of parts and components by SITC category in regional parts and components trade*
Office and adding machinery (SITC 759)	37.5
Telecommunications equipment (SITC 764)	27.7
Electric power machinery (SITC 772.29)	1.1
Switchgear (SITC 772)	12.9
Motor vehicles and accessories (SITC 784)	2.4
Carriages and cycles (SITC 786.89)	1.3
Still cameras (SITC 874.29)	1.0
Other parts and components	16.1
Total parts and components as % of manufactures trade (excluding chemicals)	26.2

Source: Ng and Yeats (2003), originally on UN Trade Statistics (UN Comtrade).

Table 11.6 Trade in parts and components in East Asia, 2001 (billions of US$)

Importer	*Exporter*			
	China and Hong Kong	*Advanced East Asia7*[a]	*Japan*	*All East Asia*
China and Hong Kong	—	19.5	14.4	33.9
Advanced East Asia 7	10.4	24.8	24.3	59.6
Japan	5.8	9.4	—	15.2
All East Asia	16.2	53.7	38.7	108.6

Source: Ng and Yeats (2003), table 8.3. Data originally from UN Comtrade.

Note

a Indonesia, Korea, Malaysia, Philippines, Singapore, Taiwan, and Thailand.

components among major East Asian countries. Hong Kong has been lumped with China, since it serves an entrepot role for much of China's trade. Singapore has its own growth linkage relationships with areas in Indonesia and Malaysia, not shown here. An important consideration in evaluating these figures is that, in general, exporters of parts and components are countries that produce these products while importers of parts and components are assemblers, countries that assemble them into finished products. The classic example is computer chips that are produced in South Korea, Taiwan, and Japan, and that are assembled into computers and cellular telephones in China. China and Hong Kong are relatively small exporters of parts and components and substantial importers. The more advanced East Asian countries and Japan are large exporters of parts and components to other East Asian countries including China.

These patterns reflect the differences in comparative advantage among the East Asian countries, specifically low labor cost in China, the Philippines, and Thailand, as compared to Japan and the high income East Asian countries like South Korea and Taiwan.

Another perspective on this trade is that sophisticated products and parts are shipped to less advanced low labor cost countries for processing and assembly. In turn, these countries supply simpler mass production goods, footwear is an example, to the more advanced parts of the region.

An East Asian free trade area

Such trading relationships are the basis for growing interest in the establishment of an East Asian free trade and regional cooperation area (Lincoln 2004). Yusuf and Evenett (2002) argue that there was little incentive for promoting intraregional trade at earlier stages of the East Asian industrialization since the countries were largely competing with each other for entry into foreign markets. As domestic markets have grown and as the elements of the supply chain have increasingly been focused on each country's comparative advantage, liberalization of trade and investments is becoming more important. The South East Asian countries (ASEAN) are already tied together into the ASEAN Free Trade Area (AFTA). Enacted in 1993, AFTA has made considerable progress at almost eliminating tariffs (a range of 0–5 percent) on all but a limited list of exempt products. ASEAN has grown from its original six members (Brunei, Malaysia, Thailand, Indonesia, the Philippines, and Singapore) to include Laos, Cambodia, Myanmar, and Vietnam.

More recently, there have been growing efforts to establish bilateral free trade deals between the East Asian countries, themselves, and with countries in other parts of the world. Singapore, which has little local production to endanger, has been a leader in these efforts, establishing free trade relationships with Japan and South Korea as well as with the Australia, the United States, India, and others. China has been seeking trade deals as well, especially with Australia, a major supplier of basic commodities, like copper and iron ore, that China needs badly. (This may be seen as old-fashioned geopolitics at its most basic level.) There are also possibilities of free trade deals between Japan, China, and South Korea (*The Economist*, February 28, 2004).

In 2002, ASEAN, pledged with China to create a China-ASEAN free trade area by 2010[55]. It is interesting to observe that such a grouping is disproportionately dominated by 1 huge country in comparison to 10 small countries. The grouping is sometimes referred to as 1 + 10. In view of the size of the economy involved, such expansions would be at once most promising and also most threatening. From the perspective of achieving scale sufficient to produce economically, the ability to sell in the large East Asian market including China without barriers offers significant advantages to the smaller East Asian countries. Already there is substantial trade between China and South Korea, for example. Moreover, many entrepreneurs in the smaller East Asian countries (many, of course, of Chinese descent) see their future as increasing involvement in the huge, rapidly growing, Chinese market, either as exporters or as investors. But competition from large-scale export producers in China and, perhaps, also in India must frighten many smaller companies in the region. China can be seen as a competitive threat, one that has already affected markets for some of the region's countries. Moreover, from the point of view of negotiating strength, opening the trade block to a big country like China, must seem to many of the countries like "going to bed with an elephant."

The various countries in the group are at different development stages and consequently, there are important complementarities between some of them. The area's production chains will take advantage of these differences and will increasingly cross national boundaries. This is likely to be especially true for the IT industries that contain components from very high up the technological ladder and that also require simple labor-intensive assembly operations.

Whether Japan becomes part of a regional economic block is an interesting question. In the past, Japan has maintained a degree of separation between its economy and those of East Asia. But in recent years, Japanese trade with East Asia, and with China, in particular, has been increasing very rapidly. Japanese firms are establishing subsidiaries in China, supplying them with Japanese-made equipment and parts. While a large fraction (perhaps 40 percent) of the goods produced remain in China, a sizeable flow goes to Japan, previously a market accepting few finished goods imports. Equally important is the growing market for Japanese machinery and equipment and electronics in the rapidly growing economy of China. The headline in the *Wall Street Journal* reads: "As Japan Recovers, An Unlikely Source Gets Credit: China" (WSJ, May 4, 2004). The article emphasizes that extraordinarily rapid growth in China has strained local capacity so that China's needs for machinery are being met from Japan. Moreover, many important components of Japanese products are assembled in China, Matshushita power shovels for example, are sourced in Japan and assembled in China.

Japan has long had an interest in being a part of an East Asian economic and political block. In 2002, Prime Minister Koizumi proposed a Japan-ASEAN comprehensive economic initiative that would include Japan and that would be linked to the other regional powers including China and Australia and New Zealand.

Such a grouping would have the potential to rival other major economic blocks like North American Free Trade Area (NAFTA) and the European Union. So far, however, Japan has found it difficult to establish bilateral trade agreements with individual countries, not to mention a broader linkage. That reflects domestic political and economic issues, for example, Japan's role in Asia before the Second World War, its protected rice economy, and the fact that Japan has been largely an exporter into the region. Today, the situation is different. Japan has increasingly sent investment into the other East Asian countries and is accepting their consumer products in its home market. Trade has become a two-way street. Geopolitical considerations, to be discussed in Chapter 13, also count, since in the absence of Japan, China will have a dominant role in a regional economic grouping. Joining an East Asian free trade association would boost Japan's position as a regional and political power.

12 IT/e-business in East Asia's future economic development

A critical issue is how the new dynamic technology economy relates to East Asia. That is, after all, a central topic of this volume. To summarize briefly, we are going to see that the impact of the ICT/e-business revolution will vary greatly in East Asia depending on the sectors of IT and e-commerce and on the country being considered.

East Asia and the new technology

For newcomer countries, dynamic competition poses some difficult challenges. An advanced level of technological expertise is required to compete effectively, to keep up with and to lead high-tech development. But advanced technology, in turn, calls for technological experience and sophistication. It is very much a chicken and egg problem. It is not easy to acquire the knowledge required to jumpstart the process of technical change in a country that has been lagging, that is, to leapfrog into the twenty-first century. But some East Asian countries have done it. Financial/entrepreneurial considerations are also important for entry into new dynamic markets. In many countries of East Asia, a tradition of entrepreneurship and family financing and international linkages among the overseas Chinese community facilitate the development of new businesses.

The role of IT in the development of the East Asian economies has a number of alternative possibilities. Much depends on what dimension of IT is being considered. The nature of traditional East Asian export products is very different from the products of the IT/e-business fields. We compare the resource and skill requirements of "old economy" export products and of the outputs of the IT/e-business economy in Table 12.1. The distinctions shown involve:

- Standardization—the degree to which the products are standardized, in popular parlance "commodities" and the extent to which they are differentiated.[56]
- Technological complexity—the extent to which products require advanced technology that is difficult to obtain in some countries.
- Labor intensity versus capital or equipment intensity in relation to labor/capital costs is a major factor in determining competitiveness.

Table 12.1 Technology characteristics and resource requirements of alternative East Asian products: standard "old economy" export products and "new economy" IT/e-business products

	"Old economy" products		"New Economy" IT/e-business products			
	Traditional export products	Hardware (low tech)	Hardware (high tech)	Software applications	Software development	e-business applications
Product	Clothing, shoes, watches	Cell phones, TVs, screens, DRAM chips	Custom chips, servers, switches	Standardized B2C and B2B software applications	Custom programs, systems integration	Vendor applications, supply chain management
Standardization	Commodity	Commodity	Diversified	Standardized/diversified	Diversified	Standardized/diversified
Technical complexity	Low tech	Low/medium tech	High tech	Low tech	High tech	Low tech/high tech
Labor/capital intensity	Labor intensive	Labor intensive	Capital intensive	Some equipment dependence	Equipment dependence	Equipment dependence
Economies of scale	Large volume	Large volume	Low/high volume	Large volume	Low volume	Large volume
Skill requirements	Low skill	Low skill	High skill/engineering	Low skill	High program skill	High/low skill
Language requirements	No English	No English	Some English	Some English	English language	Some English

- Production volume economies—because of high development costs and low marginal costs, the economies of scale associated with IT products are great, often resulting in a small number of suppliers.
- Skill requirements—there is frequently need for specialized, high level expertise.
- Language requirements—in most cases comprehension and communication in English is relevant here, though ability in other regional languages, Mandarin Chinese, for example, may be important for some purposes.

In many of these respects, the requirements of the "new economy" products are very different from what most of the East Asian countries have been accustomed to produce.

While East Asian countries have been leaders in the production of consumer IT hardware and some of them are quickly jumping into the electronic age, they have been much less successful at establishing a place in the softer dimensions of computing or in e-business.

Production of low-tech electronic hardware. In earlier stages of economic development, the focus is on manufacturing relatively simple IT products such as mobile telephones, memory chips, PCs, and related products like monitors and printers. (In Table 12.1 we refer to them as "low tech.") These are products of mass production technology that take advantage of low assembly costs in East Asia and require only limited amounts of high-tech engineering skills. Many of these products, like DRAM chips, have become "commodities," standardized products manufactured and sold by merchant fabricators. A large share of the world's production of these goods is already concentrated in East Asian countries, particularly in South Korea, Malaysia, and Taiwan. China, with its large potential domestic market and extremely low labor costs, is becoming a major producer. Management of these production operations is sometimes in the hands of foreign capitalists and joint venture partners. Increasingly foreign direct investment (FDI) has become an intra-regional transmission mechanism for technology. As we have noted, firms originating in Taiwan, Hong Kong, and Singapore have transferred much of the needed technical and management knowledge to neighboring areas of China and Malaysia. Some countries in East Asia have become the world's dominant producers of PCs, disk drives, and cell phones, supplying exports to Europe, Japan, and the United States. Some important brands of electronics have been developed in East Asia.

Production of advanced IT products. As countries gain technological sophistication, they are able to produce more technically advanced IT products, like LCD displays, servers, manufacturing equipment, and telecom switches. In Asia, originally, Japan was the leader in such products, but increasingly sophisticated products are also being produced elsewhere in East Asia. Some East Asian countries have specialized in technologically advanced products with large markets, chip set fabrication, for example and, some companies have specialized on sophisticated leading edge products—Samsung in Korea on large flat video displays. But production at the technological frontier is not yet widely distributed in East Asia outside Japan, Taiwan, Singapore, and Korea. In terms of frontier technologies, even the most advanced East Asian developing countries still lag behind the leading science centers in the United States, Japan, and in Europe.

Software program development. The story is quite different, since software development calls for very different capabilities. Software development remains largely in Western countries. It involves technical standards that have been set by early movers. It sometimes uses proprietary algorithms that developers may not want to transfer to developing countries for fear of inadequate intellectual property protection. The kind of work that calls for a high level of programming expertise is typically carried out in regional technological clusters in advanced countries. Until recently, workers with appropriate skills were not yet widely available in East Asia.

Though routine programming is being transferred into programming centers in Asia, for example, to Singapore and, recently, to Shanghai in China, software and programming services are still centered in the United States and Europe. Substantial programming operations also are carried on in other advanced countries. Most recently, the IT industry has discovered that engineers and programmers can be hired at much lower wages in developing countries. As a consequence, much more programming work is being shifted to specialized centers in Asia, in Shanghai, Israel, and other parts of the world. The burgeoning growth of software centers in India is legendary. India with its highly educated English-speaking engineers represents a serious competitive threat to East Asia in the programming fields.

While Cupertino, California, and Bellevue, Washington remain central development centers despite the dot-com crash, they will face increasing competition. According to *Business Week* (February 3, 2003) "No longer are Asian IT engineers only writing routine software applications and maintaining mature computer systems. Now they are remotely managing sophisticated networks, designing Websites, and developing software for entire business processes for big Western corporations."[57]

Application of software for administrative, accounting, and e-business computation. Data entry, simply punching written information into a data bank, was the earliest business back-office application that was transferred to foreign locations. Paradoxically, increasing use of direct electronic data collection is rapidly reducing the need to enter information manually. Today's business back-office operations such as billing, payroll, logistics, human resource management, etc. are often carried out, without human intervention, on a computer operated system.

Everyday business computer applications call for large-scale computer equipment and rapid Internet connections. Building or customizing the required applications software faces some of the same challenges that are encountered in software development. It can be extremely challenging to replace long-used paper-based and labor-intensive business systems with electronic paper-less methods, though a long leap from the abacus to a touch computer screen is always a possibility. Installation and maintenance also remain serious challenges in regions where there is a shortage of experienced computer professionals. But once a software system has been established and workers have been trained, some of these difficulties disappear. Until recently only the most advanced cities in East Asia, like Singapore and Hong Kong, could hope to develop their economies around IT/e-business processing activities like communications and financial centers. Experienced programmers and computer center operators are still scarce as is high-speed broadband communications infrastructure. But in time, as communications links are built, as more staff are trained, as the programs become more standardized and as greater familiarity with their operations is built up, other East Asian countries may also become business information processing centers.

E-business applications. The distinguishing mark of e-business is the direct electronic connection between the customer and the supplier. Some e-business transactions like stock purchases can be carried out electronically in their entirety. Others like ordering books or making other purchases over the web require physical delivery of the product, what the experts call "fulfillment." The widespread availability of high-speed computer connections for access by prospective users is the critical consideration. As a result e-business applications between businesses and between businesses and consumers are still being used and centered largely in the advanced countries. Once an e-business is operational and, presumably, effective, it has only modest requirements for sophisticated maintenance. Information must be entered and orders must be filled. Everyday operation should be simple enough to allow many unskilled people to handle procedures, either as consumers, suppliers, or operators.

However, infrastructure considerations are an important issue. Modern applications in e-business, for example, supply chain management and retail B2C, call for sophisticated communications and networking capabilities. This means that the utilization of applications programs and the development of e-business operations depend greatly on the available IT infrastructure. B2B operations require high-speed connections that are costly and difficult to set up in many developing countries. Consumer use of the Internet also faces infrastructure barriers. B2C operations call for a high level of PC penetration as well as broadband connections to provide market reach to make such operations economic. The requisite computer connections are not yet widely available in East Asia beyond Taiwan, Singapore, South Korea, and urban centers in Malaysia, China, and Thailand. Except in these areas, consumers are not yet accustomed to doing business electronically, computers are not yet widely enough dispersed among consumers, and access to the web remains difficult. Until these issues are remedied, it will be difficult to reach the majority of East Asian consumers over the Internet. This represents a serious barrier to B2C in the region.

On the other hand, while users represent only a small fraction of the region's population, their number may be substantial. By and large, customers located in the advanced countries will call on the large existing companies. These have extended their activities into East Asia. There is room for local East Asian companies to enter this field, but most will come in under the umbrella of their advanced country partners.

Some of the large computer service companies have begun to operate e-business centers in East Asia, Shanghai and Singapore, for example, and in India. Some integrate their Asian operations closely with the work in the United States, taking advantage of the fact that Asian operations are open when it is nighttime in the United States. But the centers of enterprise programming remain in the advanced countries where many programs were originally developed and where a specialized and experienced work force is readily available.

Finally, as the IT/e-business field matures, there is substantial continued work in servicing and updating the new hardware and software. This remains a challenge long after the new systems have been installed and are in use.

The Productivity gains of IT and e-business

In which of these activities and in what countries are the gains from the IT/e-business revolution in East Asia going to be realized? There will be improvements in many activities, some closely connected to IT and others less so. There will be progress throughout the entire region. But some countries may see gains for high tech and others for traditional industries.

In terms of production volume and employment, production of consumer goods represents the most important industrial activity in East Asia. Only a fraction of this output consists of IT products. There is every reason to think that consumer goods production will continue to expand for foreign markets and for the burgeoning domestic East Asian market. The sophistication of production processes is likely to improve, and, particularly, the application of IT techniques in controlling production, quality control, and logistics can be expected to expand greatly.

The largest potential productivity gains are in the conventional industries of the economy where e-business approaches can be applied. Some of these gains represent accomplishment of "old" tasks in new ways: stock brokerage transactions on the Internet. Others, for example, are activities that reduce costs through improved logistic controls and optimal supply chain management, new computerized payments systems replacing the old-fashioned letter of credit, for example. Global value chains that link manufacturing processes in many countries (ADB 2003) rely heavily on computer and communications links.

The continued expansion and upgrading of IT products output, as distinct from conventional consumer goods, is a development consistent with ongoing trends and with underlying comparative advantage. Singapore, South Korea, and Taiwan have already stepped into the hardware aspects of IT becoming leading producers and exporters of consumer electronics, computers, and parts. They are also investing in and managing production of IT-related products—assembly and fabrication of technologically standardized products like cell phones and disk drives—in neighboring countries. They are rapidly stretching their technologies into more advanced fields. Recognizing the need for entrepreneurship and technical expertise, much of the activity in this field is still done under affiliation with companies from Japan and Korea.

Implications for East Asian development planning

The new economy has profound implications for East Asian development. The IT/e-business revolution promises gains in productivity and changes the terms on which many industries operate and firms interact. It is not altogether surprising that many East Asian countries have put IT development into the forefront of their development plans.[58]

As we have seen in Chapter 11, Singapore, which has long drawn on foreign investors to augment its technological possibilities, is now promoting the local IT economy by "wiring" the island and by building the appropriate educational system. South Korea's large *chaebols* have established themselves as world brands in production of electronic products. In sharp contrast, as we have noted, Taiwan has successfully developed its IT industries in the form of smaller- and medium-sized enterprises, often drawing on foreign technologies. As in Hong Kong and Singapore, local investors have gone to neighboring China to develop production operations, an outward transfer of technology. Malaysia seeks to advance high-tech activities at the same time that it improves the situation of its rural areas. Highly focused industrial policy projects to create a Multimedia Super Corridor are intended to build a cluster of high-tech organizations. China, not as far along technologically as these smaller East Asian countries, has established its "Golden Development Plan" to advance technology and education. Thailand, Indonesia, and the Philippines also have made efforts to build strength in the IT area.

The IT fields pose special difficulties for development policy. They call for priorities that are different from export promotion of traditional products. They call for long-term investments in education, science, and infrastructure.

The challenge of becoming and remaining competitive in the high-tech hardware fields involves much more than the obvious need for high technology expertise and equipment. Suppose a country seeks to promote production of a particular type of advanced computer chip, it is necessary to obtain licenses, develop the product, test it, and achieve consistent production performance. This work calls for construction and operation of a complex "clean room" production facility. One must build commercial relationships with users of the chips and one must face the possibility that there will be competitors or that still more sophisticated chips will be developed elsewhere. Public support for specific high-tech production projects risks enmeshing countries deeply into selective industrial policies. Such policies have often failed, for technical or commercial reasons. That may reflect the fact that government officials are often guided by non-commercial considerations. Once choices are made, they may be reluctant to change course even if adverse financial results would suggest a strategy reversal. Finally, high technology projects call for international interaction, using the latest intellectual property, and applying international technical standards that are out of reach to some developing countries.

The policy challenges with regard to applications software and e-business are even more complex. Since these fields depend greatly on the availability of a trained and experienced labor force of programmers and other technical experts, they suggest a policy effort focused on education and technical training. Since they depend on suitable network infrastructure supported by broadband communication, they suggest public sector support or encouragement for Internet communication networks. Indeed, many countries in East Asia have already set up policies with this objective, as we have noted. It is not clear however, whether public support for infrastructure is the appropriate solution. Note, for example, that in many parts of the world, internet infrastructure has been supplied largely by the private sector. Ultimately, they may develop alternate systems based on cellular phones or on special access sites in convenience stores, for example.

Conclusion

A realistic appraisal suggests that there are many possibilities for improving productivity throughout the economy through the use of IT in conventional production and in IT hardware. Such developments are under way, representing an important basis for the growth in East Asia. On the other hand, other dimensions of IT and e-business are much more challenging. These are highly dynamic competitive fields that, as we have noted, call for inputs of knowledge, high-tech sophistication, risk capital, advanced infrastructure, and skilled labor. Developing policy to build a competitive position in the software and e-business fields will be a long term challenge for the East Asian countries. It will require many resources and may take many years.

13 Forecasting East Asian development in an IT world

We now turn to the future. The IT/e-business revolution is spreading rapidly across the world. In spite of the fact that important barriers remain, particularly in areas that are still on the shady side of the digital divide, East Asia will be—indeed, already is—an important participant. At the same time, globalization is moving apace, stimulated by the very gains in communication and transportation that are generated by the new technologies.

As the East Asian countries find their place in the new economy, we can expect many of them to continue their rapid pace of economic progress. Much of this growth will continue to use old-fashioned ways of doing business but some important parts will depend on the new IT and communications technologies. The basics of the East Asian development process have been discussed in Chapter 5. The principles of growth economics continue to apply in the new economy, though the composition of output and the sectors benefiting from the new technologies may be different from what prevailed in the past.

Projecting East Asian growth

Projections of Gross Domestic Product (GDP) and trade are helpful to evaluate the future position of the East Asian region. In this section, we use the theories of economic development and the development ladder to make projections for the countries of East Asia to the year 2020. We will look at the growth of China and other East Asian countries, living standards achieved in the region, and the role of IT and e-business in achieving these results.

Trend projections are a simple, though sometimes risky way to forecast long-term growth. If they are done with logic as well as statistics, they are a useful way to provide some perspective on broad future developments. We are also interested in the role of the East Asian region from a worldwide perspective and what is likely to be the importance of this region. How big and powerful will the economy of China and the other East Asian developing economies be in comparison to the United States, Japan, and the newly enlarged European Union?

We use standard trend projection procedures except that we recognize the frequently observed fact that, once rapid development has started, rates of growth depend negatively on the level of per capita income and output that has already been achieved, as indicated in our discussion of the S-curve of economic growth (Chapter 5).[59] With respect to East Asia, this means that the lower-income countries in the region continue to have high growth rate prospects. Once development has begun, sustained productivity growth can be extremely rapid, as high as 6 or 7 percent annually. This reflects the development of efficient manufacturing, the acquisition of capital and knowledge, and the shift of workers out of low productivity agriculture to more productive manufacturing-related occupations. Rapid growth in these countries reflects structural changes that are related to the growth of manufacturing for export and for domestic markets. Even though these changes may not in themselves involve advanced technological processes, they are closely linked to globalization of the world economy.

The high-income countries in the region are also likely to grow, but more slowly. There have been exceptional cases, small countries becoming high-tech specialists, Taiwan in East Asia and Ireland in Europe, for example. But generally as a country achieves a high level of per capita output, using capital-intensive production methods close to the technological frontier, a rapid pace of productivity growth becomes more difficult. Typically the mature countries show productivity growth trends between 1.5 and 3 percent annually although in some cases the potentials of the new economy have allowed some mature countries to grow more rapidly for a period especially economies like South Korea that have export markets for a large fraction of their high-tech product output. The information and communications technology (ICT) revolution will contribute to further rapid growth in some of these countries.

The future economic role of East Asia

Our estimates of the future growth of the East Asian countries allow us to make some comments on the future economic role of East Asia as compared to Japan, the United States, and the European Union.[60] The projected growth path and the resulting GDP data (in billions of 2002 purchasing power parity (PPP) dollars) are shown in Table 13.1. As we have noted earlier, the less advanced countries will continue to grow more rapidly than the East Asian countries already close to maturity. Moreover, East Asia's growth remains considerably greater than that of the United States, Europe, and Japan.

Summing up data for individual countries into regional blocks, already in 2004, Developing East Asia has a GDP of approximately $10,000 billion in PPP terms, approximately the same overall size as that of the United States and the European Union. China represents two-thirds of East Asia's GDP.[61] Looking ahead to 2020, Developing East Asia has a GDP almost twice as big as the European Union. From 2015, China alone exceeds US GDP. Japan, however, is only one-third as large economically as the United States or the European Union and the other East Asian countries are much smaller.[62]

Table 13.2 considers the implications for living standards, projections of per capita real income for the East Asian economies to 2020. For all East Asian countries, continuation of growth trends, some closely linked to the new economy, will

Table 13.1 GDP projections: East Asia and the West

	GDP						
	2004 (billions of 2002 PPP $)	*% change p.a.*	*2010 (billions of 2002 PPP $)*	*% change p.a.*	*2015 (billions of 2002 PPP $)*	*% change p.a.*	*2020 (billions of 2002 PPP $)*
China	6,678	8.1	10,856	7.0	15,406	6.5	21,322
Hong Kong, China	204	4.1	261	3.5	310	3.5	370
South Korea	851	5.1	1,153	5.5	1,518	4.5	1,901
Thailand	491	5.9	698	6.0	943	5.5	1,241
Vietnam	209	7.3	325	8.0	484	7.0	687
Indonesia	749	4.2	966	5.0	1,240	5.0	1,592
Malaysia	211	5.0	284	6.0	384	5.0	493
Philippines	396	4.9	530	6.0	715	5.5	942
Singapore	112	3.6	140	3.5	167	3.0	194
Taiwan	442	5.0	597	4.5	747	4.0	913
Developing East Asia	10,343	7.1	15,810	5.4	21,915	5.0	29,655
United States	9,686	4.0	12,314	3.5	14,668	3.0	17,042
Japan	3,100	3.0	3,711	4.0	4,533	3.0	5,266
European Union(25)	9,891	2.0	11,152	4.0	13,621	4.0	16,637

Source: Author's projections based on recent trends.

Table 13.2 GDP per capita 2004–20

	Thousands of 2002 PPP $			
	2004	*2010*	*2015*	*2020*
China	5.3	7.8	10.5	14.2
Hong Kong, China	29.4	35.7	41.9	49.1
South Korea	18.2	24.7	30.4	37.3
Thailand	8.2	11.3	14.4	18.4
Vietnam	2.7	4.1	5.5	7.3
Indonesia	3.7	4.7	5.7	6.9
Malaysia	9.3	12.1	14.5	17.2
Philippines	5.2	6.8	8.3	10.1
Singapore	28.3	32.7	36.0	39.6
Taiwan	19.9	25.2	29.8	35.4
Developing East Asia	5.8	7.8	9.7	12.0
United States	34.8	40.9	45.6	50.9
12 Japan	24.3	31.2	36.6	43.0
European Union(25)	20.8	26.5	32.4	39.5

Source: Authors calculations based on World Bank and IDB projections.

sharply increase per capita GDPs. In some East Asian countries, Singapore, South Korea, Hong Kong, and Taiwan living standards will be similar to those in the advanced countries. In China, per capita incomes will rise sharply but not yet fully to advanced country levels. It is likely that the imbalance between the eastern and western regions of China, and between urban and rural populations will persist. For the entire Developing East Asian region, per capita incomes of $12,000 (2002 PPP $) represent a sizeable improvement, but are not yet, even in 2020, at the levels of the high consumption economies of the West.

The per capita GDP figures are a reflection of the rising economic performance of the East Asian countries. While IT can be expected to play an important part in the East Asian growth process, most of the increase in real output will represent higher levels of production in conventional activities. Higher personal incomes will translate into burgeoning consumer markets.

The future role of East Asia in world trade is intrinsically more difficult to establish numerically. In an increasingly global world economy, exports from East Asia can be expected to continue to grow rapidly for some time. However, since the expansion of exports at rates much faster than the growth of the market countries represents a transitional development, projections of export growth from East Asia cannot be extended linearly for an indefinite period. The statistics for export shares (Table 13.3) indicate that already in 2001, East Asian exports represented 16.8 percent of the world exports. Exports of manufactured mass production goods and high-tech and capital goods originating in East Asia accounted for 26.7 percent and 18.4 percent, respectively, of the international market and are increasing extremely rapidly, in view of the high rates of growth (between 20 and 30 percent annually) seen in recent years, particularly for Chinese exports of manufactures. How large the share of East Asia in world trade of manufactures will ultimately be will depend greatly on what happens to production costs in East Asia and in the advanced countries, exchange rates, and world trade policies. A numerical estimate would be risky, but it is likely that East Asia will account for an increasing share of world trade for some time to come. Eventually, as living standards and wages in the East Asian countries rise further, the production of manufactures for export markets may shift again to lower-wage countries elsewhere in the world, but that may be some decades in the future.

The East Asian challenge

As China's GDP grows along with that of other East Asian countries East Asia will be playing an increasing role in the world's economic power structure. This is the geopolitical, perhaps better, geoeconomic perspective.

An historical view has led some social scientists to warn of potential conflict between regions of the world. *Geopolitics*, as a mode of analysis, is no longer as fashionable as it was during the first half of the twentieth century.[63] But some social scientists still use a geopolitical perspective to evaluate how the power blocks of the world economy compare with each other in the future. The issue is how the new economy changes the international balance of power.

Huntington (1996), for example, raises the specter of "The Clash of Civilizations" between the West and a massive East Asian region including Japan as well as China.[64] Fears of economic confrontation have recently had some popular support in connection with the bid by Chinese government-backed oil company, Cnooc, to acquire the midsize American oil and gas producer, Unocal.[65] The *New York Times* headline reads, "Who's Afraid of China Inc.?" (July 24, 2005)

Table 13.3 Share of world exports by product class and country

Percent of world exports 2001

	China and Hong Kong	Indonesia	Korea	Malaysia	Philippines	Singapore	Thailand	Total
Raw food	4.5	1.0	0.7	0.5	0.4	0.5	2.9	10.5
Processed agricultural products	3.3	1.8	0.8	2.2	0.4	0.8	1.1	10.4
Fuels	1.9	3.0	1.7	1.8	0.1	1.9	0.4	10.8
Industrial materials	4.9	0.5	2.4	0.7	0.1	1.3	0.6	10.5
Manufactured mass products	18.2	2.2	2.8	1.0	0.5	0.5	1.5	26.7
High-tech and capital goods	7.9	0.4	3.1	2.0	0.8	3.1	1.1	18.4
Total	7.9	1.0	2.6	1.5	0.6	2.1	1.1	16.8

Source: United Nations Comtrade.

The concern was with the specific deal, but in the background are broader issues of maintaining United States' international hegemony, strategic competition for increasingly short energy supplies, and other concerns about unfair Chinese competition and the impact of globalization on American industry.

The idea of international competition and economic and political power is not a new one. About 40 years ago, the French journalist Jean-Jacques Servan-Schreiber wrote *The American Challenge* chronicling the threat that American multinationals posed for European business. Twenty years later, the situation had changed. JJ-SS, as he became known, published a new book, *The World Challenge*. In one sense, this was a remarkably prescient book, recognizing the transfer of physical production activities to labor-saving machinery in the West and to production sites in East Asia and promoting the advancement of education and "informatics" for "developing the faculties of every man and every woman...because in face of the new era which is beginning, we are all under-developed." On the other hand, the prediction grossly missed its mark, because what JJ-SS saw as a threat to the advanced industrial countries in Europe and North America was the growing economic power of Japan! Today, in important respects, the world has changed again. If he were to write today, JJ-SS would see the challenge in the development of East Asia and, particularly, of China. His message about the need for educational and technological development might well be the same.[66]

The rapid economic growth of the East Asian region and its large size, particularly of China, raises the possibility that it could become a power block, one that might confront the West politically as well as economically.

A view of such confrontational groupings is summarized in Figure 13.1, where the size of the rectangles representing each region corresponds roughly to their GDP in 2004 and in 2020.

China will become the world's largest economy. It will dominate the rest of East Asia. In contrast, the Western economies, now the dominant group, will grow only slowly and will represent a less important share of world GDP in 2020 than they represent now.

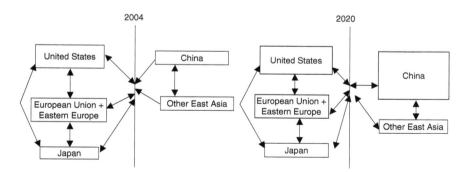

Figure 13.1 Economic/political relative size and relationships in 2004 and 2020.

There is no doubt that China, and perhaps the entire East Asian block, will play a more important part in world political and economic negotiations in the future than it has in the past. Size of GDP is not the only consideration but it is an important one. With greater size come greater political/military clout. One cannot be certain about the relationship between the major powers in the future. With higher income and technology come increasing needs for energy that cannot be satisfied by locally available resources. With higher levels of trade, East Asia will have greater impact on industries in other parts of the world and will be more concerned with maintaining its export outlets. On the other hand, economic conditions in China will be more closely linked to the business cycle elsewhere in the world, particularly in the countries where Chinese exports go. Recent discussions about China's undervalued exchange rate are an illustration of the conflicts growing out of the interdependence between East Asia and the rest of the world.

The East Asian challenge today is a very different one from the Japanese challenge in the 1980s. Japan was a relatively small economy, one that was highly urbanized and that had achieved substantial industrialization. Limited in its domestic market, Japan developed rapidly by pursuing a policy of export promotion, one that, in contrast to pre–Second World War days, stressed quality and performance. While the Japanese economy relied on private enterprise all along, government planning in the form of the "visions" of Ministry of International Trade and Industry (MITI) and its administrative guidance influenced the structure of industrial development. In the 1970s, lacking low-wage workers and seeing costs rise with wage increases and appreciation of the yen, Japanese industry sought to achieve a high level of technical proficiency, meeting and, in some cases, exceeding Western technology standards. Moreover, Japan was a largely "closed" economy. Foreign technology was used—indeed, improved on—but Japanese industry relied largely on domestic capital and management, limiting the inflow of foreign direct investment (FDI). It is only a small exaggeration to say, "The Japanese did it by themselves." But the Japanese boom ended in the early 1990s and, the economy has stubbornly resisted efforts to renew rapid growth. Moreover, Japan now has a very different relationship to East Asia. "Japan and China are so complementary" says retired business consultant and author Kenichi Ohmae. "A greater, stronger, more successful China helps Japanese industries sharpen their focus on what they're good at" (*New York Times* May 18, 2004).

As we have noted in Chapters 5 and 8, other East Asian countries, most clearly Korea, Taiwan, and Singapore, initially followed a "Japanese" development strategy with a substantial degree of success. These countries are relatively small and, like Japan, started with a high level of education, relative to other countries in East Asia. These countries have jumped full force onto the IT bandwagon producing high technology electronic products for the world. At the same time, Taiwanese businesses have become an entrepreneurial force in neighboring China.

In contrast, Chinese development is an altogether different story. China started as an agricultural economy with a small part of its enormous population in manufacturing industry or concentrated in urban centers. After giving up its Soviet-inspired centrally-planned approach, opening its economy in the late 1970s,

China's transition toward industrial prowess has been facilitated by foreign investment and entrepreneurship, some of it from Taiwan and Hong Kong and not so foreign after all. Businesses are attracted by the size of the domestic market and by China's cost advantages. China will continue to pose a competitive challenge, worldwide, particularly in standardized consumer products like clothing and consumer electronics. China is acquiring foreign technology at a rapid rate. But it is not yet a high-tech economy. Its competitive primacy is likely to remain in mass production. It will continue to be closely linked by trade with its markets in the West and with other East Asian countries, trade links that depend greatly on high-speed communication and low-cost transportation.

In turn, the United States, Western Europe, and Japan will be increasingly IT and service economies, relying on IT, communication, and services for a large share of their GDP. Manufacturing has already diminished its share of GDP and is likely to account for a still smaller share of output as the twenty-first century evolves. East Asia, too, will develop its IT, communications, and service sectors. But, importantly, it will continue to be the location of manufacturing industries. These will include electronics and equipment sectors related to IT like chips and computers.

Conclusions

These developments signal a geographic rearrangement of production between the West and East, the result of globalization. The ties between the world's trading blocks are getting closer as the volume of trade rises and as the integration of production systems increases. This integration is clearly a consequence of the transportation and communication improvements resulting from the IT revolution. The implication is complementarity rather than conflict between the two regional blocks. While many possibilities for conflict remain,[67] there have been and will continue to be significant advantages for East Asia and the West. East Asia will see increasing trade, a further upgrading of its production technology and its living standards. The West will continue to see manufactured products available at low cost. Many people, but not all, view this as an offset against the need to adjust labor force and production facilities to the new world economy.

14 What will advance the new economy in East Asia?

The rapid development of East Asia has depended as much, if not more, on private initiatives as on government policies. In this section, we consider what will advance the ICT/e-business economy in East Asia. We consider first the private entrepreneurial efforts that can advance the new economy and how private firms can take advantage of the new technologies. Then, we will consider public strategies. It goes almost without saying that the public and private approaches are closely interrelated, the setting for private entrepreneurial effort is established by public authorities. But development also depends on the response by private business to public policy. This is particularly true because of the unique aspects of the new technologies, their rapid evolution, their high level of competitiveness, their externalities, and their need for advanced education and skills.

Private strategies

Private entrepreneurship has been the dominant force driving East Asian development. Business managers from the East Asian countries themselves as well as foreign direct investors have developed numerous IT related enterprises. Local entrepreneurial effort has originated in all the East Asian countries. In many East Asian countries, private businesses, often owned or directed by local families, have been responsible for much technical upgrading. Perhaps surprisingly, in China, even firms that ultimately are owned by provincial or central government authorities have engaged in considerable entrepreneurial activity. Finally, from farther afield, many United States, European, and Japanese companies have entered into joint-venture agreements or have established fully owned subsidiaries in many countries of East Asia.[68]

So far, most of these operations have involved production or assembly operations for conventional consumer products like clothing. Some have been electronic products like computers and cell phones. The production of heavier, more capital-intensive products, like automobiles, is burgeoning in China, first for the domestic market and, before long, for export. Significant technical upgrading is under way. Some East Asian firms have been able to establish dominant positions in the world market for highly sophisticated products, for flat screens, for example, and China has become a center for building cell phones and computers.

So what is the appropriate East Asian business strategy with regard to IT and e-business? Competitiveness must clearly be the first consideration. East Asian competitiveness is not only a matter of low labor costs and favorable exchange rates. As the East Asian experience demonstrates, the product specifications and quality meeting world market standards are a central consideration. In a world of rapid technological and product change, business managers must be on their toes to keep up with the latest developments in technology, in product markets, and in the competitive environment. In looking to the future, managers must evaluate all dimensions of high-tech or e-business projects from the perspective of whether they can be carried out successfully from a commercial perspective: whether they will they make a profit over a short- or medium-term horizon, whether they satisfy a market, abroad or at home.

Small- and medium-size private business firms have considerable flexibility. They can operate with speed and originality, qualities that are highly useful in "new technology" operations. They are more likely to introduce "disruptive" technologies and products. Large international firms are less nimble but often have "deep pockets," well-known trademarks, widespread international markets, and sophisticated technical and management experience. They may want to extend a platform of existing technology. They can frequently leverage their knowledge to extend successful techniques in one region into new markets. Such skills are particularly important when complex high technology operations or sophisticated programming systems for international logistics, accounting, or other dimensions of management are involved.[69]

Many high technology and, to a lesser extent, e-business initiatives have good prospects in East Asia but many are also high risk operations with payout over a long-term future period. Possible issues involve:

- The suitability and size of international and domestic markets—will consumers in the chosen market have sufficient incomes to buy the product?
- The availability of the requisite infrastructure—are the broadband or cell phone communications networks sufficient to support advanced systems?
- The level of available technology—while technology can often be transferred from abroad, this involves local requirements for skilled technical employees and the requisite supplies of parts and supplies and maintenance of sophisticated equipment.
- Labor supply and skills—will a suitable supply of labor with sufficient technical skills and competitive wages be available?
- Cultural issues—handling of cultural or language questions so as to facilitate successful operations management.
- High costs of capital and exchange rate and solvency risks associated with international transfer of capital.
- Intellectual property risks—in frequent cases, transferred technology, even to affiliated firms, shows up in the hands of competitors.

Much depends on the nature of the IT project being proposed. The assembly of inexpensive television sets in China is an altogether different project from the production of highly sophisticated chips or flat panel displays in South Korea. An e-business website is likely to have a very different market potential in Singapore, a small but "connected" country, than in China, a huge country with sparse Internet connectivity.

Entering new IT fields or utilizing IT is often a promising strategy. In a rapidly changing world, one where IT technologies increasingly relate to production and its management, few firms can afford to ignore the potentials of the new systems. Competitive advantage lies with the firm that can consider all technological and market alternatives. It is important to be informed, to have personnel or consultants with appropriate knowledge and experience, and to consider all relevant possibilities. Enterprises operating in East Asia must seek to be close to the technological frontier, but perhaps not too close in order to make use of the comparative advantage available in the region. This may call for more labor-intensive production methods in East Asia than would be utilized in the United States. IT-related activities may involve improvements in management, logistics, and production processes. They may refer to new technically more sophisticated products, or they may involve new methods of marketing and distribution and customer relationships over telecommunications and/or over Internet connections. Such approaches are highly appropriate to some East Asian countries where rapid progress in IT is being made. Singapore, Taiwan, and South Korea come to mind. Even though the digital capabilities of other East Asian countries, including China, Indonesia, or Vietnam, are not as far advanced, IT and e-business approaches may offer opportunities in these large and rapidly growing countries.

On the other hand, it is important also to remain focused on a firm's principal activity—a cement producer is not likely to be an Internet company but may use Internet services for a variety of activities (however, see note 69). And, firms may recognize the potentials of forming joint ventures or other forms of affiliation to enter new "unknown" markets.

The possibilities for business strategy in alternative parts of the IT fields can be summarized as follows:

In production of hardware, East Asian manufacturers have gained a strong position. This is no longer just a matter of assembly and production of simple hardware. While the countries in the region differ greatly, as we have noted, they are gaining increasing sophistication. The links between suppliers and producers, that are so vital in high-tech industries are being established, not only in Taiwan and South Korea, but in China and Thailand, as well. New, more advanced products at the edge, technologically, are being developed and manufactured in the region and are being marketed worldwide under Asian trademarks as well as those of Western multinational firms. Strategically, East Asia offers great opportunities in production of increasingly sophisticated IT products.

Software development is more challenging. East Asian competitiveness is much harder to establish. This is because the development of new software calls for advanced programming skills and a highly detailed knowledge of practice in the field for which the programs are being built. Ability to communicate in

English and close contacts with the existing programming community are also important.

Software applications, usually involving customization of exiting programs, may be somewhat easier to transfer overseas, particularly for local use. It is premature to write off East Asia in the softer aspects of IT business. In China, in particular, efforts are being made to develop home-grown standards and programs. These will provide opportunities for programming for the Chinese market.

E-business represents a real conundrum for East Asia. On one hand, there is a huge potential market—1.5 billion Chinese speaking people, for example. On the other hand, custom and computer connectivity mitigate against e-business, at least in the immediately foreseeable future. It is simply unlikely that very large numbers of people in East Asia will turn overnight to purchasing books and other goods, ordering tickets, trading securities, running their bank accounts, etc. on the web. With exceptions of the most advanced countries and urban centers, customary use of small shops and transactions using human contact may persist longer in East Asia than in the West.

Public sector strategies

It is not premature to make judgments about the success of public planning and support policies in East Asia. All of the East Asian countries have made spectacular progress. In some countries, active government support appears to have paid off. In others, the failure to implement effective policies may have been a barrier to still more rapid growth or to continuation of the growth trajectory.

The strategies of public planning, state enterprises, and export promotion (EP) that were effective at early stages of industrialization and that produced rapid expansion of export manufacturing may not be as powerful for the next stage of development. With respect to Singapore, *The Economist* (November 30, 2002: 56) writes "an awareness is sinking in among the island's ruling elite that a model that turned a swamp into metropolis may not work as well when it comes to turning the metropolis into a citadel of the 'knowledge economy'."

The likelihood that IT policies will be successful appears to depend greatly on the nature of the policy: whether it is consistent with a country's comparative advantage, whether it is flexible rather than narrowly technical- or product-specific, and whether it makes adequate provision for infrastructure and education. The setting in which the policies are applied may also be important considerations. This includes: technology plans that are appropriate to the country's stage of development, entrepreneurial culture, and availability of venture financing.

What can the East Asian economic planners do to take advantage of the IT/e-business opportunities? One approach is to create a "vision," a study of the potentials and policy alternatives of a country's IT possibilities. Such a planning exercise frequently joins government officials with leaders in the business community in a common effort. Such an exercise may provide useful guideposts for business as well as for government policy. But because of technological uncertainties, politics, and bureaucracy, it is not always possible to make such a plan realistic or to implement it successfully. Drawing on such a "vision" of the future to implement specific policy measures favoring IT and Internet activities is even more risky and difficult than the traditional industrial policy plans that guided development in Japan and some East Asian countries in earlier decades.

The implications for public policy of alternative possibilities in the IT field are:

IT products remain a mainstay of East Asian economic advancement. The continued promotion of IT hardware production—consumer goods, parts, and gradually more sophisticated high-tech products—for export markets and for the growing domestic markets is a logical step. As incomes rise and as labor becomes more expensive, it is logical to turn toward more technically sophisticated products that call for higher levels of technology and more qualified workers. Such products may be complete consumer electronics, or specific parts or subassemblies, like chips and screens. Product assembly is frequently carried out in lower-income countries like the Philippines. An international production chain may profitably link producers located at various stages of the development ladder. On the high end, IT products may extend to machinery and capital goods embodying advanced IT controls.

Much depends on the ability of the East Asian countries to acquire the technology and develop the manpower that are necessary for the more advanced and more profitable steps of the production chain. Some countries like Korea, Taiwan, and Singapore have been eminently successful in this direction. Foreign direct investment (FDI) and alliances with multinational firms can be encouraged as a good source of capital and technology from the advanced industries. Domestic capabilities must be also upgraded to enable indigenous firms to compete and to prevent an "enclave" phenomenon. Building technology parks or geographic "clusters" associated with a technical university has been useful strategy.

Software and e-business activities are less likely to respond to direct public sector intervention, except possibly for e-government initiatives. So far, only Singapore, South Korea, and Taiwan have the facilities and human capital that can fully support the softer aspects of IT and e-business. There is, moreover, substantial competition in these fields from India, where widespread competence in the English language offers significant advantages. The development of the soft IT fields will require focused policy initiatives. Physical facilities are a matter of investment and many East Asian countries are moving rapidly to build Internet spines and related telecom facilities. Private businesses have been major movers in this respect in most countries, although government-owned or controlled firms still dominate in some countries, China, for example. But, perhaps surprisingly, many of these state- and provincially-owned enterprises are showing a remarkable amount of entrepreneurial and innovational spirit. With public sector encouragement, some large foreign companies like Intel and Microsoft are building research centers in China. Significantly, some of these will focus on software and testing and development projects rather than on basic research. In any case, there is still much to be done to provide rapid Internet access widely for business and consumers, a constraint, particularly, for the lower-income countries.

The real challenge to policy-makers will be to build human capital, to develop a population of technical experts, entrepreneurs, and a computer-literate population of users. Significant progress is being made. It will not be possible to skip steps in this regard. Secondary school education as well as more advanced technical education must be built up. Universities and technical schools must reorient their instruction toward applications and use computerized procedures. In the academic world, computer methods will be used when computers are available, but computers are not likely to be made available until computer methods are widely used. It will take extensive planning and resources to create an environment that favors the development of IT/e-business economies in East Asia.

15 Summary and conclusions
How will the IT/e-business revolution help to sustain East Asian economic growth?

We now turn to our initial question: "How will the IT/e-business revolution help to sustain East Asian economic growth?" Let us first summarize briefly the principal conclusions about future developments that we can draw so far.

The ICT/e-business revolution is making an important contribution to globalization and to East Asian growth. The revolution in communication and transportation has been a central element in permitting globalization: increased international competition, changes in the location of production, logistic control of a complex supply chain, and international entrepreneurship and investment. We are witnessing a new international division of labor where manufacturing will be centered in East Asia. Much of this manufacturing will remain in conventional products for international and domestic markets. The new microelectronics-based industries are also a growing part of East Asian manufacturing.

East Asia's rapid growth is likely to continue for many more years. The process of globalization, worldwide, and the development ladder process in East Asia are far from complete. It is not certain, of course, how much longer East Asian growth can be based on exports to the West, though the pace of these exports has not slowed and new classes of goods—even services—are being added. On the other hand, the potentials of the East Asian market itself, as living standards in the region rise and as intra-regional trade increases are enormous. Forecasters typically slow growth projections, assuming that growth becomes more difficult the closer a country's industry is to the technological frontier. Nevertheless, we project an East Asian economy significantly bigger than that of the United States or the European Union by 2020.

Increasingly East Asia will become a center for IT products production, particularly for electronics directed at the consumer market. East Asian countries are already the dominant suppliers for PCs, cell phone, LCD screens, and digital cameras, a specialization that is likely to continue into the future.

How much East Asian development will be based on the softer parts of IT is uncertain. In the context of the world marketplace, the larger East Asian countries may not have broad competitive advantages in these fields, though low wages and some skilled workers offer some opportunities in applications programming and some other offshoring activities. Higher-level programming and

Internet development activities are likely to continue to be centered in the advanced countries of the West.

East Asia is participating in e-business and related non-business e-activities, particularly with respect to international supply chains but, with exceptions, the development of e-business is not likely to be the engine for East Asian growth. From a worldwide international perspective, many East Asian countries do not have comparative advantage in these activities. All countries in the area are hoping to cross the digital divide and to advance e-business and related activities, but, except for cellular communication, progress lags behind the Western countries where these technologies were developed. In view of the long time it takes to build appropriate infrastructure and to develop a clientele of active users, it is likely to be many years before e-business will claim a large part of East Asian consumer transactions.

The nature of the contribution of IT differs among the East Asian countries. Improved information and a more effective competitive playing field will affect most of the countries in the region. Broadly, the impact in East Asia is likely to follow the pattern of the development ladder. The advanced countries will produce and develop increasingly sophisticated high-tech products or high-level consumer goods. The low-wage East Asian countries have become *the* producers of consumer goods for the entire world market: for the advanced countries and, as their living standards rise, for their own regional market. These developments are likely to continue, a step at a time.

Development, globalization, and location of manufacturing

East Asian development has represented a symbiosis between the needs of advanced Western countries and the abilities of developing countries of East Asia. It has produced a new division of labor among the world's producers. The flow of consumer products from East Asia to the United States, Europe, and, in recent years, increasingly, also to Japan is largely matched by a flow of raw materials, capital goods, information, entrepreneurship, and foreign direct investment (FDI) from the advanced countries toward East Asia. The changes in patterns of trade have been going on for many years.

A parallel symbiotic relationship links the countries of East Asia intra-regionally as simple manufacturing production has moved from higher cost countries to those where labor costs are still low. Parts and assembled consumer goods are increasingly being shipped from one East Asian country to others, from Taiwan and Korea to China, for example, as supply chains cross international boundaries. Flows of capital and entrepreneurship also move within the region. Indeed, East Asia is rapidly becoming an integrated trading region in its own right, a fact that is recognized by movements to further develop and extend an East Asian free trade area that may eventually include China and Japan.

As we have noted, rising living standards in East Asia, the immense and rapidly growing markets for household equipment, automobiles, and consumer electronics in China, are coming just in time to absorb the products of the vastly expanded production potential of the region. In other words, East Asia is increasingly becoming a customer for its own products.

The broadening of interaction between East Asia and the rest of the world and within the East Asian region itself, has greatly increased the range and scale of competition. In turn, competitive forces have helped to raise the efficiency of production, to improve quality by meeting or beating world market product specifications, and to stimulate the pace of product differentiation and development.

The fundamental changes in industrial operations and world trade are not all, in themselves, only the result of the new high-tech technologies. But they have been greatly facilitated by the decline in transportation and communication costs for which advanced new technologies are responsible. From the perspective of communication, we are living in one simultaneous world that makes possible logistic control of the supply chain with efficiencies never before achieved. And it does so almost without regard to the distances involved. In this sense the IT revolution has made possible the global transformation that continues to change the world economy.

Globalization and IT as the engines of East Asian development?

Where this transformation of the world economy will end is still an open question. It would be interesting, indeed, to see clearly into the future and to be able to respond unequivocally to our question about IT as the engine of sustained growth in East Asia. The ICT/e-business revolution has many dimensions. Some of these like communication and transportation are critical in advancing the division of labor between the Western countries and East Asia. Others, like the development of advanced programming and e-business, may be critical to the future of the most advanced countries, in the West and in East Asia, but less central for the larger developing East Asian countries.

There is little doubt that most of the East Asian countries will seek to compete in the IT fields. Some will find this road to renewed progress, while others still have substantial room to advance themselves through conventional mass production methods. All of them are gaining as computer controls and high-tech communication facilitate the integration of the global and East Asian regional markets.

Notes

1 Introduction: the challenge of sustaining East Asian growth

1 The term comes from the World Bank (1993) book, *The East Asian Miracle: Economic Growth and Public Policy*.
2 A saying that has been attributed to Prince Metternich in the nineteenth century, who is reputed to have said that "when Paris sneezes, the rest of the world catches cold." More recently, a headline in the *Financial Times* (April 14, 2003) says: "Asia sneezes and the world catches cold." The reference is to SARS, but the point is that the outbreak of this virulent disease was impeding travel and sales in Asia so that some people feared that the world would lapse back into recession.
3 An interesting example is how the recent elimination of multi-fiber agreement apparel import quotas resulted in an enormous increase in Chinese clothing exports to the United States, presumably, at the expense of other producing countries.

2 The ICT/e-business revolution: a new economy?

4 Thurow writes of the first industrial revolution related to steam power and the second related to electricity. Historians of technology may number them differently, however. For example, the middle of the twentieth century was undoubtedly also a period of revolution with the introduction of electro-mechanical controls.
5 The Ethernet, the networking protocol on which the Internet is based, was originally developed in 1975 by Robert Metcalfe at Xerox's celebrated PARC research lab. Apparently, somewhat to Metcalfe's surprise, with many complex upgrades, the Ethernet protocols still serve at the basic approach governing international data transfer.
6 In American economic history, the classic example is Francis Cabot Lowell's trip to study cotton weaving machinery in Lancashire in 1810. On the basis of the information gathered, machinist Paul Moody was able to produce an improved loom, which Lowell and his brother-in-law Nathan Appleton were to use in the first fully integrated cotton mill in Lowell, MA, starting the American cotton cloth industry to compete with established mills in Britain. Today, the industry has moved on to East Asia.
7 Feenstra (1998) gives a similar numerical example with regard to Mattel's Barbie doll whose cost of production and materials in China also accounts for little more than 10 percent of its final retail value.
8 The analogy to philosopher Herbert Spencer's "survival of the fittest" and Charles Darwin's theory of evolution is not accidental. An entire new field, called "evolutionary economics" has been built around these ideas.
9 Gordon sees increased productivity as a statistical mirage, the result of measurement errors, respectively, in price indexes and measurement of hours worked. Kiley argues that large adjustment costs offset gains in productivity.

10 Numerous recent studies have considered the determinants of productivity growth and the role of IT in Europe, for example, Bowman *et al.* 2004; OECD 2003; and Jorgenson 2005.

3 Globalization: a linked world

11 Most economists and some, but not all, politicians support free trade. But many do not take into account that importing goods, albeit more cheaply than producing them at home, carries severe social costs for workers who have to be retrained and employed. There is also a strong opposition to globalization in developing countries, some of whom see it as damaging to their position in the world economy. As a result there is an extensive literature, pro and con. For some discussion, see Bourguignon *et al.* 2002; Stiglitz 2002; Fischer 2003; and Bhagwati 2004.

12 For a discussion of using price differentials as a way of measuring barriers to globalization, see Bradford and Lawrence 2004.

13 Feldstein and Horioka (1980) found that for most countries saving and investment were closely correlated, suggesting that there were not significant capital flows between countries.

14 An important point is that the economists' traditional Heckscher-Ohlin approach to international trade relationships assumes a fully integrated international market for trade in goods and autarchic international markets for resources like capital and labor.

15 The theory of economic geography, Krugman (1991), would call for locational specialization, because of economies of scale, availability of natural resources like minerals, linkages between producers along the supply chain, and other clustering advantages. But there would be no geographic specialization as a result of comparative costs based on the unequal availability of labor, capital, or knowledge.

16 This is even though the potentials for exporting Chinese-built cars are huge. In 2005, Honda is beginning to export cars from its Chinese plant to the European market.

4 East and Southeast Asia: a dynamic but diverse region—overview

17 East Asia and the Pacific includes the low- and middle-income countries of East Asia. The Pacific component is a miniscule part of the total. Japan, South Korea, Singapore, and Australia are considered high-income countries, and are not included.

18 Note that growth at 7 percent annually implies a doubling of income every ten years. Some of the East Asian countries have more than doubled their income first in the 1970–80 period, again from 1980 to 1990 and again from 1990 to 2001. By the beginning of the twenty-first century, at this rate of growth, average income would be eight times what it was 30 years earlier in 1970.

19 The data for China are best treated as an aggregate of China, Hong Kong, and Macao, since there has been transshipment and substitution in production between China and its related territories.

20 The World Bank categories for 2001 are as follows:

Low-income	GNI per capita of $745 or less
Lower middle income	GNI per capita of $746 to $2,975
Upper middle income	GNI per capita of $2,975 to $9,205
High-income	GNI per capita of $9,206 and above
	(World Bank 2003)

21 An important caveat with regard to these numbers is that they are supposed to measure sustainable growth, *after* allowing for catch-up to advanced country technology. It is not clear how such an adjustment can be made with any accuracy.

22 One way of viewing these discrepancies is according to the OECD.

> Shanghai has a per capita GDP level, expressed in PPP, equivalent to that of South Korea or Argentina. Fujian has a GDP equivalent to that of South Africa or Thailand. Lastly, Tibet's GDP is equivalent to that of Cameroon, and Gansu's to that of Mozambique.
>
> (OECD 2001: 4)

23 Another example of the role of cultural considerations is the extremely high rate of saving that is typical of the East Asian countries (Perkins 2000). On the other hand, a recent article (Modigliani and Cao 2004) suggests that China's high saving rate can be explained by rapid growth rather than by cultural factors. See also, Adams and Prazmowski, 2004.

24 See also Inkeles, *One World Emerging: Convergence and Divergence in Industrial Societies*, 1998.

25 The Chinese term, a "socialist market economy" appears on the surface to be an oxymoron, but perhaps not.

5 Development economics, the ITC revolution, and East Asian growth

26 The term "dismal science" is attributed to philosopher–writer Thomas Carlyle. Most economists assume that he was referring to the Malthusian idea that living standards were kept in check by subsistence. In fact, however, he used the term to scorn economists like David Hume who explained the world in terms of "supply and demand" in a debate where Carlyle supported the institution of slavery in the West Indies. Robert Dixon (1999) "The Origin of the Term 'Dismal Science' to Describe Economics," University of Melbourne Research Paper 215, available at http://www.economics.unimelb.edu.au/tldevelopment/econochat/dixonecon00.html, accessed October 20, 2005.

27 For a discussion see Barro and Sala-i-Martin (1995).

28 Kato adds

> not least because some policy makers did not welcome a questioning of the exceptional nature of regional growth performance which they had been attributing to the unique importance of "Asian values" [and also] because they predicted an end to the miracle.
>
> (2004: 3)

29 The data behind this figure may be of interest:

	Manufactures as % of GDP (2001)	*Change in manufactures as % of GDP (1990–2001)*	*Growth % p.a. (1990–2001)*
China	51	9	10.0
Hong Kong	14	−11	3.8
Indonesia	47	9	3.8
South Korea	41	−2	5.7
Malaysia	49	6	6.5
Philippines	31	−3	3.3
Singapore	32	−2	7.4
Thailand	40	3	3.8

30 Westphal (2002) elaborates on these terms and provides an extensive discussion of the role of knowledge acquisition in East Asian development.

31 Others have referred to assimilation of technology as imitation (Saito 2000), but assimilation seems a more appropriate term since a good deal of adaptation to local economic and cultural conditions may be necessary.
32 For an excellent discussion of the results of research on the pros and cons of FDI, see Lipsey, 2003.

6 From miracle to meltdown and beyond

33 There is an extensive literature on the East Asian financial crisis. An interesting summary for the general reader is Blustein (2001). The academic literature is summarized in Corsetti *et al.* (1998).
34 Subtitle to Chapter 4, "The East Asian Crisis" in Stiglitz (2002), 89.

7 The digital divide

35 His reference is to Joseph Schumpeter's classic discussion of competitive innovation as "creative destruction"; that is, new, more advanced, products drive out the old.

8 The role of government in East Asian development

36 A fascinating and comprehensive discussion is Blustein (2001).
37 There is an extensive literature on the possibilities and on the appropriate mix of domestic and international stabilization policy. For a discussion of alternative exchange rate regimes see Frankel (2003).
38 Import substitution (IS) was the center of Brazil's early development policy. More recently a curious example relating to IT was the Brazilian policy experiment during the early 1990s banning the use of computers with the DOS operating system. The hope to build a domestic computer industry working with a homegrown operating system was not realized. Along similar lines, today, the Chinese government is promoting the use of Linux in place of Windows in all government operations.
39 The desire to sell products in world markets has important implications of exchange rate policy. An undervalued exchange rate favors exports and discourages imports. Undervaluation of the exchange rate is observed for many East Asian economies. (See for example our discussion of East Asian competitiveness in Chapter 10.)
40 Pack who studied this topic, concludes:

> In contrast to other cases of interventionist development strategies, Korea and Japan had vastly better experiences, having generated higher growth rates than many economies that pursued import-substituting industrialization... The simplest explanation is that policies in both countries induced significant competition.
>
> (2000: 63)

> But later he points out that "in view of the minor benefits and the potentially adverse effects on the financial sector and the neglected industrial sectors, countries should be exceptionally cautious before embarking on such policies."
>
> (2000: 64)

41 For a historical discussion of the political economy of Singapore's development, see Rodan (1989).
42 For a discussion of the role of the government in the development of Taiwan's industries and, more recently, the push toward liberalization, see Hsueh *et al.* (2001).
43 The changing pattern of the chaebols and their links to government, from entrepreneurial paternalism to diversified international competitors, is described in Ungson *et al.* (1997). Government policy is for the chaebols to specialize and to increase their already high focus on high technology.

9 Science, IT, and communications policies for East Asian growth

44 However, one should not underestimate the importance of standard setting. For example, failure to establish one universal standard for cellular telephones in the United States has meant the proliferation of various nonconforming systems and delayed nationwide accessibility.

45 European union international scientific cooperation policy, *Science and Technology in Korea* (2004) http://europa.eu.int/comm/research/iscp/countries/korea/ko-doc2.pdf, accessed October 21, 2005.

46 Lall says:

> where the appropriate skills, institutions, and infrastructure are present, free-market policies can stimulate investment and competitiveness in activities with 'easy' learning. However, where learning costs are high and specialized skills and information are involved (as in industrial and technological deepening) more selective policies are required after an initial, 'entry-level' stage of industrial development.
>
> (1996: 67)

47 At one point this project employed more than half of Indonesia's engineers.

10 Trends in East Asian high-tech export performance and competitiveness

48 This chapter is based on Adams and Shachmurove (2005).

49 The production stages include the following SITC production categories. The third column shows the category's primary resource requirement.

Category	SITC categories	Resource intensity
1. Raw food	00–09	Land
2. Processed agricultural goods	11–29, 41–43	Land, labor
3. Fuels	32–35	Natural resources
4. Industrial materials	51–59, 67–69	Natural resources, capital
5. Manufactures (mass production)	61–66, 81–85	Labor, capital
6. High-tech and capital goods	71–79, 87–89, 91–97	Capital, technology

50 For example, the three-digit category 776 (Transistors and valves) accounts for only $4.9 billion, though it too is growing rapidly at 22.3 percent per year.

51 For reasons of consistent coverage, deflation was done on the basis of the CPI. Alternative measures of prices, more appropriate in this case, gave approximately the same results. Comparison against the Japanese yen and the Euro would show even greater depreciation for the Chinese and East Asian currencies since the US dollar has depreciated relative to the yen and the Euro.

52 Next to the United States, China has become the world's largest FDI recipient.

11 Presaging the future: developing trends

53 European firms send operations to countries that are closer to home, like Hungary, and the Czech Republic. (Romania is a major center of programming for European companies.)

54 *USA Today* estimates that jobs leaving the United States amounted to approximately 100,000 in 2000 and would grow to almost 600,000 by 2005.

55 A similar but broader project has been proposed by the APEC (Asia Pacific Economic Cooperation) group that has sought, so far unsuccessfully, to implement a pledge to free trade between all the Asia-Pacific countries.

12 IT/e-business in East Asia's future economic development

56 An interesting paradox of the new technologies is the fact that tremendous economies are associated with standardization and scale. On the other hand, the new technologies also facilitate the customizing of the product to individual customer specifications.

57 *Business Week* notes that the salary in India for a database manager is $500 per month. His US counterpart earns up to $10,000 month. With respect to China, the discrepancy may be even larger.

58 For discussions of high tech, telecommunications, and e-business policy in East Asia, see ADB (2003), International Telecommunications Union, various case studies http://www.itu.int/ti/casestudies, accessed October 21, 2005 and Westphal (2002).

13 Forecasting East Asian development in an IT world

59 Statistical regressions using cross-country data for East Asia suggest that for every 100 percent increase in per capita income the annual growth rate will be lower by 0.4–0.6 percentage points.

60 Our focus is on economic considerations. Historical experience and political and military considerations often influence the role and power of countries on the world scene. Note, for example, the troubled relationship between China and Taiwan.

61 In purchasing power parity (PPP) terms. On an exchange rate basis (the World Bank's Atlas method), East Asian GDP remains much smaller than that of the United States or the European Union.

62 Other long term projection studies, for example, Wilson and Purushothaman (2003), show a similar catching up of aggregate income for the big developing economies— Brazil, Russia, India, and China, what they call the BRICs. Their estimates are somewhat lower than ours, since they are presented in terms of US exchange rate dollars rather than in PPP terms, delaying the time when the statistics show these economies to be bigger than the economies of the advanced countries.

63 This is for obvious reasons. Geopolitics was seen as a rationale for the expansion of empire, particularly for the territorial ambitions of Germany and Japan prior to the Second World War (Klare 2003).

64 It should be noted that, in another respect, Huntington is remarkably prescient since he also predicts conflicts focused on the Middle East.

65 The considerable outcry is surprising considering that Unocal's principal assets are offshore gas deposits in Southeast Asia. It was anticipated that Unocal's reserves of oil and gas in the United States would be sold off or exchanged for energy properties located overseas.

66 For a somewhat similar view, see Friedman 2005. Paul Krugman's column (*New York Times* June 27, 2005) is entitled "The Chinese Challenge." But, in line with a Chinese bid for US gas producer Unocal, Krugman's concern is with Chinese competition for scarce energy resources.

67 For example, with regard to energy and other resources.

14 What will advance the new economy in East Asia?

68 It is interesting to note that Japanese firms have tended to establish subsidiaries while many of the Western firms have operated through joint ventures.

69 Cemex, a Mexican cement producer is an interesting example. Using its skills in Internet based logistics, Cemex was able to expand to become the world's third cement producer. It has also been commercializing its computer programs. So far the company only has limited activities in East Asia IMD (2003) *Cemex: Global Growth through Superior Information Capabilities*, Lausanne: IMD International. IMD-3-0953.

References

Adams, F. Gerard (1998) "The East Asian Development Ladder," in *East Asian Development: Will the East Asian Growth Miracle Survive?* (eds) F. G. Adams and S. Ichimura, Westport, CN: Praeger, 3–18.

Adams, F. Gerard and Heidi Vernon (1998) "The 1997 East Asian Crisis: Will the East Asian Growth Miracle Survive?" in *East Asian Development: Will the East Asian Growth Miracle Survive?* (eds) F. G. Adams and S. Ichimura, Westport, CN: Praeger, 195–209.

Adams, F. Gerard and L. R. Klein (1983) (eds) *Industrial Policies for Growth and Competitiveness*, Westport, CN: Lexington Books, D.C. Heath.

Adams, F. Gerard and Peter A. Prazmowski (2003) "Why Are Saving Rates in East Asia So High? Reviving the Life Cycle Hypothesis," *Empirical Economics*, 28, 2, 275–289.

Adams, F. Gerard and Tayyeb Shabbir (forthcoming) "Investment, Growth, and Productivity During the East Asian Financial Crisis" (To appear in a book edited by L. R. Klein and T. Shabbir).

Adams, F. Gerard and Yochanan Shachmurove (2005) "Trade and Development Patterns in the East Asian Economies," unpublished.

Adams, F. Gerard and Yochanan Shachmurove (forthcoming) "Why Is China So Competitive? Measuring and Exploring China's Competitiveness," *The World Economy*.

Akamatsu, K. (1962) "A Historical Pattern of Economic Growth in Developing Countries," *The Developing Economies* (March–August), Preliminary issue 1, 3–25.

Allen, Douglas (2002) "Meet the New China," *International Journal of Business*, 7, 3, 35–49.

Anuwar, Ali (1992) *Malaysia's Industrialization: The Quest for Technology*, Singapore: Oxford University Press.

Arrow, Kenneth J. (1962) "The Economic Implications of Learning by Doing," *Review of Economic Studies*, 29, 155–173.

Asian Development Bank (2003) *Asia's Growth Strategies for the 21st Century*, Manila: ADB (draft).

Baily, Martin N. (2002) "The New Economy: Post Mortem or Second Wind?" http://www.iie.com/Publications/papers/baily02102.pdf, accessed October 11, 2005.

Baily, Martin N. (2003) "The Sources of Economic Growth in OECD Countries: A Review Article," *International Productivity Monitor*, 7 (Fall), 1–5.

Baily, Martin N. and Diana Farrell (2004) "Is Your Job Headed for Bangalore?" *Milken Review*, 4, 33–41.

Balassa, Bela (1979) "Changing Pattern of Comparative Advantage in Manufactured Goods," *Review of Economics and Statistics*, 61, 2, 259–266.

Barro, Robert J. and Xavier Sala-i-Martin (1995) *Economic Growth*, New York: McGraw-Hill.

Basu, Susanto, J. G. Ferald, N. Oulton, and S. Srinivasan (2003) "The Case of the Missing Productivity Growth: Or, Does Information Technology Explain Why Productivity Accelerated in the United States but not in the United Kingdom?" Chicago, IL: Federal Reserve Bank of Chicago, Working Paper 2003–8.

Bhagwati, J. N. (2004) *In Defense of Globalization*, New York: Oxford.

Blustein, Paul (2001) *The Chastening: Inside the Crisis that Rocked the Global Financial System and Humbled the IMF*, New York: Public Affairs.

Bourguignon, F., Dalia Marin, Anthony J. Venables, Alan L. Winters, Francesco Giavazzo, Diane Coyle, Paul Sealright, Thierry Verdier, Kevin H. O'Rourke, Raquel Fernandez, and Richard Portes (2002) "Making Sense of Globalization," CEPR Policy Paper 8, London: CEPR.

Bowman, D., B. Madigan, A. de Michelis, S. D. Oliner, D. L. Reifschneider, and D. E. Sichel (2004) "Productivity Growth, Information Technology, and Monetary Policy," *Economie Internationale*, 98, 89–95.

Bradford, Scott and R. Z. Lawrence (2004) *Has Globalization Gone Far Enough? The Costs of Fragmented Markets*, Washington, DC: Institute of International Economics.

Browning, John and Spencer Reiss (1998) "The Encyclopedia of the New Economy," *Wired Magazine*, http://www.wired.com/wiredmagazine/wired/reprints/encyclopedia.html, accessed October 12, 2005.

Brynjolfsson, E. and L. Hitt (2003) "Computing Productivity: Firm Level Evidence," *Review of Economics and Statistics*, 85, 4, 793–808.

Business Software Alliance (2003) Eighth Annual BSA Global Software Piracy Study, Washington, DC.

Calvo, Guillermo A. and Frederic S. Mishkin (2003) "The Mirage of Exchange Rate Regimes for Developing Countries," NBER Working Paper No. 9808, June.

Calvo, Guillermo A., Alejandro Izquierdo, and L.-F. Mejia (2004) "On the Empirics of Sudden Stops: The Relevance of Balance Sheet Effects," NBER Working Paper No. 10520, May.

Chenery, H. and M. Syrquin (1989) *Patterns of Development 1950–1983*, New York: Oxford.

Chin, M. D. and Robert W. Fairlie (2004) "The Determinants of the Global Digital Divide: A Cross-Country Analysis of Computer and Internet Penetration," Working Paper 10686, Cambridge: NBER, http://www.nber.org/papers/w10686, accessed October 21, 2005.

Choung, W. I., G. C. Kwon, H. S. Jun, and M. J. Jeong (2002) "Improving the Roles of the National Assembly for the Development of Science and Technology in Korea," *STEPI Newsletter*, vol. 1, 1.

Christenson, Clayton M. (2000) *The Innovator's Dilemma*, New York: Harper Business.

Coase, Ronald (1937) "The Nature of the Firm," *Economica*, 4, 386–405.

Collins, Susan M. and Barry P. Bosworth (1996) "Economic Growth in East Asia: Accumulation Versus Assimilation," Brookings Papers in Economic Activity, 135–203.

Corsetti, G., P. Pesenti, and N. Roubini (1998) "What Caused the Asian Currency and Financial Crisis?" *Temi di Discussione*, 343. Rome: Banca d'Italia.

Crafts, Nicholas (1999) "East Asian Growth Before and After the Crisis," *IMF Staff Papers*, 46, 2, 139–146.

Dasgupta, S., S. Lall, and D. Wheeler (2001) "Policy Reform, Economic Growth, and the Digital Divide," World Bank Working Paper 2567, Washington, DC: World Bank.

Dent, Christopher M. (2002) *The Foreign Economic Policies of Singapore, South Korea and Taiwan*, Cheltenham, UK: Edward Elgar.

ESCAP (2004) *Bulletin on Asia-Pacific Economic Perspectives* 2004/05, Bangkok, Thailand: United Nations Economic and Social Council for Asia and the Pacific.

Feenstra, Robert C. (1998) "Integration of Trade and Disintegration of Production in the Global Economy," *Journal of Economic Perspectives*, 12, 4, 31–50.

Feldstein, M. and C. Horioka (1980) "Domestic Saving and International Capital Flows," *Economic Journal*, 90, 358 (June), 314–329.

Fischer, Stanley (2003) "Globalization and Its Challenges," *American Economic Review Papers and Proceedings*, 93, 2, 1–32.

Frankel, J. A. (2003) "Experience of and Lessons from Alternative Exchange Rate Regimes in Emerging Economies," February, KSG Working Paper Series No. RWPO3-011, http://ssrn.com/abstract=413162, accessed October 14, 2005.

Friedman, Thomas L. (2005) "It's a Flat World, After All," *New York Times Magazine*, April 3, 33–40.

Fukuyama, Francia (1995) *Trust*, New York: The Free Press.

Ghernawat, Pankaj (2003) "Semiglobalization and International Business Strategy," *Journal of International Business Studies*, 34, 2 (March), 138–152.

Gordon, Robert J. (2000) "Does the 'New Economy' Measure Up to the Great Inventions of the Past," *Journal of Economic Perspectives*, 4, 14, Fall, 40–74.

Hamilton, Alexander (1791) "Report on Manufactures," Communication to the House of Representatives, December 5.

Harrison, L. E. and C. P. Huntington (2000) (eds) *Culture Matters*, New York: Basic Books.

Hobday, M. (1995) *Innovation in East Asia: The Challenge to Japan*, Aldershot, UK: Edward Elgar.

Hsueh, L., C. Hsu, and Dwight H. Perkins (2001) *Industrialization and the State: The Changing Role of the Taiwan Government in the Economy, 1945–1998*, Cambridge, MA: Harvard University Press.

Hughes, Helen (1995) *Achieving Industrialization in East Asia*, Cambridge, UK: Cambridge University Press.

Huntington, Samuel P. (1996) *The Clash of Civilizations and the Remaking of World Order*, New York: Simon and Schuster.

IBM (2005) *Understanding Our Company*, an IBM Prospectus, Armonk: IBM.

Inkeles, Alex (1998) *One World Emerging: Convergence and Divergence in Industrial Societies*, Boulder, CO: Westview.

International Telecommunication Union (2001, 2002) Internet Diffusion Case Studies, Geneva: ITU, http://www.itu.int/ti/casestudies, accessed October 13, 2005.

Iqbal, F. and William E. James (2002) (eds) *Deregulation and Development in Indonesia*, Westport, CN: Praeger.

Johnson, Chalmers (1982) *MITI and the Japanese Miracle: The Growth of Industrial Production, 1925–1975*, Stanford, CA: Stanford University Press.

Jorgenson, Dale W. (2001) "Information Technology and the U. S. Economy," *American Economic Review*, 91, 1, 1–32.

Jorgenson, Dale W. (2002) *Economic Growth in the Information Age*, Cambridge, MA: MIT Press.

Jorgenson, Dale W. (forthcoming) "Accounting for Economic Growth", in *Handbook of Economic Growth* (eds) P. Aghion and S. Durlauf, Amsterdam: North Holland.

Jorgenson, Dale W., M. S. Ho, and K. J. Stiroh (2002a) "Growth of U. S. Industries and Investments in Information Technology and Higher Education," Paper presented at Conference on Income and Wealth, April, Washington, DC.

Jorgenson, Dale W., M. S. Ho, and K. J. Stiroh (2002b) "Projecting Productivity Growth: Lessons from the U. S. Growth Resurgence," *Federal Reserve Bank of Atlanta, Economic Review* (third quarter), 1–13.

Kaminsky, G. L. and C. M. Reinhart (1999) "The Twin Crises: The Causes of Banking and Balance-of-Payments Problems," *American Economic Review*, 89, 473–500.

Kato, T. (2004) "Can the East Asian Miracle Persist?" http:www.imf.org/external/np/speeches/2004/120204.htm, accessed October 14, 2005.

Khan, Haider A. (1999) "Corporate Governance of Family Business in Asia," ADB Institute Working Paper No. 3, Manila: Asian Development Bank.

Kiley, Michael T. (1999) "Computers and Growth with Costs of Adjustment: Will the Future Look Like the Past?" Federal Reserve Board, Finance and Economics Discussion Paper Series 1999–36.

Kim, Linsu (1997) *Imitation to Innovation: The Dynamics of Korea's Technological Learning*, Boston, MA: Harvard Business School Press.

Klare, Michael (2003) "The New Geopolitics," *Monthly Review*, 55, 3 (July/August), http://www.monthlyreview.org/0703klare.htm, accessed October 13, 2005.

Kojima, Akira (2002) *Look Japan*, 48, 561, December 22.

Kojima, K. (2000) "The 'Flying Geese' Model of Asian Economic Development: Origin, Theoretical Extensions, and Regional Policy Implications," *Journal of Asian Economics*, 11, 375–401.

Kravis, Irving, Alan Heston, and Robert Summers (1978) *International Comparisons of Real Gross Product*, Baltimore, MD: Johns Hopkins University Press.

Krugman, Paul (1991) *Geography and Trade*, Cambridge, MA: MIT Press.

Krugman, Paul (1994a) "Competitiveness: A Dangerous Obsession," *Foreign Affairs*, July/August , 73, 2.

Krugman, Paul (1994b) "The Myth of Asia's Miracle," *Foreign Affairs* (November/December), 73, 62–78.

Kumasaka, Y. (2003a) "The Pirates of the Software Seas: Software Piracy Ranked by Country and Region," ITE Column, July 24, http://www.iteconomy.com

Kumasaka, Y. (2003b) "Outsourcing of White-Collar Jobs Abroad," ITE Column, August 12.

Lall, S. (1996) *Learning from the Asian Tigers*, New York: St. Martin's Press.

Lall, S. (1999) *Promoting Industrial Competitiveness in Developing Countries: Lessons from Asia*, London: Commonwealth Secretariat.

Landes, David (2000) "Culture Makes Almost All the Difference, in *Culture Matters* (eds) E. Harrison and C. P. Huntington, New York: Basic Books, 2–13.

Lau, L. J. (1998) "The Sources of East Asian Economic Growth," in *East Asian Development* (eds) F. G. Adams and S. Ichimura, Westport, CN: Praeger, 41–68.

Lau, L. J. (2000) "Economic Globalization and the Information Technology Revolution," presentation, http://www.stanford.edu/~ljlau, accessed October 11, 2005.

Lee, W.-Y. (2001) "To Evaluate Korea's Current Technological Competence and Future Potential in Comparison," Seoul, Korea: Science and Technology Policy Institute, http://www.stepi.re.kr:8080, accessed October 21, 2005.

Levy, Frank and Richard Murnane (2004) *The New Division of Labor: How Computers are Creating the Next Job Market*, Princeton, NJ: Princeton University Press.

Lincoln, Edward J. (2004) *East Asian Economic Integration*, Washington, DC: Brookings Institution Press.

Lipsey, Robert E. (2003) "Home and Host Country Effects of Foreign Direct Investment," http://www.nber.org/books/isit02/

Liu, Z. (2002) "Foreign Direct Investment and Technology Spillover: Evidence from China," *Journal of Comparative Economics*, 30 (3), 579–602.

Mahmood, I. and J. Singh (2003) "Technological Dynamism in Asia," *Research Policy*, 32 (5), 1031–1054.

Malthus, T. R. (1798) *An Essay on the Principle of Population*, http://www.ac.www.edu~stephan/malthus/malthus0.html, accessed October 11, 2005.

Mill, J. S. (1848) *Principles of Political Economy*, London: Longmans and Green, 1940 edition.

Modigliani, Franco and S. L. Cao (2004) "The Chinese Saving Puzzle and the Life-Cycle Hypothesis," *Journal of Economic Literature*, 42, 1, 145–170.

Ng, Francis and Alexander Yeats (2003) "Major Trade Trends in East Asia: What Are the Implications for Regional Cooperation and Growth?" World Bank Policy Research Working Paper 3084, Washington, DC: World Bank.

OECD (2001) *The New Economy: Beyond the Hype*, Paris: OECD, http://www.oecd.org/dataoecd/2/43/2380415.pdf, accessed November 21, 2005.

OECD (2003) *The Sources of Economic Growth in the OECD Countries*, Paris: OECD.

OECD Territorial Development Service (2001) "Regional Disparities and Trade and Investment Liberalisation in China" in OECD-China Conference: Foreign Investment in China's Regional Development: Prospects and Policy Challenges, October 11–12, 2001, Xi'an, Chinaq.

Oliner, S. D. and D. E. Sichel (2000) "The Resurgence of Growth in the Late 1990s. Is Information Technology the Story?" *Journal of Economic Perspectives*, 14, 3–22.

Oliner, S. D. and D. E. Sichel (2002) "Information Technology and Productivity. Where Are We Now and Where Are We Going?" Federal Reserve Bank of Atlanta, *Economic Review* (third quarter), 15–44.

Pack, Howard (2000) "Industrial Policy: Growth Elixir or Poison?" *World Bank Research Observer*, 15, 1, 47–67.

Pack, Howard and Larry Westphal (1986) "Industrial Strategy and Technological Change: Theory versus Reality," *Journal of Development Economics*, 22, 1, 87–128.

Perkins, Dwight H. (2000) "Law, Family Ties, and the East Asian Way of Doing Business," in *Culture Matters* (eds) L. E. Harrison and C. P. Huntington, New York: Basic Books, 232–243.

Porter, Michael (1990) *The Competitive Advantage of Nations*, New York: Macmillan.

Porter, Michael (2000) "Attitudes, Values, Beliefs, and the Microeconomics of Prosperity" in *Culture Matters* (eds) L. E. Harrison and C. P. Huntington, New York: Basic Books, 14–28.

Pye, Lucian W. (2000) " 'Asian Values': From Dynamos to Dominos" in *Culture Matters* (eds) L. E. Harrison and C. P. Huntington, New York: Basic Books, 244–255.

Rodan, Gary (1989) *The Political Economy of Singapore's Industrialization: National State and International Capital*, London: Macmillan.

Rogoff, Kenneth (2003) "The IMF Strikes Back," *Foreign Policy* 134 (February), http://www.foreignpolicy.com/Ning/archive/archive/134/rogoff2.qxd.pdf, accessed October 11, 2005.

Romer, Paul M. (1986) "Increasing Returns and Long Run Growth," *Journal of Political Economy*, 94, 5, 1002–1037.

Romer, Paul M. (1990) "Endogenous Technical Change," *Journal of Political Economy*, 98, 5, Part II, S71–S102.

Rostow, W. W. (1960) *The Stages of Economic Growth*, Cambridge, UK: Cambridge University Press.

Saito, Mitsuo (2000) *The Japanese Economy*, Singapore: World Scientific Publishing Co.

Schumpeter, Joseph A. (1942) *Capitalism, Socialism, and Democracy*, New York: Harpercollins, 1984 edition.

Schumpeter, Joseph A. (1975) *Capitalism, Socialism, and Democracy*, 3rd edn, New York: Harper & Row.

Servan-Schreiber, J.-J. (1969) *The American Challenge*, New York: Atheneum.

Servan-Schreiber, J.-J. (1981) *The World Challenge*, New York: Simon and Schuster.

Smith, Adam (1776) *The Wealth of Nations*, Digireads.com

Solow, R. M. (1957) "Technical Change and the Aggregate Production Function," *Review of Economics and Statistics*, 39, 312–320.

Stern, J. J., Kim J., Dwight H. Perkins, and J. Yoo (1995) *Industrialization and the State: The Korean Heavy and Chemical Industry Drive*, Cambridge, MA: Harvard University Press.

Stiglitz, Joseph (2002) *Globalization and Its Discontents*, New York: W. W. Norton.

Summers, Robert and Alan Heston (1991) "The Penn World Table (Mark5): An Expanded Set of International Comparisons, 1950–1988," *Quarterly Journal of Economics*, 106, May, 327–368.

Thompson, E. R. (2003) "Technology Transfer to China by Hong Kong's Cross-Border Garment Firms," *Developing Economies*, 41, 1, 88–111.

Thurow, Lester (2003) *Fortune Favors the Bold*, New York: HarperCollins.

Trefler, Dan (2003) "Trade and Production in the World Economy," Paper presented at meetings of LINK, United Nations, New York.

Ungson, G. R., R. M. Steers, and S-H. Park (1997) *Korean Enterprise: The Quest for Globalization*, Cambridge, MA: Harvard Business School Press.

Vernon, Raymond (1966) "International Investment and International Trade in the Product Cycle," *Quarterly Journal of Economics*, 80, May, 190–207.

Vernon, Raymond (1975) "The Product Cycle Hypothesis in a New International Environment," *Oxford Bulletin of Economics and Statistics*, 41, 255–267.

Wade, Robert (1990) *Governing the Market: Economic Theory and the Role of Government in East Asian Industrialization*, Princeton, NJ: Princeton University Press.

Warschauer, Mark (2002) "Reconceptualizing the Digital Divide," *First Monday*, June, http://www.firstmonday.dk/issues/issue7_7/warschauer, accessed October 11, 2005.

Weber, Max (1904–5) *The Protestant Ethic and the Spirit of Capitalism*, London: Routledge, 2001 edition.

Westphal, L. (2002) "Technology Strategies for Economic Development in a Fast Changing Global Economy," *Economics of Innovation and New Technology*, 1 and 2.

Wilson, D. and R. Puroshothaman (2003) "Dreaming with BRICS: The Path to 2050," Goldmaqn Sachs Global Economics Paper No. 99.

Wolf, Martin (2004) *Why Globalization Works*, New Haven, CT: Yale University Press.

World Bank (various) *World Development Indicators*, Washington, DC: World Bank (available on line).

World Bank (various, annual) *World Development Report*, Washington, DC: World Bank.

World Bank (1993) *The East Asian Miracle: Economic Growth and Public Policy*, New York: Oxford University Press.

World Economic Forum (2003, 2004) *Global Information Technology Report 2002–3 and 2004–5*, New York: Oxford University Press.

World Economic Forum (2004) *The Global Competitiveness Report*, New York: Palgrave Macmillan.

Young, A. (1995) "The Tyranny of Numbers: Confronting the Statistical Realities of the East Asian Growth Experience," *Quarterly Journal of Economic*, 110, 641–680.

Yusuf, S. (2003) *Innovative East Asia: The Future of Growth*, Washington, DC: World Bank.

Yusuf, S. and S. J. Evenett (2002) *Can East Asia Compete?: Innovation for Global Markets*, Washington, DC: World Bank.

Index

For Product Safety Concerns and Information please contact our EU
representative GPSR@taylorandfrancis.com
Taylor & Francis Verlag GmbH, Kaufingerstraße 24, 80331 München, Germany

www.ingramcontent.com/pod-product-compliance
Ingram Content Group UK Ltd.
Pitfield, Milton Keynes, MK11 3LW, UK
UKHW021611240425
457818UK00018B/507

* 9 7 8 0 4 1 5 6 4 7 3 0 4 *